Imranali Panjwani is a tutor and PhD candidate in the Theology and Religious Studies faculty at King's College London. Educated at the University of Sheffield, The College of Law and Al-Mahdi Institute in Birmingham, he has worked for the Centre for Islamic Shi'a Studies in London as its research co-ordinator.

'During the rule of Saddam Hussein's Ba'th Party, studies of Iraq's Shi'a community, whether historical or contemporary, were few and far between. In *The Shi'a of Samarra: The Heritage and Politics of a Community in Iraq*, Imranali Panjwani has addressed this problem in compiling an impressive group of essays on the history, religious significance and politics of a city that is central to Shi'ism. Rather than viewing Samarra as a site of sectarian conflict and political decay, the volume's contributors offer much hope for the future of Iraq. In an exceptionally creative manner, this volume uses the notions of place and geographical space to demonstrate not only Samarra's great contributions to Shi'i scholarship, but the manner in which its heritage has enriched all Iraqis. This collection is a must-read for all scholars of Iraq, whatever their disciplinary specialisation.'

Eric Davis, Professor of Political Science, Rutgers University

'The authors and compiler of this volume are to be thanked for placing Samarra in its true historical focus, bringing an appreciation of the ways in which the city and its monuments resonated through the history of the region.'

Charles R. H. Tripp, Professor of Politics, School of Oriental and African Studies (SOAS), University of London

THE SHI'A OF SAMARRA

The Heritage and Politics of a Community in Iraq

EDITED BY
IMRANALI PANJWANI

WITH A FOREWORD BY
CHARLES R. H. TRIPP

I.B. TAURIS
LONDON · NEW YORK

Paperback edition published in 2017 by
I.B.Tauris & Co. Ltd
London • New York
www.ibtauris.com

Hardback edition first published in 2012 by
I.B.Tauris & Co. Ltd

ISBN: 978 1 78453 744 9
eISBN: 978 1 78672 982 8
ePDF: 978 0 85772 145 7

A full CIP record for this book is available from the British Library
A full CIP record is available from the Library of Congress

Library of Congress Catalog Card Number: available

Typeset by Newgen Publishers, Chennai
Printed and bound by CPI Group (UK) Ltd, Croydon, CR0 4YY

MIX
Paper from responsible sources
FSC® C013604
FSC www.fsc.org

To all those who lost their lives due to the rage of others and never got an opportunity to express their talents for the prosperity of humanity. May God bless the languages and colours that never were.

CONTENTS

ILLUSTRATIONS

Chapter 2 The Shrine in Its Historical Context

Chapter 3 Rebuilding al-Askariyyain Shrine

Every attempt has been made to gain permission for the use of the images in this book. Any omissions will be rectified in future editions.

ACKNOWLEDGEMENTS

The publication of this book represents a great deal of hard work, patience and effort by a whole host of people. It would not be appropriate to begin this book without mentioning their names and contributions. The idea of discussing the heritage and politics of Samarra was born out of the 'Samarra: Heritage & Culture' conference held in February 2009 in the School of Oriental and African Studies (SOAS), London. Along with the director of the Centre for Islamic Shi'a Studies (CISS), Sayyid Fadhil Bahrululoom, Sajad Jiyad, a CISS researcher, put in a great deal of effort towards organising the conference and coming up with its theme. Some staples and papers later, a short booklet was produced which summarised the arguments of the conference's speakers – Peter Sluglett, Alastair Northedge, Usam Ghaidan, Reidar Visser, Søren Schmidt and Pascal Missak Abidor. A special mention must go to Alla Hassan for his contribution; Muhammad Daraji, Ghanem Jawad and Ja'far al-Ahmar greatly helped organise the conference and finally, Jawad Baraka and Hadia Saad, along with the rest of the conference staff, gave further exposure and administration to the conference. It was from the intentions, ideas and work of the aforementioned people and the unassuming booklet produced afterwards, that this book was born.

I would also like to thank those who contributed to the book after the conference - Charles Tripp for writing the foreword, Sayyid Qamar Abbas for stepping in to write an article for part II of the book, Amal

Imad for contributing her piece on citizenship, Vahid Majd for his translation of Ziyarah al-Nahiyah al-Muqaddasah (published by the Naba Cultural Organisation), Syed Rizwan R. Rizvi of www.ziaraat.com and Eric Davis for reviewing the book. Editing and compiling all the articles has been an arduous process but this would not have been achieved if it had not been for the patience and support of the team at the CISS. On behalf of the whole team at the CISS, we appreciate our publishers, I.B.Tauris, especially Iradj Bagherzade's interest in this book and Maria Marsh's and Nadine El-Hadi's support during the stages of publication. On a personal note, I would like to thank my dear family and teachers at Al-Mahdi Institute, Birmingham, for their continued kindness. Thank you and may God reward you all.

All of the efforts above have been part of the continual progress of the Centre for Islamic Shi'a Studies, which was set up in July 2007 in London. The CISS was formed to bring the Shi'i hawza tradition and Western academic tradition closer to each other as well as foster greater understanding of Islam. It aims to produce research on traditional and contemporary issues specifically from the Shi'i perspective and promote a better understanding of the Shi'i faith, its people and heritage in academia and society.

Finally, the views of the authors in this book are entirely their own and do not reflect the views of the Centre for Islamic Shi'a Studies. I have done my utmost to review the manuscript and check for any errors. Should there be any, I accept full responsibility and kindly ask the reader to forgive them.

Imranali Panjwani
Editor
Centre for Islamic Shi'a Studies, London

FOREWORD

Charles R. H. Tripp

For many people outside Iraq the town of Samarra is most likely to have entered their consciousness recently as the site of one of the spectacular acts of violence that helped to push Iraq into a sectarian civil war in the years 2006–7. The destruction of the great dome of al-Askariyyain shrine in February 2006 and the blowing up of its two minarets in the following year, were triggers, but also symptoms of the sectarian conflict that became so bloody and marked a feature of Iraqi politics in the wake of the US-led invasion and occupation of the country in 2003.

Because of the deliberately provocative and symbolic aspect of this act of destruction, and because of the civil conflict of which it formed a part, it seemed to represent for many the depth of sectarian hatreds in Iraqi society. All too often it was portrayed as being only the most recent manifestation of the seething historical enmities between the Shi'i and the Sunni communities – an enmity which was read backwards as having been an indelible part of the both the Shi'i and the Sunni heritage in the lands that were to become the modern state of Iraq since the fateful battle of Karbala in 61/680.

The truth is somewhat different and hinges less on sectarian identities than on political ambitions and strategic miscalculations, although the consequences both for al-Askariyyain shrine in Samarra and for countless thousands of Iraqis were terrible enough. By having the courage to look at those events head-on and to use Samarra and what it has stood for in Islamic and Iraqi history as a device to explore what it means both to be Shi'a and indeed Iraqi, this book succeeds in refocusing our attention on the potential in both legacies. It is a potential that can be realized in building for future, involving not simply the physical reconstruction of al-Askariyyain shrine but also the reconstruction of a truly national community in Iraq.

As some of the essays in this collection remind us, the challenges, at least in the sphere of reconstructing communal trust, are great and there is no guarantee that they will succeed. But they are also by no means pre-ordained to fail. Indeed it could be argued that the chasm that opened up before all Iraqis in 2006–7, regardless of their religious or ethnic identities, served as a terrible warning of what might be in store, causing even the most ruthlessly ambitious of political actors to draw back from the brink and to find other means of dealing with their compatriots than with the gun and the bomb. In that sense, it is possible that Samarra will stand as a reminder of what might have been, a turning point, although it did not seem so at the time, of Iraq's long journey back to the re-establishment of a civic polity.

The authors and compilers of this volume are to be thanked therefore for placing Samarra in its true historical focus, bringing an appreciation of the ways in which the city and its monuments resonated through the history of the region. Like all cities, it saw its days of glory and decline, although as a site of pilgrimage as one of the Atabat it has retained its lustre in the eyes of the Shi'i community in particular because of its association with Imam Ali al-Hadi and Imam Hasan al-Askari, as well as with the Occluded Imam Muhammad al-Mahdi. Nevertheless, with the shifting politics of the Abbasid Empire and the return of the Abbasid Caliphs to the former capital Baghdad, the court and the patronage that had been so important for the expansion and embellishment of the city moved away, representing a significant loss and inevitably diminishing its importance. When the course of the Tigris moved westwards, away from Samarra some eight hundred years ago, it deprived the city of yet another pillar of its economy, making it all the more dependent upon the pilgrim traffic that now constituted its lifeblood.

In its more modern history, it was Samarra's prominence within a universe of Shi'i devotion that may have helped to suggest to those Shi'i scholars – primarily from the Jabal Amil – who were dissatisfied with what they found in Najaf, that the city and its shrines could become a centre of learning, aimed at the renewal of Shi'i thought. As a dream it was not to be realised. The city and the community were too small and marginal to form the basis of such a plan. The gravitational pull of the long established centres of learning was too strong to allow Samarra to emerge as a contender. Equally, the need to relocate in order to modernise was made redundant by the transformations in Shi'i thought that were taking place under the stimulus of the rapid social and economic changes experienced by all Iraqis in the twentieth century.

In fact, for the residents of Samarra, where the Shi'i community was in the minority, it was to be the joint effort to construct a modern state that was to take up most of their energies. This was an effort that crossed sectarian lines and united – as well as divided – the inhabitants of Samarra, as it did in other parts of Iraq, following the many trends that were so characteristic of the plural voices of Iraq's rich and complex society and political debates. An integral part historically of the region of al-Iraq al-Arabi, Samarra's inhabitants found it natural to identify with the twentieth-century state of Iraq and all of its vicissitudes. As a community, they had their ideological differences, reflecting the larger disputes of Iraqi politics, drawn into them by the forces that were shaping Iraqi history and subjected, like all Iraqis, to the increasingly repressive order of the Iraqi state in the late-twentieth century.

This laid the foundations for the political conflicts that have so disrupted the current condition of Samarra, as of all Iraq, with terrible violence, so memorably inscribed in the ruins of al-Askariyyain shrine. It is all the more important therefore that this book should become known to a wider public who might otherwise think that this was an inescapable part of the Iraqi condition. On the contrary, as the contributions brought together here indicate, the history of Samarra not only brings a very different and richer perspective to our understanding of the trajectory of Iraq and of Iraq's many communities, but it also suggests that it is in the power of the Iraqis – whether identifying with a religious community or not – to reconstruct a future on foundations solid enough to withstand the violence of those whose political ambitions have blinded them to their common humanity.

INTRODUCTION: CONTEXTUALISING THE SPIRITUAL AND INTELLECTUAL HERITAGE OF THE SAMARRAN SHI'I IMAMS

Imranali Panjwani

The destruction of any city brings about a sense of loss of what could have been: life, family, talent, knowledge, culture, heritage and a place in the world's heart as a representation of the diversity and growth of humanity itself. This is precisely the spirit upon which this book is based: the notion that Samarra was one such city which had the thriving potential (and still does) of contributing its unique heritage to the world. There is a sense of melancholy but also hope and passion associated with the city. Sadness, at the Abbasid ruins of the pre-Samarra to its eventual shift into the post-Abbasid Samarra of today, which is known for the *ziyarah* (visitation) to the shrine of the tenth and eleventh Shi'i Imams, Ali al-Hadi and Hasan al-Askari (and the house of the twelfth concealed Shi'i Imam, Muhammad al-Mahdi). Even this holy shrine has not been without casualties and strife. The two explosions at the shrine in 2006 and 2007 debilitated the city and brought sectarian conflict once more to the fore.

Interestingly, however, there is a growing optimism for the city – a tone which permeates virtually all of the contributions in this book.

This optimism is rooted in the rebuilding of the shrine through the co-operation of the residents of Samarra – whether they are Shi'a, Sunni or Kurds. This is a fact sometimes forgotten in both the media and history, and the opposite seems to be reported – that there always has been sectarian conflict in Samarra, and indeed in other parts of Iraq. The reality is the peaceful coexistence of different sects and cultures with conflict as an exception. The role of UNESCO in recognising the heritage of Samarra and helping the restoration of the city is also a significant step towards rebuilding its future. This brings us to the question of precisely what Samarra was and what it can contribute today. Many of the writers in the book have touched upon various aspects of the city: the architecture and history of the shrine, the Abbasid and post-Abbasid Samarra, the scholarship of Mirza Shirazi, the lives and political period of the tenth and eleventh Shi'i Imams, sectarianism and finally, citizenship and identity. I think this is a testament to the diversity of the book. My introduction is arranged in two parts. The first will explain the structure and key themes of the book and the second consists of my own humble contribution in contextualising the spiritual and intellectual heritage of the tenth and eleventh Shi'i Imams who resided in Samarra (with a final reference to the twelfth Shi'i Imam).

Themes of the book: Samarra, Shi'a, heritage and politics

The most central themes of the book are 'Samarra', 'Shi'a', 'heritage' and 'politics', which I shall explain in turn. Samarra is a town in northern Iraq with a population of 205,664.[1] Literally, Samarra comes from *Surra Man Ra'a* (delighted one who beholds it) and is one of the most well-known cities in Iraq, famous for its archaeological sites. Iraq is divided into 18 different governates. Samarra stands on the east bank of the Tigris in the Salah al-Din governate, named after the famous Muslim warrior-ruler, Salah al-Din Yusuf ibn Ayyub (known in Western history as Saladin). Saladin was a ruler of Egypt but he originated from Kurdistan, just to the north of the Samarra district. He fought against the European crusaders and recaptured Jerusalem.[2] As Sajad Jiyad in Part I of the book will explain, the 'old' Samarra was the Abbasid Samarra where Mu'tasim, the eighth Abbasid caliph, relocated the capital in 221/836.

However, due to difficulties in expanding the city and political strife, the Abbasids returned to Baghdad and established their palaces there, an issue explored in Alastair Northedge's Chapter. The Samarra they left eventually turned into ruins and it was not until 333/945 that the first official building housing al-Askariyyain shrine was built by the Hamdanids and later the Buyids. The 'new' and current Samarra, therefore, was essentially a shrine city symbolising the Shi'i faith through the burial places of the tenth and eleventh Shi'i Imams, Ali al-Hadi and Hasan al-Askari. There are now renewed efforts at rebuilding this shrine which Usam Ghaidan will elaborate on.

The 'Shi'a', literally meaning follower or aid, 'are the party of Ali b. Abi Talib, peace be upon him, who are also called *Shi'atu Ali*, peace be upon him, during the life of the Prophet, peace be upon him, and his family, as well as after his life. They were known for supporting him [i.e Ali] and believing in his *Imamah*. Among these were al-Miqdad b. al-Aswad, Salman al-Farsi, Abu Dhar Jundub b. Junada al-Ghafari, Ammar b. Yasir, and whoever agreed with Ali, peace be upon him. They were the first Muslims to be called with this name, although the word Shi'a is an old term since the Shi'a of Ibrahim (Abraham), the Shi'a of Musa (Moses), the Shi'a of Isa (Jesus), and the other prophets, peace be upon them ...' [3]

In this context, the Shi'i faith and its people go back to not only the Prophet's nomination of Ali b. Abi Talib as his successor but Ali b. Abi Talib's own values, which in the eyes of the Shi'a, then and today, made him a central figure of leadership; he is understood to be an exemplar of morality and knowledge to the extent that the Prophet is reported to have famously said, 'I am the city of knowledge and Ali is its gate.'[4] It is particularly interesting that the intellectual and spiritual legacy of Ali b. Abi Talib carried on through his progeny with all the Imams exhibiting patience during tribulation and disseminating guidance to thousands of students.[5] I would like to expand on this point later in the introduction but at this juncture, it is important to mention the tragedy of Karbala since it is an innate part of Shi'i identity in Samarra and wider Iraq, as well as Shi'i identity in general.

Ali al-Hadi and Hasan al-Askari represent the last of the Twelver Imams and their shrines are a source of visitation, Shi'i values and history of oppression which the earlier Imams faced, a central issue tackled by Sayyid Qamar Abbas' article in Part II of the book. The survival of the Shi'i faith as well as the principles of Islam can be attributed to the efforts of Ali b. Abi Talib's son, Husayn. In 61/680, Husayn stood up against the corrupt ruler, Yazid b. Mu'awiyah. Yazid's reign as caliph in Arabia had resulted in civil strife, instability, indignity and a corruption of basic Islamic and moral principles. Furthermore, Yazid demanded allegiance from the people to obey his kingship. Husayn, his family relatives and few followers (together numbering 72) refused on the basis that they saw the notions of good and evil being manipulated. It was at this point that Yazid decided to force Husayn to accept his allegiance or be killed. In the end, Husayn and his small band of men, women and children (including a few-months old baby) were deprived of water for several days and murdered on 10 Muharram 61\10 October 680 in Karbala, Iraq (known as the Day of Ashura) by a vastly larger and superior army. The remaining women and children were tortured and enslaved. The Day of Ashura marks a great day of mourning and remembrance for Shi'i Muslims around the world. Husayn's shrine is located in Karbala, Iraq where it is visited by numerous pilgrims throughout the year.[6]

The fact that the tragedy of Karbala still resonates with Shi'i Muslims today and the shrines of the Imams after Husayn (who were also martyred), is arguably due to the martyrdom of Husayn. It is perhaps aptly summed up by a narration of Husayn's descendent and great grandson, Ali b. Musa al-Ridha (the eighth Shi'i Imam) who said,

> ... O Ibn Shabib! Muharram is the month in which the people of the Age of Ignorance had forbidden committing any oppression and fighting in. However, this nation did not recognize the honour of this month or the honour of their own Prophet(s). In this month, they killed the Prophet's offspring, they enslaved the women and took their belongings as booty. God will never forgive them. O Ibn Shabib! If you wish to cry, then cry for Husayn who was slaughtered like a sheep and was killed along with the members of this household. Eighteen people were martyred along with al-Husayn who had no equal on earth. The seven heavens

> and the earths mourned for his martyrdom. Four thousand angels descended to the earth to assist him. They will remain at this shrine with wrinkled hair until the Riser (Muhammad Al-Mahdi) rises. Then they will be among those who will assist him. Their slogan will be 'Revolt for al-Husayn!'[7]

Significantly, the language of the eighth Imam in particular places of this narration is graphic both in its meaning and the sound of the Arabic, exemplifying the absolute inhumanity of the martyrdom and his own grief. For example, he says Husayn was 'slaughtered like a sheep is slaughtered' *(dhubiha kama yudhbahu al-kabsh).* In terms of *ilm al-balagha* (science of literary expression), he has used the equivalent of the following English literary devices: simile, alliteration, imagery and emphasis. He also says, 'Revolt for al-Husayn!'. The plainness and directness of the language used here shows his cry for justice. It is precisely the continual remembrance of Karbala through mourning and literature, even many years after Husayn's martyrdom, which forms the religious, communal and social identity of the Shi'a in Iraq and around the world.

The third central term of this book, 'heritage', has evolved over the last 30 years. Initial definitions, dictionary and legal, have suggested land, property, possessions, architecture, natural habitats and environmental beauty. For example, the UNESCO Convention concerning the Protection of the World Cultural and Natural Heritage (1972) divides heritage into 'natural' and 'cultural' categories. Article 1 defines cultural heritage in terms of 'monuments', 'groups of buildings' and 'sites.'[8] Article 2 defines natural heritage in terms of 'natural features consisting of physical and biological formations', 'geological and physiographical formations' and 'natural sites.'[9] Approximately 30 years later, UNESCO saw the need to expand the concept of heritage to 'intangible heritage' via the Intangible Heritage Convention (2003). At the time of adoption, the Director-General of UNESCO, Koichiro Matsuura, commented, 'I was surprised, upon my arrival in UNESCO, to note the relatively low priority given to living heritage compared to the strong focus on the tangible part of the world's cultures ...'[10]

Realising this void, Article 2 of the Intangible Heritage Convention (2003) states, 'The term "cultural heritage" has changed content considerably in recent decades, partially owing to the normative instruments developed by UNESCO. Cultural heritage does not end at monuments and collections of objects. It also includes traditions or living expressions inherited from our ancestors and passed on to our descendants, such as oral traditions, performing arts, social practices, rituals, festive events, knowledge and practices concerning nature and the universe of the knowledge and skills to produce traditional crafts . . .'[11]

In discussions over the title of this book, several words were brainstormed with regards to the best way in which a faith or a community's history could be explored and appreciated. 'History' and 'case study' were among the words to denote some kind of examination of Samarra's past to differentiate many books that used merely 'politics' to describe the situation of the Middle East. However, we came to the conclusion to use 'heritage' in order to convey the broadest possible meaning of the word, in line with the Intangible Heritage Convention (2003), and to bring out the lives and legacies of historical figures, as per Part II of the book. In particular, the articles of Sayyid Fadhil Bahrululoom and Pascal Missak Abidor bring out the scholarly heritage of Samarra through jurists such as Mirza Shirazi.

'Politics', the other major word in the title (denoting the art of governance, administration and societal structure), will always continue to dominate current discussions, partly due to sensationalist media coverage and partly due to directed government policies. This is a concept we are surrounded with but have we ever investigated the historical places, streets, city developments and influential figures of countries or minority groups that provide clarity to the very things we debate about? John Pilger, in commenting on the regressive state of Iraq since 1989, acutely highlights this question via the schools of Iraqi children,

> . . . she took me to a typical primary school in Saddam city, where Baghdad's majority and poorest live. We approached along a flooded street, the city's drainage and water distribution system having collapsed since the Gulf War bombing. The headmaster, Ali Hassoon, guided us around the puddles of raw sewage in the

> playground and pointed to the high-water mark on the wall. 'In the winter it comes up to here. That's when we evacuate. We stay for as long as possible but, without desks, the children have to sit on bricks. I am worried about the buildings coming down.'[12]

One may ask what kind of intellectual heritage can be passed onto children when it is constantly destroyed through war and oppression fuelling only sectarianism, a theme predominantly tackled by Peter Sluglett and Reidar Visser in Part III. This book aims to challenge the reader to appreciate a broader conception of not just the Shi'a in Samarra and wider Iraq but the Middle East in general and the international policies affecting it. In this respect, Amal Imad explores international involvement and the effect this has on the internal politics of Iraq.

Having given a brief explanation of these four central concepts, when we consider the title of the book in its entirety, *The Shi'a of Samarra: The Heritage and Politics of a Community in Iraq*, we are focusing on the livelihood, way of life, spirit, scholarship, legacy and modern currents that have characterised the Shi'a of Samarra; a faith community with an enduring bond with the Prophet and his family, their sufferings and their shrines which continue to be a source of spirituality and inspiration for millions of visitors around the world. The book's motivation is aptly summed up by Ali b. Abi Talib who stated, 'There is no greater wealth than wisdom, no greater poverty than ignorance; no greater heritage than culture and no greater support than consultation.'[13]

The contribution of holy figures today

In this vein, I would like to devote the rest of this Introduction to the theme of spiritual and intellectual heritage. Considering that the contributions in this book have tackled issues ranging from architecture and scholarship to the political life of the tenth and eleventh Imams and sectarianism in Samarra, I would humbly like to focus on the spiritual and intellectual contribution of Ali al-Hadi and Hasan al-Askari today with a final reference to Muhammad al-Mahdi. It is interesting that to date there are very few books in Western academia which deal with the intellectual heritage of the Twelver Shi'i Imams.[14]

More than that, both in eastern seminaries and Western universities, very few tend to focus on practically contextualising the contribution of the Twelver Shi'i Imams to contemporary problems like human rights, bioethics, terrorism, economic issues such as the recession, government issues such as the cash for honours scandal, pluralism and more.[15] Before delving into the lives of the Samarran Shi'i Imams, it is necessary to place holy figures in an appropriate academic context.

The definition of 'holy' is an association with 'sacredness', 'purity', 'God' and 'virtue.'[16] When we use the term 'holy figures', we are naturally indicating sacred persons with high virtues, often in a Godly or religious context. As such, saints, prophets and Imams come under this category but the problem is that we *only* associate these figures as existing within a purely religious and/or theological framework relevant only to their followers. How often have we found academic deliberation on the teachings of Moses, Jesus or Muhammad (apart from biographical works)? What happens when philosophers such as Aristotle and Kant are elevated to a status akin to Prophets? By venturing into this territory, I am fully aware that some academics may believe I am confusing academic thinking with religious thinking, the latter firmly rooted in beliefs. I wonder, is this distinction valid when it comes to the contribution of holy figures today or have we, as academics, chosen to compartmentalise holy figures? Over ten years ago, research into hagiography or the study of holy figures was minimal: 'unfortunately no adequate general guide to the history, study, and use of hagiography exists in English'[17] but today, it appears to be a growing field of research, often met with some resistance.[18] I would like to offer two reasons as to why I believe there has been this resistance, which will provide my epistemological basis for this Chapter.

The first is that investigating the deeds and works of holy figures can point to a greater humanitarian vision of elevating society from a lower form of existence to a higher one. Extracting this vision or at least parts of this vision can always be a difficult task due to historical and epistemological constraints. At times, the most common option is to choose a reductionist methodology in compartmentalising the figure thereby procuring a safer and more certain analysis. Despite the merits of this position, it does not secure the essence and living framework of the figure. From a holistic perspective, I think it is extremely significant to create a broader system of coordinates that allows us to understand and even empathise with the meanings, events and personal actions of historical figures. Why were these figures oppressed? What did they succeed in? How did they impact the individuals around them? Why did they attract students and followers which survive till today? This would, at the least, position the holy figure in a wider human context. It is interesting that any attempt to derive values, epistemic methods and relevance of a religious figure is now termed as apparently hagiographical and proselytising yet there is, I think, a deeper significance of theology, religious figures and religion in general within a sociological perspective, particularly a postmodern one. William Hart aptly summarises this tension in academia, 'the house of religious studies is full of strange beds and even stranger bedfellows. One often finds oneself in a strange bed, embraced by a stranger, not knowing how one got there or how to get out. No wonder so much effort goes into policing the boundaries between the scholarly self and the dogmatic other, between the academic study of religion and the promotion of an ecclesiastical agenda in the guise of scholarship. For when this boundary is blurred, there can be a dreadful and palpable sense of violation.'[19]

In this vein, Richard Roberts, in his book *Religion, Theology and the Human Sciences*, tackles several important questions related to the corporate management of education to yield skills and commodities rather than true academia, the need for practical theology in allowing religious believers to connect with their own tradition and figures, the disintegration of identities in an ever-changing postmodern society where unassailable human truths are not recognised and the role of religion in offering positive, societal renewal. It is his last point which interests me because I wonder whether there can be a critical investigation of religious tradition and its saintly figures with a view to contributing to constructive moral, social and transcendental values that help form rooted identities in human beings. According to him, society today is controlled by managerial modernity where everyone conforms resulting in a loss of meaningful human identity. In addition, religion and its contribution have been marginalised in the face of secularisation. This has led to a 'societal transcendental in which all other realities appear to subsist. Such totalisation, which has now grasped much main-line religion within its cold, fruitless embrace, closes off deeper sources for the renewal of the human condition.'[20] Human beings then become vagabonds:

> the vagabond does not know how long he will stay where he is now, more often than not it will not be for him to decide when the stay will come to an end ... What keeps him on the move is a disillusionment with the last place of sojourn and the forever smouldering hope that the next place he has not visited yet, perhaps the place after next, may be free from the faults which repulsed him in the places he has already tasted ... The vagabond is a pilgrim without a destination, a nomad without an itinerary.[21]

What Richard Roberts is perhaps getting at is the loss of important facets of religion which we previously associated ourselves with and which have given a positive growth to society. Although he is rightly critical of those within a faith tradition who have been dogmatic, losing touch with a religion's essential values, he still brings out the religiosity which society may need: 'part of the collapse of socialisation can be associated with the disappearance of the ritual, experiential and mythic means of connecting the particular individual to the universals of cosmos, community and even the family.'[22] It is here that an evaluation of a holy figure's life within the context of his moral code and religious framework can offer society some intrinsic values which are being lost – values central to the way we interact with each other, build relationships, form communities, lead societies and conceive of what is meaningful to us.[23] The heritage of the Samarran Shi'i Imams is within this argument rather than a simplified hagiographical one because of their capacity to serve primary human needs through their spirituality.

The second reason, which has been acknowledged before by both Muslim and non-Muslim scholars, is the issue of Orientalists and Orientalism which has influenced the way in which academics think about Islam and its holy figures. Edward Said, in his seminal book *Orientalism*, stated,

> The closeness between politics and Orientalism or to put it more circumspectly, the great likelihood that ideas about the Orient drawn from Orientalism can be put to political use, is an important yet extremely sensitive truth. It raises questions about the predisposition towards innocence or guilt, scholarly disinterest or pressure-group complicity, in such fields as black or women's studies. It necessarily provokes unrest in one's conscience about cultural, racial or historical generalisations, their uses, value, degree of objectivity, and fundamental intent. More than anything else, the political and cultural circumstances in which Western Orientalism has flourished, draw attention to the debased position of the Orient or Oriental as an object of study ...[24]

Although there has been a change within academia over the last 30 years in the study of Islam, his words still have a strong resonance today because the study of Islam, whether in the context of Middle Eastern Studies or Humanities, still has a position within an Orientialist context that is not considered for its own independent analysis and methodology, which has been substantiated by the *Siddiqui report* (2007).[25] Perhaps a humble challenge for academics within the scope of Islamic studies is to consider the study of Islam within its own methodology, whether this yields merits or demerits with particular interpretations. At least that way, Islamic sciences and the contributions of holy figures would be appreciated from their own perspectives first with due consideration given to seminary training, thinking and terminology. This would involve acknowledgement of subjects such as *ilm al-fiqh* (the science of jurisprudence), *ilm al-hadith* (the science of narration) and *ilm al-mantiq* (the science of logic), which offer the classical framework needed to comprehend and develop the study of Islam, the solutions it can offer and the challenges it faces. It would also harmonise the subjects, figures and ideology of Islam with the context it finds itself in; whether this is geographical, intellectual, political, moral or social. Finally, this would yield greater understandings between different religious and secular systems from Islam's intellectual core. From this understanding, we can appropriately discuss the heritage of the Samarran Shi'i Imams.

The spiritual heritage of Ali al-Hadi

With this in mind, what kind of heritage of Ali al-Hadi can one appreciate today? Born in Madinah on 212/828 and martyred in Samarra in 254/868 owing to poison administered by al-Mu'tazz, the Abbasid caliph, means Ali al-Hadi only lived approximately 40 years. One of the recurring themes within al-Hadi's relatively short life is the spiritual and moral way in which he dealt with his oppressors. Al-Mufid reports an interesting incident between al-Hadi and al-Mutawakkil, the Abbasid caliph in Samarra. The Abbasid caliphs had a history of oppressing the Twelver Imams, their values and scholarship and al-Mutawakkil was no different. There are numerous reports about al-Mutawakkil attempting to assassinate al-Hadi, humiliate him, search his house and even incite him to immoral doings.[26] However, on occasion, al-Mutawakkil required al-Hadi's help and guidance. Al-Mufid states, 'al-Mutawakkil became ill with boils which appeared on him. He was on the point of death. No one dared touch him with a knife (to cut them away). His mother vowed that if he was preserved she would give a great deal of wealth from her fortune to Abu al-Hasan Ali b. Muhammad (al-Hadi), peace be on them.'[27] Al-Fath b. Khaqan advised al-Mutawakkil to go to al-Hadi for a solution and al-Mutawakkil sent al-Fath to do so. Al-Hadi informed al-Fath to 'take the dregs of the fat from a sheep. Mix it with rose-water and put it on the boils. It will be beneficial, if God permits.'[28] Al-Mutawakkil tried this remedy and it worked. His mother was overjoyed and sent ten thousand dinars under her seal to al-Hadi.

However, what transpired after al-Hadi helped al-Mutawakkil was highly dubious. Saeed of al-Mutawakkil informed him that al-Hadi had money and weapons, which were a threat to his government. Al-Mutawakkil sent Saeed, the chamberlain, to break into al-Hadi's house at night and search for the money and weapons. When Saeed reached there trying to break into the house, he saw al-Hadi on his prayer mat. On seeing Saeed, al-Hadi surprisingly gave him a candle and informed him where the rooms of the house were. After searching the rooms, Saeed could only find the ten thousand dinars that was given to al-Hadi by al-Mutawakkil's mother. When Saeed returned with the dinars and al-Mutawakkil saw his mother's seal, he called his mother to account for this money and his mother duly informed him of her vow to gift money to al-Hadi if al-Mutawakkil was cured of boils. On hearing this, al-Mutawakkil ordered Saeed to return the money and any other property to al-Hadi. When Saeed did, he felt ashamed and informed al-Hadi, 'Master, it grieves me to have entered your house without your permission but I was ordered (to do it).' Al-Hadi replied by quoting from the Qur'an, "Those who do wrong will come to know by what a (great) reverse they will be overturned [26:227].'"[29]

The incident above is interesting for several reasons. It demonstrates the forgiving nature of al-Hadi who had no cause to help his oppressor, the medical knowledge he possessed to cure al-Mutawakkil's boils, the use of patience instead of aggression when Saeed began his unilateral search, the reliance on honesty to reform Saeed and al-Mutawakkil and finally, scriptural reasoning in order to respond to Saeed's indirect apology. These facets of al-Hadi's character exemplify his fundamentally pious nature which directed his conduct. From this small example, perhaps we can deliberate that the heritage of al-Hadi is two-fold. The first is the reformation of society through sacrificial conduct by which people's consciences are awakened. Al-Hadi chose to help his oppressor, thereby removing his anger and replacing it with genuine human concern for a fellow man's well-being. This was decidedly humanitarian and charitable but achieved only through his own moral struggle. It may seem far-fetched to think that goodness in others, even dictators, can be achieved through fleeting moments of reflection on other's moral conduct or through a sense of natural moral instinct. However, according to Charles Taylor, this instinct is part of the human condition and often forgotten today. He says,

> ... much of contemporary philosophy has ignored this dimension of our moral consciousness and beliefs altogether and has even seemed to dismiss it as confused and irrelevant ... we are dealing here with moral intuitions which are uncommonly deep, powerful and universal. They are so deep that we are tempted to think of them as rooted in instinct, in contrast to other moral reactions which seem very much the consequence of upbringing

> and education. There seems to be a natural, inborn compunction to inflict death or injury on another, an inclination to come to the help of the injured and endangered. Culture and upbringing may help to define the boundaries of the relevant 'others' but they don't seem to create the basic reaction itself. That is why eighteenth-century thinkers, notably Rousseau, could believe in a natural susceptibility to feel sympathy for others.[30]

The second aspect of his heritage is the way in which he dealt with rulers, government policies and spies. The notion of claiming that a person, group or country is a threat due to possession of money and weapons sounds strikingly familiar to the arguments advanced in support of invading Iraq in 2003. However, the reaction of al-Hadi was to intellectually and practically engage with al-Mutawakkil, keeping a distance but never compromising his moral code in order to help his enemy. It seems there was no political motivation in al-Hadi's actions. His response to Said was a cordial but firm method to get the message across to both Said and al-Mutawakkil about their wrongdoings, which are fraught with consequences. Beyond any theories of leadership and governance, al-Hadi's aim as an Imam or leader himself appeared to be neither revenge, defamation, political gain, material enterprise nor control of the masses but the spiritual growth of society through constant moral engagement, passive leadership and intellectual discourse.

The intellectual heritage of Hasan al-Askari

Having described the spiritual heritage of al-Hadi, I would like to shift the focus to the intellectual heritage of his son, Hasan al-Askari. Born on 232/846 in Madinah and like his father, martyred by poison by al-Mu'tamid on 260/874, al-Askari lived an even shorter life of 28 years. Prima facie, it may seem that no particular intellectual influence could be fathomed from this Imam. However, upon researching several history books within the scope of Islamic history and Islamic philosophy, I humbly found a glaring omission – al-Askari's intellectual influence on the Muslim philosopher and polymath, Abu Yusuf Ya'qub ibn Ishaq al-Kindi, popularly known as al-Kindi or al-Kindus.

Al-Kindi was born on 185/801 in Kufa, Iraq and lived through the lifetimes of the eighth, ninth, tenth, eleventh and twelfth Shi'a Imams.[31] Al-Kindi died on 259/873 in Baghdad, Iraq. One may be intrigued as to whether or not and if so, how al-Kindi intellectually engaged with these five Imams, most of who were in the same region as he was.[32] It is here that there is a notable incident recorded in history about exchanges between Hasan al-Askari and al-Kindi.

In one of these incidents, al-Kindi believed that verses of the Qur'an were contradictory to each other and wrote a book about this. The news of al-Kindi's views soon reached Hasan al-Askari through al-Kindi's students. Al-Askari told one of al-Kindi's students,

> 'Is there no wise man among you to prevent your teacher al-Kindi from that which he has busied himself with in the Qur'an?' The student said, 'We are his disciples. How is it possible for us to object to him, whether in this matter or another?' Imam Abu Muhammad (Hasan al-Askari) said to him, 'Would you inform him of what I say to you?' The student replied, 'Yes.' Imam Abu Muhammad informed him, 'Go to him, be courteous with him, and show him that you will help him in what he is doing. When he feels comfortable with you, say to him, is it possible that the speaker of this Qur'an means other meanings than what you think them to be? He shall say that it is possible because a man understands when he listens. If he answers that, you say to him, how do you know? He might intend other than the meanings you apply, and so he places other than it's (the Qur'an) meanings.' The student went to his teacher, al-Kindi and did as the Imam told him. Al-Kindi said to his student, 'I ask you by Allah to tell me where you have got this from!' The student said, 'It came from my own mind and I mentioned it to you.' Al-Kindi replied, 'No, it is not in your capacity to think in this manner. Could you tell me where you have obtained this?' He said, 'Imam Abu Muhammad asked me to say that...' Al-Kindi said, 'Now you speak the truth. This (argument) would not come from anywhere except from that house (the Ahl al-Bayt)...' After that, al-Kindi burnt his book.[33]

The above exchange is important for several reasons. Firstly, it shows Hasan al-Askari had a direct impact on the philosophy and religiosity of al-Kindi. In the key compilation, *History of Islamic Philosophy*, Felix Klein-Frank states 'al-Kindi is generally held to have been the first Muslim philosopher'[34] and 'al-Kindi's arguments go ultimately back to the late school of Alexandria'[35] and finally, 'it is generally held that al-Kindi's philosophy is in harmony with the Muslim creed.'[36] However, one humbly feels these statements can be challenged because had it not been for al-Askari's arguments, al-Kindi's philosophy would not have been in harmony with the Muslim creed for he believed the Qur'an contained contradictions. Secondly, al-Kindi appreciated the epistemology of al-Askari which led him to burn his own book. This impacted al-Kindi's own level of philosophical interpretation and logic, particularly in the understanding of the Qur'an. Arguably, al-Askari's influence must also be factored in the origin of al-Kindi's arguments, not just the late school of Alexandria.

Finally, the fact that al-Askari and indeed, the Imams before him, taught many students, begs the question of how to characterise holy figures who are also scholars. For example, Ali b. Abi Talib is credited to be the first exegist (*mufassir*) due to the knowledge he obtained about verses of the Qur'an from the Prophet, some of which is present in Nahj al-Balagha.[37] Or the fifth and sixth Imams were experts in both jurisprudential and theological fields as well as science, medicine and maths to the extent that Jabir b. Hayyan (also known as Geber, the father of chemistry and pioneer of algebra) was the sixth Imam's student.[38] Practically, one could link Muslim philosophy to al-Askari first, before al-Kindi because al-Kindi might have produced a very different form of Islamic philosophy had it not been for al-Askari's arguments. I have only cited one incident between al-Askari and al-Kindi due to the word-limit of the introduction but sadly, it is also due to evidential constraints. One wonders whether more exchanges were recorded between these two figures, especially considering how well-known they were and being present in the same region. We do, however, have *Tafsir al-Askari* in existence which, despite some debates about its authenticity, may give an idea of al-Askari's interpretation of the verses of the Qur'an. What the above incident shows is that the intellectual heritage of al-Askari is unfortunately buried in history and needs to be brought out and contextualised today.[39] The influence which he had on Islamic and other sciences can be seen from such incidents as well as his narrations.

The union of al-Hadi's and al-Askari's spiritual and intellectual heritage can be seen in al-Askari's son, Muhammad al-Mahdi, the twelfth living but concealed Shi'i Imam who was born on 255/869 in Samarra. There are many books which deal with the life, proofs and signs of al-Mahdi, which go beyond the parameters of these pages.[40] According to the Shi'a, Muhammad al-Mahdi is the saviour of humanity and will return according to God's will to restore peace and justice to humanity at a time of great discord and injustice; and that Hasan al-Askari desperately protected his son as there were many people who wanted to destroy him and what he represented.[41] Here, one can argue the continuing heritage of these Samarran Imams is that al-Mahdi's role as the awaited Imam represents the ever growing moral, social and intellectual aspirations of humanity. Philosophically, a human being's need for prosperity and happiness is perhaps a natural and innate feeling and this can come about through the actualisation of normative conditions such as justice and dignity. The arduous efforts of al-Hadi and al-Askari to bring about what they understood to be conditions of justice and dignity through their intellectuality and spirituality are perhaps an enduring heritage for humanity. The martyred scholar, Sayyid Muhammad Baqir al-Sadr, aptly sums ups up this sentiment:

> The concept of the Mahdi is not just the embodiment of an Islamic doctrine possessing a religious character but rather signifies a universal aspiration of mankind with the variety of its religions and creeds. It represents an innate aspiration through which people, despite the variety of their beliefs and their means of recourse to the Unseen *(ghayb),* perceive that there is, for all mankind on the earth, a promised day wherein the divine messages with their momentous significance will be fulfilled and their ultimate objective will be realized, bringing the long and arduous human journey through history to its ultimate destination.[42]

In terms of the style of transliteration used, the book has adopted a style based loosely on the *International Journal of Middle Eastern Studies* (IJMES). This is a fairly simplistic style to avoid complex fonts and signs when transliterating an Arabic word into English. Finally, the dates used in the book are both in *After Hijri* (AH) and *Common Era* (CE) format to give an accurate sense of the time period of events but dates from nineteenth century onwards, which are relatively recent, will not be given in *After Hijri* format.

Notes

1. United Nations Office for the Coordination of Humanitarian Affairs & Inter-Agency Information and Analysis Unit, July 2009. http://www.iauiraq.org/reports/GP-Thi-Qar_v1.pdf
2. Lamb, Harold. *The crusades: the flame of Islam.* (New York, 1930), pp. 31–39.
3. Al-Nawbakhti, Hasan., *Kitab Firaq al-Shi'a* (London, 2007), pp. 60–61.
4. Al-Tusi, Ja'far., *Amali al-Tusi* (Qum, 1984), p. 558 and al-Amili, Al-Hur., *Wasail al-Shia* (Qum, 1993), vol 27, p. 34. See also al-Majlisi, Muhammad Baqir., *Bihar al-Anwar*, (Beiruit, 1983), vol 99, p. 106, al-Nisapuri, Abdullah al-Hakim., Al-Mustadrak *'al al-Sahihayn*, (Beirut, 1983), vol 3, pp. 126–7 and ibn Kathir, Ismail., *Al Bidayah wa al Nihayah*, (Beirut, 1993), vol 7, pp. 358–359.
5. For example, with regards to Ja'far al-Sadiq, the 6th Shi'a Imam who taught Abu Hanifa and Malik b.Anas (the founders of the Hanafi and Maliki Sunni schools of thought), al-Mufid states he was, 'the most celebrated, the greatest in rank and the most illustrious of them in (the eyes) of both the non-Shia (al-amma) and the Shi'a (al-khassa). The people transmitted on his authority the religious sciences which travellers carried with them (around many countries) and thus his fame was spread throughout the lands. The learned scholars have transmitted on the authority of no other member of the House (ahl al-bayt) as much as they have transmitted on his authority … they were four thousand men.' Al-Mufid, Muhammad., *Kitab Al-Irshad – the Book of Guidance.* (London, 1981), p. 408.
6. For further sources on the martyrdom at Karbala, see Mikhnaf, Yahya ibn., *Kitab Maqtal Husayn* (London, n.d) http://www.sicm.org.uk/knowledge/Kitab%20Maqtal%20Husayn.pdf. See also al-Tabari, Muhammad., *Tarikh al-Tabari*, (New York, 1988).
7. Al-Saduq, Muhammad., *Uyun Akhbar Al-Ridha* (Qum, 2006), vol 1, p. 560.
8. Article 1, UNESCO Convention concerning the Protection of the World Cultural and Natural Heritage (1972) http://whc.unesco.org/archive/convention-en.pdf
9. Article 2, Ibid

10. 'UNESCO's Cultural Heritage Convention "fully operational"', UNESCO Press Release No. 2009-109, 7th October 2009. http://portal.unesco.org/culture/en/ev.php-URL_ID=39849&URL_DO=DO_TOPIC&URL_SECTION=201.html
11. *'What is intangible cultural heritage?'*, UNESCO. http://www.unesco.org/culture/ich/index.php?pg=00002
12. Pilger, John., *The New Rulers of the World* (London, 2002), p. 70.
13. Radhi, Shareef., *Nahj al-Balagha (The Peak of Eloquence) Sermons of the Commander of the Faithful, Imam Ali b. Abi Talib* (New York, 1986), saying no. 54. http://al-islam.org/nahj/
14. By the twelve Shi'i Imams, I do not mean Twelver Imami thought, which is essentially the work of Shi'i scholars from the post-ghayba period (10th – 11th centuries) and beyond, of which there is still a scarcity. One of the recent works in this field is Bayhom-Daou, Tamima., *Shaykh Mufid* (London, 2005). I am also not referring to the history and theology of the Shi'i school of thought which has been covered by authors such as Wilfred Madelung, Etan Kholberg and Moojan Momen. I am specifically referring to the teachings and works of the twelve Imams themselves and their contribution to knowledge and society. For example, despite the vastness of *History of Islamic Philosophy* by Syed Hossein Nasr and Oliver Leaman (Routledge, 2003), only half a page is dedicated on p. 122 to the Shi'i Imams' contribution to philosophy. For recent contributions in the field of the teachings of the twelve Imams, see Lalani, Arzina., *Early Shi'i Thought: The Teachings of Imam Muhammad al-Baqir* (London, 2004), Shah-Kazemi, Reza., *Justice and Remembrance: Introducing the Spirituality of Imam Ali* (London, 2007) and Panjwani, S & Panjwani, I., *Islamic Metaphysics in Bioethics: Animal-Human Experimentations* (London, 2010).
15. It was however refreshing to see the Edgware District Reform Jewish Synagogue hold an event in January 2010 entitled, *'The Banking and Business Crisis: Does Islam & Judaism have an Answer?'* The event tried to demonstrate the practicality of the two faiths and their doctrines in creating solutions for business ethical dilemmas. See: http://www.hujjat.org/index.php?option=com_content&view=article&id=311&Itemi
16. Holy. (n.d.). *Collins English Dictionary - Complete & Unabridged 10th Edition.* Retrieved September 19, 2010, from Dictionary.com website: http://dictionary.reference.com/browse/holy
17. Head, T (1999). *An introductory guide to research in medieval hagiography.* http://www.the-orb.net/encyclop/religion/hagiography/guide1.htm
18. See Watson, C. (2004), *Old English Hagiography: Recent and Future Research.* Literature Compass, 1. http://onlinelibrary.wiley.com/doi/10.1111/j.1741–4113. 2004.00100.x/abstract

19. Cady, Linell and Brown, Delwin., *Religious Studies, Theology and the University: Conflicting Maps and Changing Terrain*, 'From Theology to theology: The place of "God-talk" in Religious Studies' by William D. Hart (New York, 2002), p. 93.
20. Roberts, Richard H., *Religion, Theology and the Human Sciences* (Cambridge, 2002), p. 305.
21. Bauman, Zygmunt., *Postmodern Ethics* (Oxford, 1993), p. 240.
22. Roberts: *Religion, Theology and the Human Sciences*, p. 300.
23. Anthony Giddens makes an interesting comment about the destructive nature of postmodernism, 'postmodernism is decentred; there is a profusion of style and orientation. Stylistic changes no longer "build on the past", or carry on a dialogue with it, but instead are autonomous and transient. Any attempt to penetrate to a "deeper" reality is abandoned and mimesis loses all meaning.' Giddens, Anthony, 'Uprooted Signposts at Century's End', *The Times Higher Education Supplement*, 17, (January 1992), pp. 21–2.
24. Said, Edward W., *Orientalism* (London, 1985), p. 95.
25. See *The Siddiqui Report – Islam at Universities in England* (tenth April 2007) which outlines the areas of Islamic studies teaching and research at universities that needs to be improved. http://www.mihe.org.uk/mihe/detail.php?page=179&s=15
26. al-Mufid: *Kitab Al-Irshad*, p. 502 and p. 506. For a fuller list of incidents, see Husayn, Jassim., *The Occultation of the Twelfth Imam: A historical background* (London, 1982), ch: 2.
27. Ibid, p. 499.
28. Ibid, p. 500.
29. Ibid, p. 501. For further information on such incidents, see Ashub, Ibn Shahr. *Al-Manaqib Al Abi Talib* (Najaf, 1956)., vol 3, p. 526 and Al-Yaqubi, Ahmad., *Tarikh al-Ya'qubi* (Beirut, 1960), vol 3, p. 217.
30. Taylor, Charles. *Sources of the Self: The Making of the Modern Identity* (Cambridge, 2008), pp. 4–5.
31. The following dates and regions are relevant: Ali b. Musa al-Ridha (eighth Imam) born in Madinah on 148/765 and died as a martyr in Mashhad on 203/818. Muhammad b. Ali al-Taqi (ninth Imam) born on 195/811 in Madinah and died as a martyr on 220/835 in Kadhimayn. Ali al-Hadi (tenth Imam) born on 212/828 in Madinah and died as a martyr on 254/868 in Samarra. Hasan al-Askari (eleventh Imam) born in Madinah on 232/846 and died as a martyr in Samarra on 260/874. Finally, Muhammad al-Mahdi (twelfth Imam) was born on 255/869 in Samarra – present.
32. See al-Saduq, M., *Uyun al-Akhbar* for the eighth Imam's (Ali b. Musa al-Ridha) scholarly debates in the court of al-Ma'mun in Baghdad.
33. Ashub, Ibn Shahr. *Al-Manaqib Al Abi Talib* (Najaf, 1956)., vol 3, p. 526. See also Al-Majlisi, Muhammad Baqir., *Bihar al-Anwar*, (Beiruit, 1983), vol 10, p. 392,

al-Amin, Muhsin., *A'yan al-Shi'a*, (Beirut, 1983), vol 10, p. 308 and Qurashi, Baqir Shareef., *The Life of Imam Hasan al-Askari* (Qum, 2005), p. 163.

34. Nasr, Sayyid Husayn and Leaman, Oliver., *History of Islamic Philosophy* (Routledge, 2003), p. 165.
35. Ibid, p. 170.
36. Ibid, p. 173.
37. For example, 'Ali is with the Quran, and the Quran is with Ali. They shall not separate from each other till they both return to me by the Pool (of Paradise)' - hadith cited in al-Nisapuri, Abdullah al-Hakim., *Al-Mustadrak 'al al-Sahihayn*, (Beirut, 1983), v3, p. 124. See also Radhi, Shareef., *Nahj al-Balagha (The Peak of Eloquence) Sermons of the Commander of the Faithful, Imam Ali b. Abi Talib.* (New York, 1986) http://al-islam.org/nahj/ For further information on Ali's knowledge of other fields such as law, see Bahmanpour, Muhammad., 'The Book of Imam Ali (Kitabu Ali): al-Jamiah', *Journal of Shi'ite Islamic Studies*, 1:1 (2008), pp. 3–28.
38. Al-Muzaffar, Muhammad., *Imam al-Sadiq* (Qum, 1998), p. 149. For further information on al-Sadiq's medical and scientific knowledge, see Newman, Andrew & Ispahany, Batool., *Islamic Medical Wisdom: The Tibb al-Aimma* (London, 1990).
39. In my trip to the British Science Museum's special exhibition of 2010 entitled: '1001 Muslim Inventions', it was commendable to see Muslim inventors, scientists and polymaths being recognised for their contribution to civilisation, in particular to Western science. However, it was also sad to see that there was no mention of the twelve Shi'i Imams' contribution to science, considering that the Imams taught some of these inventors. See http://www.1001inventions.com/
40. See, for example, al-Tusi, Ja'far., *Al-Ghayba* (Qum, 1911), al-Majlisi, Muhammad., *Kitab al-Ghaibah: The Book of Occultation* (Qum, 2003), al-Nu'mani, Abu Zaynab., *Al-Ghayba: Occultation* (Qum, 2003), al-Amini, Ibrahim., *Al-Imam al-Mahdi: The Just Leader of Humanity* (London, 1996) and for a full list, refer to Husayn: *The Occultation of the Twelfth Imam*, ch: 1.
41. For a full list of these attempts, see Husayn: *The Occultation of the Twelfth Imam*, ch: 2.
42. al-Sadr, Muhammad Baqir., *A Discussion concerning the Mahdi.* Al-Tawhid Journal. (Beirut, 1990) http://www.al-islam.org/al-tawhid/default.asp?url=mahdi/discussion.htm

PART I

HISTORY OF THE SHRINE AND CITY IN SAMARRA

CHAPTER 1

SAMARRA: SHI'I HERITAGE AND CULTURE

Sajad Jiyad

Since the establishment of the city by the Abbasids as their new capital in the ninth century, Samarra has had a notable Shi'i presence. Starting with the forced emigration of the tenth and eleventh Shi'i Imams, Ali al-Hadi (212/828–254/868) and Hasan al-Askari (232/846–260/874), the city was inhabited and later developed by their followers.

This Chapter addresses the key events in the timeline of the city and how centuries of deliberate and unrelenting demographic challenges have changed the sectarian makeup of Samarra. Key elements of the infrastructure of the modern city such as bridges, mosques, schools and markets are shown to have been built by Shi'i residents. The local noblemen – in particular those with a role in overseeing the shrines of the Imams and many of the tribal groups living in and around Samarra, are identified as being Shi'a.

I aim to dispel the myth that the Shi'i inhabitants of Samarra have always been a minority, and made up of non-Arabs. Rather, my argument is that the Shi'a are responsible for developing the city and contributing to its heritage. This is exemplified by the significance of the shrines of the tenth and eleventh Shi'i Imams and the fact that the city is the birth place and last known residence of the twelfth Shi'i Imam, Muhammad al-Mahdi (255/869–). The chapter concludes with several key statements on the identity of Samarra as a religious and cultural capital of the Shi'a.

The origins of the city of Samarra

In the year 221/836, the eighth Abbasid caliph, Muhammad al-Mu'tasim, relocated the capital of his empire to a recently re-established city north of Baghdad. This city came to be known as Samarra. His legion of personal bodyguards, the Turkish slave-soldiers referred to commonly as the *ghilman*[1], had gained increasing power over the caliphate. This had led to riots, resentment and unrest among the Arab courtiers and general population in Baghdad. He also wished to emulate his successors in building a new city as a mark of his rule. In addition, the city of Baghdad stifled him to the point that he is claimed to have detested it.

Al-Mu'tasim had been planning the move for some time and had ordered construction projects to start in an area around the canal called *Qatul Abi al-Jund*. Interestingly, his father, Harun al-Rashid (164/763–193/809), the fifth Abbasid caliph, had tried to build a town called *al-Mubarak* in the same area in anticipation of the need to relocate the capital of the caliphate. However, the soil proved inadequate for large-scale buildings and the project was abandoned unfinished in 180/796. This was also the same obstacle that al-Mu'tasim faced and the site was left for more suitable ones. In view of this problem, al-Mu'tasim decided to move the bulk of his regular army to Samarra where there would be specific camps for soldiers, quarters for officers, elegant residences for generals and palaces for himself. The roads were wide (perhaps a deliberate move on al-Mu'tasim's part in light of the previous problems his father faced during construction), the city became functional quickly and it seems that the planners and engineers had done their job well.[2]

The area around Samarra was suitable for hunting, contained clean air and possessed lush and untouched landscape that was a world away from the hustle and bustle of Baghdad, which had become the pre-eminent city of the world.[3] The people familiar with the area around Samarra told the caliph's retinue that its name from ancient times was *Surmarrati*.[4]

This was later rendered into Arabic as *Surra Man Ra'a* by the courtiers of the caliph and eventually to the shortened *Samarra* for convenience.[5] However, *Surra Man Ra'a* can still be read in works (particularly Ottoman era works and even Shi'i *fiqh* and *hadith* books) written many years after Samarra become the formal name.

Initially the move to Samarra became a relocation for al-Mu'tasim's army but this was accompanied with the formal transference of the capital of the Islamic caliphate from Baghdad, along with the administrators and civil servants who ran it. The plentiful land soon attracted all the important courtiers and those hoping to profit through real estate or retail by proximity to the court of the caliph. In effect, this meant that the caliph and his entourage were the principal beneficiaries of this huge property development. The administration of the caliphate purchased vast lands from Christian monks and other landowners and proceeded to gift these or sell them to those close to the hierarchy. Al-Mu'tasim's move to the area of Samarra had now given enormous value to lands that were previously ignored. The question was whether the subsequent caliphs could maintain Samarra as their capital and keep the *ghilman* as servants rather than as kingmakers.

Al-Mu'tasim hoped this move would give him a chance to break with the stifling court bureaucracy that had developed since al-Mansur (95/714–158/775), the second Abbasid caliph and saw its peak with the Barmakids during the time of Harun al-Rashid. However, since the Turks which al-Mu'tasim had come to favour were not competent in running the state's affairs, it meant that the viziers and clerks in Baghdad would have to follow him to Samarra. The outcome of this would be a clash between the administrators who followed in the steps of the Barmakids and the Sahl family (themselves following the model set by the Sassanid court viziers) and the new elites, i.e the Turks who now also had interests to protect. It was this volatile mix which the subsequent caliphs had to deal with and in particular, it became increasingly difficult for Samarra to retain its status as the capital city of the Abbasid Empire for very long.

Al-Mu'tasim commanded personal loyalty of the Turks and was firmly in control over them. His successors could not rule over them with the same authority and either favoured them too much to the dislike of the civil servants or did not favour them and thus incurred their wrath. It was no surprise that four of the later Abbasid caliphs were murdered by Turkish soldiers and this led to a tense and unstable environment in Samarra. Finally, the decision to return to Baghdad was taken by al-Mu'tadid (242/857–289/902), the sixteenth Abbasid caliph, in 278/892 and the capital of the Abbasid empire was moved once again. This sudden move meant Samarra was left without a source of revenue because the agriculture in the area was not well developed and without the caliph and the civil servants, the population dwindled drastically.

The city of al-Mu'tasim and al-Mutawakkil (205/821–246/861), the tenth Abbasid caliph, soon became a city of ruins and a new town to the south started developing. This attracted many people because of the shrines of two descendants of the Prophet, al-Hadi and al-Askari who were revered by the Shi'i community. Figures 1–5 clearly show the old city of Samarra as being located to the north of the new one. The excavations of Hertzfeld and others have confirmed that the old city was left to become ruins and was not lived in after the Abbasids left it to return to Baghdad. Therefore, to claim that the Samarra of today

Figure 1 Modern map of Iraq showing the location of Samarra

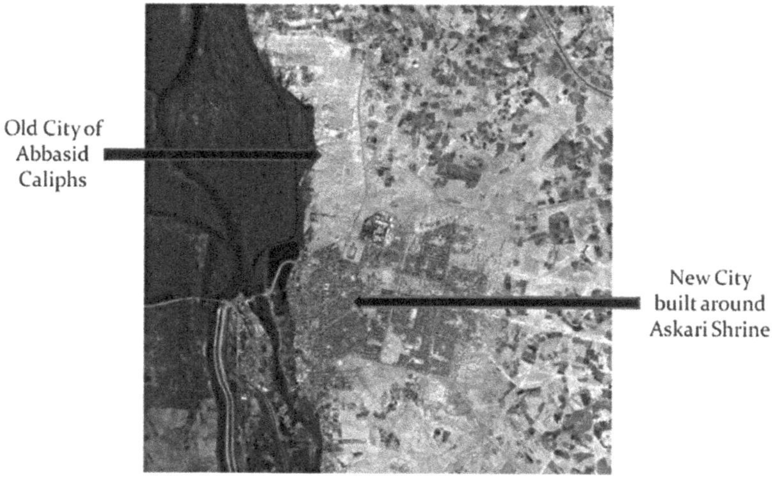

Figure 2 Satellite image showing old and new Samarra

Figure 3 Outlines of the remains in the old city of Samarra

was that of al-Mu'tasim is incorrect. It is, in fact, a new city of about 200 years in its current layout and in its original form, and dates to the first official building of al-Askariyyain shrine by the Hamdanids and then the Buyids, around the year 333/945 onwards.[6]

Figure 4 The modern city centred around the al-Askariyyain shrine

Figure 5 Aerial Photograph taken in 1917 clearly showing the modern city encircled by the city walls that were built through the donations of the Shi'i pilgrims[7]

Al-Hadi and al-Askari in Samarra

The Abbasids had a history of conflict with the Shi'i Imams, starting with al-Mansur and his imprisonment and poisoning of Ja'far al-Sadiq (83/702–148/765), the sixth Shi'i Imam. The Imams were largely based in Madinah and this distance from Baghdad posed a problem for the caliphs. Madinah was also a city that did not lean to the Abbasids and the presence of the Imams during the *hajj* (pilgrimage) season in Makkah further added to the suspicions of the rulers that the rebellions of the Alawids were being co-ordinated or supported by the Imams. Thus each of them chose to deal with the Imams in a particular way – mostly through imprisonment.[8]

Al-Mutawakkil was fervently opposed to the Shi'i and their Imams and had to contend with the popularity of Ali al-Hadi, the tenth Shi'i Imam. Outright execution or assassination was too risky, imprisonment did not seem to do the job and there was a fear of the backlash from the general populace who were inclined to the descendants of Prophet Muhammad. Therefore, al-Mutawakkil decided upon a new strategy, not too dissimilar from the one employed by al-Ma'mun (169/786–217/833), the seventh Abbasid caliph. Al-Ma'mun's tactic was to discredit the eighth Shi'i Imam, Ali b. Musa al-Ridha (148/765–203/818) and monitor him by bringing him to the capital and appointing him as an adviser or special guest. Al-Mutawakkil, however, developed this tactic further by reducing the exposure and freedom of Ali al-Hadi. This allowed al-Mutawakkil to constrain al-Hadi's relationship with the local people and maintain a watchful eye on the Imam. Thus, al-Mutawakkil summoned al-Hadi from Madinah ostensibly to be near the caliphate. Ali al-Hadi was not allowed to return to Madinah and his son, Hasan al-Askari, was also kept under surveillance until his death.[9]

The following is the account of the historian Donaldson on the Imams in Samarra,

> Al-Hadi was summoned to Samarra by al-Mutawakkil and kept there under house arrest until his death, reported to be by poison. The house which he had bought and lived in was surrounded by the camps of soldiers (al-Askar) and he was buried in the courtyard of his house. Al-Askari was also said to have been poisoned under the orders of the caliph, Mu'tamid. He was buried next to his father. The shrine over their graves is unique because it is the only shrine of an Imam that was actually their house and not a graveyard or land owned by them. The twelfth Shi'i Imam, al-Mahdi, was born in Samarra and was last seen there. This fact is especially important to the Shi'i awaiting his return. The restricted portion that was still inhabited in the fourteenth century was approximately the same as the modern Samarra and

> was a part of the camp of Mu'tasim. Here the Imams, Ali Naqi and his son, Hasan, had been allowed to live and hence they were called the *Askariyyain* or the "dwellers in the camp". It was here also that both of them were buried.[10]

From the quote above, we see that the tenth and eleventh Shi'i Imams essentially lived under house imprisonment in the middle of the army barracks. In this way, the caliph would ensure hardly any visitors could get through to see the Imams and any movements into and out of the house were watched and controlled carefully. Their house became their prison and thus became their shrine. The return of the Abbasids to Baghdad left the shrine of the Imams as the only site of significance in the city. The few brave Shi'a that managed to visit the Imams during their life also came to their shrines after their deaths. Still, the fact that Samarra was also where the twelfth and final Shi'i Imam, Muhammad al-Mahdi, resided and eventually disappeared from, gave special importance to Samarra.

Samarra in later times and Shi'i presence

What has been said by Ibn Battutah and others regarding Samarra in the Middle Ages is that it became a shrine city built and populated by the Shi'a and frequented by pilgrims who were major contributors to the local economy.[11] The tribes around the area included some who were Shi'a at the beginning such as the 'Ijli clan and also those that became Shi'a over the years, particularly from the sixteenth century onwards. Thus, the pre-modern history of Samarra as a shrine city built and populated by the Shi'a appears to be seldom disputed.

Ya'qubi describes how the land of Samarra was a desolate place, which he also calls a desert.[12] This is significant in the context of the Abbasid development of the town as they sought to make it a capital city out of essentially nothing. When this mission failed, due to both political and geographical reasons, it was clear that the city was going to fall into ruin. Hence, the Abbasid Samarra eventually turned into ruins because the city's existence depended on the Abbasids' presence. Once they left, the city gradually perished. This is the very city that Hertzfeld and others have excavated. In contrast, modern-day Samarra is a different city singled out by the tombs of the Imams which attracted visitors and settlement, leading to the shrine city it is today. Professor Northedge, the current authority on Samarra, mentions two significant points on this issue:

> Between 274/887–8 and 281/894–5, there are several reports of looting the city, after which Samarra ceases to be mentioned frequently in the chronicles; one presumes therefore that a major depopulation occurred at this time ... Al-Muktafi attempted to resettle Samarra in 290/903 but found al-Jawsaq a ruin ... From the fourth/tenth century onwards, Samarra became a pilgrimage town.[13]

Although the date that the capital was relocated to Baghdad is given as 279/892, the attempted resettlement of only 11 years is a very short period and one expects the city to still be functioning and full of civilian life. However, we find that the landmark palace of Abbasid authority in Samarra was already a ruin. This gives credence to the notion that the old or Abbasid Samarra became a ghost town and that the new one became Samarra instead, chiefly serving as a centre for pilgrimage. Indeed, Ibn Jubayr, the Arab geographer, who visited Samarra in 580/1185, is puzzled to see ruins instead of the grandeur of the Abbasid presence.[14]

The building of the thirty-forth Abbasid caliph, al-Nasir li-Din Allah (552/1158–621/1225), in 606/1209, which shows several additions to the Imams' shrines in order to appease the Shi'a[15], demonstrates the importance attached to the shrines by the authorities. It further indicates that Samarra had become a recognised site for *ziyarah* (visitation) akin to Najaf and Karbala. Finally, it shows that there were Shi'a living in Samarra and these residents influenced the development of Shi'i religious heritage.[16]

This *ziyarah* to the shrines has continued throughout history and Ibn Battuta mentions Samarra being in ruins, save for the area in which there is a *mashhad* dedicated to the twelfth Imam of the Shi'a.[17] The town itself does not seem to have had a major role aside from being a shrine city as it was only in 1834 that it became walled to stop the looting from marauding tribes in the countryside around the area of Samarra.[18] The donation that paid for the building of the wall came from a Shi'i patron who no doubt wished for better security for residents as well as visitors (most refer to the donations of affluent Shi'a in India though there is another narration mentioning a donation from Sayed Ibrahim al-Qazwini, a famous scholar in Karbala who contributed to the building).[19]

The picture we get from the above analysis is of two distinct cities and it is only the shrine city of Samarra that survives today. Accounts of history from tenth to eighteenth centuries are scarce without much detail beyond the emphasis on the shrines and the extensive ruins surrounding them. However, this improves in the nineteenth century with the various travels of officers from the British Empire, officers such as Commander Felix Jones in 1846. His account is important because it adds to what Rich has recorded in the first half of the nineteenth century well before the move of the *hawza* (religious seminary) there and confirms the Shi'i presence and population of Samarra,

> The modern town, situated on the cliffs forming the left bank of the Tigris, is now encircled by a strong wall built at the expense of the influential Shiah population from India. When I visited it in 1843, this wall was just begun. The town was previously open, and suffered much from the demands of the Bedouins. They used to encamp outside and threaten to pillage the place if their demands were not complied with; it is, however, now secure and free from such visits. It is, however, on the whole, a miserable town, and owes its importance chiefly to two handsome tombs surmounted by cupolas, the larger being that erected over the remains of the Imam Hasan Askari. It has recently been repaired, and, I believe, was formerly covered with gold, similar to the cupolas at Kadhimein, Kerbela, and Najaf; it is now perfectly white, the present funds not being sufficient to give it its former splendour. The smaller cupola, or that of the Imam Mehdi, is very pretty, being beautifully enamelled with yellow and white flowers on a bluish-green ground. Mehdi was the last of the imams revered by the Shi'ihs, and is said to have disappeared from the earth at this spot. Pilgrims from all parts of Persia resort to this place annually. I am informed that 10,000 is the yearly average of the number of those who visit this sacred

> spot, but I am inclined to believe this amount is even under the truth ... The modern town comprises about 250 houses, with a Sunni population slightly under 1000.[20]

Jones also mentions some of the tribes living in this area – namely the Shimmar Arabs and the Ubaid that he describes as Bedouin though we know large numbers also settled and lived in Samarra.[21] These tribes are of mixed sectarian make-up with some well-known Shi'a being among them. The *dhabit* (officer) of Samarra he mentions is Sayyid Husayn who the Ottoman government paid to farm his land.[22]

Wallis Budge recalls in his book, *By Nile and Tigris,* his visit to Samarra and the ruins he encounters:

> ... in these days Samarra is famous because it contains the tombs of the tenth Imam Ali al-Hadi and his son Hasan, the eleventh Imam ... In the fourteenth century the town was a mere mass of ruins, as Abul Fida (p. 300) and Ibn Battutah (ii, 132) testify. Later it was occupied by Shi'a and the bulk of the population today are members of this sect. The tombs of the Imams are

City walls built by Shi'a pilgrims
THE WALLS OF THE ANCIENT MOSQUE OF MUSTASIM, AND THE MODERN CITY OF SAMARRAH IN THE BACKGROUND
Facing p. 249]
[Royal Air Force Official—Crown Copyright Reserved

Figure 6 A clear demarcation of the new and old Samarra shown in the RAF photo

> maintained by the offerings of the pilgrims, who are also called upon to pay for the upkeep of the walls.[23]

Kinneir recalls his visit of 1813 and mentions after passing through the various ruins leading to the modern town of Samarra that it is a village and has a population of 2000.[24] Aside from the ruins, all that remains of this town are the shrines dedicated to the Shi'i Imams.[25] In an account of travels attributed to Muhammad b. Sayyid Ahmad Husayni in the year 1237/1822[26], he mentions that the annual visitor numbers of the Shi'i Arabs and non-Arabs to the shrines were roughly 30,000. This obviously correlates with what Felix Jones mentions about the numbers of visitors far exceeding 10,000 people. For a city whose population was estimated to have been less than 5000, it highlights the importance of the town and how its development has been driven by the visitation of the Shi'a to the shrines of the tenth and eleventh Imams.

Le Strange in his book, *The Lands of the Eastern Caliphate*, recalls how Samarra fell into ruin once the Abbasid caliphs left:

> The glory of Samarra, however, naturally came to an end with the return of the caliphs to Baghdad, and its many palaces rapidly fell to ruin. Later authorities add little to our knowledge of Samarra, and after years it came to be chiefly inhabited by Shi'ihs; for here were the tombs of the tenth and eleventh Imams and where the twelfth Imam had disappeared. Mustawfi adds that Samarra was for the most part a ruin, only in part inhabited and this is confirmed by Ibn Battutah who was here in the year 1330.[27]

Lycklama a Nijholt, the Dutch explorer, in his book *Voyages en Russie*, describes his journey to Samarra on 16 April 1867 and gives various accounts of the geographical setting and historical architecture of the town as well as its ruins. He goes on to describe the modern town and compares its present size with the former grandeur of the Abbasid one and says the current town has a population of 400 families.[28] Furthermore, John Ussher in his book, *London to Persepolis*, states that his visitation of 19 January 1864 of Samarra shows it was not a small place and in fact was inhabited by a large population.[29] This again reinforces the view that the shrines of the Imams were a major reason for the increasing popularity of settling in Samarra.

From the above evidence, we can establish that the Samarra of the Abbasids became ruins whilst the area in which the Imams were buried became a pilgrimage site which was inhabited by Shi'i people. The latter shrine city of Samarra was a small town – possibly a village up until the middle of the nineteenth century when it started to attract more settlement with the building of walls and improvement in facilities. Secondly, the population at the turn of the ninetenth century was around 2000 and by mid-nineteenth century, it became 5000. Thirdly, the number of visitors to the city was in the region of 30,000 in the early to mid-ninetenth century and fourthly, the Shi'a made up the majority of the population before the twentieth century.

The fourth point above requires more deliberation. Jones in his 1846 visit mentions that there were 250 houses and that the Sunni population was under 1000. The visit in 1822 of Muhammad b. Sayed Ahmad Husayni shows that the population is 2000. Therefore, if absolutely no population growth occurred, then Samarra had a slight Shi'i majority population by the mid-nineteenth century (disregarding any small number of non-Muslims living there). However, the descriptions by visitors just after the 1840s show that Samarra had a relatively significant population. Therefore, it is safe to say some population increase must have occurred between 1822 and the mid-1800s. Post 1870s is not for discussion here since all the sources (Budge as an example) mention that the bulk of the population was Shi'a. This is significant because the relocation of the *hawza* by the scholar, Muhammad Hasan Husayni al-Shirazi (popularly known as Mirza Shirazi), occurred in 1874 and contrary to the widely held view that Mirza Shirazi brought the first groups of Shi'a to Samarra, the above analysis shows he only added to the existing majority of the Shi'i population living there.[30]

Nijholt mentions in 1867 that there were 400 families residing in Samarra. We know that houses and families were used interchangeably by the visitors because families resided in houses and it is assumed that those residing in a house are one family since there is no specific census date being taken by these visitors. This shows a clear pattern of population growth from 1822 to 1846 to 1867 with the gaps between these dates fitting accurately my aforementioned analysis. Modern data has shown that urban Iraq has an average household of seven or eight people.[31] Semi-urban and other areas had numbers above this.[32] Non-urban populations in the late-twentieth century had an average family size of 12.[33] Without doubt, families in a house were larger in the nineteenth century since building houses was a more costly task and family sizes were naturally larger. However, I am willing to assume that it is not beyond 12 persons per family because more research needs to be done to show that the family size was larger than this number.

In 1822, the population of Samarra was 2000 and in 1846 the number of houses was 250 and in 1867 it is 400. Using an average number of 12 persons for the size of a family, this gives us a population of 3000 in 1846 and 4800 in 1867. These figures seem reasonable given the intervals and fit in with the numbers one would have expected for a village becoming a town. In 1846, Jones mentions that the Sunni population was under 1000, so the Shi'i population would be approximately 67 per cent. This reinforces my argument of the Shi'a being a majority in Samarra before the arrival of Mirza Shirazi. The sheer number of visitors also supports this view since their numbers cannot be supported without a decent resident population. Of course, this needs further investigation using historical records, particularly from visitor accounts I have not included here and from the Ottoman-era administrative records. Still, I would argue it is reasonable to say that there is sufficient evidence to show the Shi'i have always been a significant component of the population of Samarra pre-1870s.

Mirza Shirazi in Najaf and Samarra

It is probably beyond the scope of this Chapter to mention the details of the residency of Mirza Shirazi in Samarra and the many achievements that came with it. Several sources have shown the tensions of the late Ottoman administration that he had to deal with, the numerous improvements to the city's such infrastructure that he made and

Figure 7 Mirza Shirazi leading the congregational prayer at al-Askariyyain Shrine

the general scholarly output of the city that all later scholars would refer to him as *al-mujaddid* (the renewer). However, some account of his time in Samarra is necessary because of the legacy that remains there till this day and the various attempts by successive administrations to limit the influence and presence of the Shi'a in and around Samarra.

Sayyid Muhammad Hasan, the son of Sayyid Mahmud Husayni al-Shirazi, was born on 25 April 1815 in Shiraz. He started basic studies at the age of four, studying and writing Arabic language and grammar, Qur'an and Farsi. At the age of six, he began studying Islamic sciences and by the age of 15, he had begun to teach *al-Lum'ah al-Dimashqiya*[34] as well as other classical legal and religious texts. He left for Isfahan at the age of 17 where he received private tuition from Shaykh Muhammad Taqi al-Isfahani, author of the commentary of *al-Ma'alim* and Shaykh Ibrahim Kalbasi. By the age of 20, he had received an *ijaza* (permission) to perform ijtihad (the employment of effort to derive a law from its sources) from the latter. At this time he began to teach in Isfahan and within a short period he became known as one of the primary teachers of *hawza* studies in Iran.

In the year 1843, he went on pilgrimage to the holy shrines of Iraq and after visiting Najaf, he planned to return to Isfahan to continue his teaching. He did not see a need to remain in Najaf and the story goes he entered Najaf a *mujtahid* (jurist). However, a meeting with Shaykh Murtadha al-Ansari convinced him to stay, whereupon

Shaykh Ansari brought up a complex *fiqh* (jurisprudence) issue and then went into dialectic, alternating between two positions and showing the strength of evidence for both arguments. The depth of the discussion Ansari entered into impressed the young Shirazi, convincing him there is more to learn in Najaf and he sought residency there soon afterwards. Mirza Shirazi learnt under Ansari for over 20 years and in that time he became his top student.[35]

Upon the death of Shaykh Ansari in 1864, the senior scholars of Najaf gathered in the house of Shaykh Habib Allah Rashti to nominate a successor to the position of *marja-i taqlid* (source of imitation). All were in agreement that the most learned of Ansari's students was Mirza Shirazi, so they sent for him and informed him of their discussion. He refused the nomination, saying others (in particular Shaykh Husayn Ashtiyani) were more capable of the demands of issuing *fatwa* (formal legal opinion) for the people. The reply was that not only were skills in *fiqh* important but also skills in leadership and decision-making, which the senior scholars believed Mirza Shirza had. Upon insistence, he reluctantly accepted the position and the people were informed that *taqlid* (imitation in law) was to be done for Mirza Shirazi, both for his being the most knowledgeable and the most capable. His following grew year by year and as other *maraji* passed away, he became the sole source of emulation for the Shi'a. He taught many of the next generation of *mujtahids* and

Figure 8 A close-up of the previous image showing Mirza Shirazi with some of his students

Figure 9 Some of the seminary classes being taught at the school that Mirza Shirazi built in Samarra. One of the famous teachers here was Shaykh Muhammad Hasan Kubba, from the notable Arab Iraqi family

explained many of the opinions of Shaykh Ansari in treatises, reports and through teaching. As the years went by, his fame spread far and wide, people would come to Najaf hoping to visit him, and his position as the spiritual leader of the Imami Shi'i was unquestioned.

As Mirza Shirazi became a scholar of high repute, he moved to Samarra on September 1874 and began to establish a prominent *hawza*, which produced numerous Shi'i scholars. Although it is difficult to establish the reason for Mirza Shirazi's migration to Samarra, it appears that several factors influenced his decision: the political difficulties in Najaf which prevented him from furthering his own scholarship, a genuine concern for the city of Samarra and its Shi'i scholarship and finally, a matter of coincidence that shifted his stay from temporary residence to a permanency owing to the rising number of students that followed him to Samarra. He perhaps felt that Samarra provided him with a number of opportunities and freedoms to guide the Shi'i community which Najaf did not afford him. Whatever the reason, the migration not only cemented Mirza Shirazi's position as a leading scholar of his time but elevated the city of Samarra to a centre of scholarship. Hundreds of students migrated to Samarra to learn under Mirza Shirazi and this brought economic growth, city developments and further attraction to the shrine. Some of Shirazi's notable students include al-Akhund al-Khurasani, Sayyid Kadhim al-Yazdi and Mirza Husayn al-Na'ini.

However, with the move of the *hawza* to Samarra and the increase in the traffic of scholars and students alike, the Ottoman government at the instigation of some of the prejudiced locals started to pursue

Figure 10 Mirza Shirazi's students. Other prominent students whose pictures are difficult to obtain are Sayyid Ismail al-Sadr, Mirza Husayn Nuri and Shaykh Muhammad Ali al-Jamali

hostile and inflammatory policies.[36] On more than one occasion, rioting broke out and the Shi'a were attacked by gangs and Ottoman security officials. Mirza Shirazi always played the role of peacemaker in these incidents but it was difficult for him to convince the Ottoman officials that he had no ulterior mission or motive in moving to Samarra apart from teaching. One of the responses from the Ottomans was to send a Shaykh al-Islam who was to be a guide for the Sunni population in and around Samarra to defend against a perceived effort by Mirza Shirazi to convert the populace to Shi'ism. Another was to build two new Madrasahs that were to teach Sunni Islam, the larger of which opened in 1898 and was headed by Shaykh Muhammad Saeed al-Naqshabandi, of the Sufi order.[37] These schools were funded by the Ottoman Sultan Abdul Hamid II himself and teachers and students were paid salaries to attend, in contrast to the Shi'i schools which relied only on the support of the *marja*.[38] The government also appointed new officials alongside the existing Shi'i ones in running the affairs of the shrine.[39]

Samarra in the modern era

Without doubt the legacy of Mirza Shirazi in Samarra has continued until today, his contribution to the infrastructure, scholarly heritage and prestige of the city is instantly recognisable. There is a detailed description of his patronage in an account of Samarra by Shaykh Mahallati[40], including the first bridge crossing into the city of Samarra, several schools, a hospital, housing for students and accommodation for pilgrims. Kadhim al-Dujaili, writing in *Lughat al-Arab* almost 100 years ago, after recalling some of the building work of Mirza Shirazi, laments his death and says that, were he alive, Samarra would have regained all its glory in previous times.[41]

I would like to have included here a whole section dedicated to the brutal demographic reshaping that occurred during the time of the Ba'athists and also the discrimination against the Shi'a generally in the post-Ottoman era. However, constraints on space and also scope force me to forego this intention, though something must be mentioned of this here.

The massacres committed by the previous regime have been well documented but there is more to the sectarian hatred than mass graves. There is the issue of the deportations, people falsely accused of being non-Iraqi being exiled to the borders, having their money, possessions and lands stolen by the authorities. In north of Baghdad, jobs were often denied to the Shi'a, lands and properties confiscated, Shi'a were often denied the rights afforded to the non-Shi'a, as well as occasions of subtle and not-too-subtle harassment by local Ba'ath party officials. These are the issues that are much harder to find documented and only those resident in Samarra would be able to recall such incidents.

In a series of interviews with Sayyid Salih Dhul Ri'asatain, whose family, particularly his father Sayyid Husain, are custodians of the al-Askariyyain shrine (they hail from the *al-Bu Salih* tribe which settled in Samarra from the nomadic areas and have been the custodians for generations), important details about the demographics of Samarra came to light. He informs us of how the custodianship of the shrines has always been in the families of Shi'i notables, centuries before Mirza Shirazi (corroborated by Mahallati in his work) and that various tribes residing in and around Samarra are Shi'a (the *Ash'isha, al-Bu Abbas* and *al-Bu Adhim* are all from Sayyid descent). This is in addition to the non-Sayyid tribes that are also Shi'a fully or mixed, such as *al-Bu Darraj*[42] and *al-Bu Eisa*, a lot of whom are nomadic residing just outside Samarra.[43] He recalls details of the work that has taken place at the shrine throughout history, such as the identity of the labourers, the gift bearers, the calligraphers and so on. All those he mentions are Shi'i residents of Samarra who had lived before Mirza Shirazi and continued to do so after his death.

This is in response to the attempts to portray the Shi'i presence in Samarra as being recent and only due to Mirza Shirazi and thus weakened after his death. Dhul Ri'asatain repeatedly makes this point but says that the general Sunni civilian population of Samarra knows the real history of the town, is thoroughly integrated and intermarried with the Shi'i population and is not distinctive at all. It is only the attempts by the Ottomans, some elements in the monarchical government and then the destructive Ba'athist authorities that have attempted to change the historical narrative of Shi'i Samarra.[44]

Recognising the heritage of Samarra

While this chapter cannot be a comprehensive account of the history and heritage of Shi'i Samarra, it does allow for a useful reminder and overview of the origins and development of the town from its humble surroundings as an army camp, house of three Shi'i Imams and enclave for visitors to their tombs. The rich architectural history is also worthy of mention and the utmost care and attention is necessary in preserving what remains of some of the thousand year old ornaments and structures affiliated with the shrines. Though the bombings of 2006 and 2007 have destroyed such a significant part of this, the designation by UNESCO of Samarra as a World Heritage Site and its subsequent role in the repair and rebuilding efforts might still go a long way in achieving the goal of protection and preservation.

The role of religious tourism cannot be overemphasised with regard to the development of Samarra and, as it originally was built and enlarged due to the continuous stream of pilgrims throughout the ages, the need for facilities, infrastructure and even marketing is more important today. There is also a need to recognise the contribution of the Shi'i Muslim population in Samarra and around the world in contributing to its legacy. The efforts of Mirza Shirazi, while no doubt significant, are by no means the only contributions to the development of Samarra by a scholar or even a resident. The Shi'i community prides itself on the role it has played in preserving the name of Samarra and allowing the former glory of the old Abbasid town to be seen through the magnificence of the shrines of al-Hadi and al-Askari.

The people of Samarra have always lived together under the shade of the shrines and owe the importance of the town and its very lifeblood to the presence of the Imams there. In these times, there is a need to reflect on the history of this town and appreciate its religious significance, so that more efforts can be made to restore it to its previous splendour. Books, scholars, thought and culture have been produced in Samarra; this needs to be recognised and promoted in order that Samarra will once again symbolise a city of unity and hope for the Iraqi people.

Notes

1. Likened to the Praetorian guard of the Roman Emperors.
2. Northedge, Alastair., 'Samarra', *Encyclopaedia of Islam*, 2nd edition, (Leiden, 1995), pp. 1039–41.
3. Ibid.
4. There is an oft-quoted story of al-Mu'tasim meeting Christian monks while hunting in the area and them retelling him a prophecy that a king would build and live in this area with his sons to which al-Mu'tasim is said to have at once declared that king to be him.
5. Though some argue after the abandonment of the city by the Caliphs, it was mockingly named Saa' Man Ra'a or displeased who beholds it. See the entry on Samarra in al-Hamawi's geographical encylopoedia: al-Hamawi, Ya'qut., *Kitab Mu'jam al-Buldan.* F.Wustenfield (ed), 6 vols, (Leipzig, 1866–70).
6. Northedge: 'Samarra', *Encyclopaedia of Islam*, pp. 1039–41.
7. Beazeley, George Adam., 'Aerial Oblique of Samarra - Surveys in Mesopotamia During the War', *The Geographical Journal*, 55 (Feb 1920), No. 2.
8. al-Mufid, Muhammad., *Kitab Al-Irshad – the Book of Guidance,* (London, 1981), pp. 411–13.
9. Ibid, pp. 500–101.
10. Donaldson, Dwight M., *The Shi'ite Religion: a history of Islam in Persia and Irak* (London, 1933), p. 244.
11. Ibn Battuta, Muhammad., *The travels of Ibn Battuta*, (London, 2003), pp. 48–9.
12. al-Hamawi: *Kitab Mu'jam al-Buldan*, p. 260.
13. Northedge: 'Samarra', *Encyclopaedia of Islam*, p. 1040.
14. Al-Khalili, Ja'far., *Mawsu'at al-Atabat al-Muqaddasa* (Beiruit, 1987), vol 12, p. 185.
15. Northedge: 'Samarra', *Encyclopaedia of Islam*, p. 1041.
16. Al-Khalili: *Mawsu'at al-Atabat al-Muqaddasa,* vol 12, p. 143.
17. Ibid, p. 186.
18. Northedge, Alastair., Ibid.
19. Mahallati, Zabih Allah., *Maathir Al-Kubara Fi Tarikh Samarra* (Qum, 2005), vol 2, p. 46.
20. Jones, J F., 'Steamship Voyage to the North of Baghdad, in April 1846'. *Journal of the Royal Geographical Society of London,* 18 (1848), pp. 7–8.
21. Ibid.
22. Ibid.
23. Budge, Wallis., *By Nile and Tigris* (London, 1920), p. 114.

24. Kinneir, John MacDonald., *Journey through Asia Minor, Armenia and Koordistan* (London, 1818), p. 471.
25. Ibid.
26. Al-Khalili: *Mawsu'at al-Atabat al-Muqaddasa*, vol 12, p. 299.
27. Le Strange, Guy., *The Lands of the Eastern Caliphate.* (New York, 2006), p. 56.
28. Al-Khalili: *Mawsu'at al-Atabat al-Muqaddasa*, vol 12, p. 305.
29. Ussher, John., *A Journey From London to Persepolis* (London, 1865), p. 436.
30. A classic example of this view is found in al-Sara.
31. Oxford Research International., *National Survey of Iraq*, (November 2005), p. 2. http://www.oxfordresearch.com/resources/Iraq+Nov+2005+Baseline+Frequencies.PDF
32. See *Pattertico's Pontifications: Civilian Casualities in Iraq*: http://patterico.com/2004/11/09/civilian-casualties-in-iraq-a-question/
33. Land Reform and Ecology in Post revolutionary Iraq Author(s): Robert A. *Fernea Source: Economic Development and Cultural Change*, Vol. 17, No. 3 (Apr., 1969), pp. 356–81. See also *Results of the Baseline Farming Systems Survey Conducted in Ninevah Governorate, Iraq* (August 2005). The survey was conducted in July/August 2005, for the ICARDA-Iraq-Australia Project funded by ACIAR) on 'Better crop germplasm and management for improved production of wheat, barley and pulse and forage legumes in Iraq'.
34. *al-Lum'ah al-Dimashqiya* was written by Muhammad Jamal al-Din al-Makki al-Amili (1334–85), commonly referred to as *Shahid Awwal* (the first martyr) as he was the first martyred scholar of Islam. Shahid Awwal wrote al-Lum'ah, a textbook of jurisprudence still being taught in seminaries today, in seven days whilst awaiting his martydom in prison.
35. Mahallati: *Maathir Al-Kubara Fi Tarikh Samarra*, vol 2, p. 55.
36. Ibid, p. 180.
37. Ibid.
38. Saint-Elie, Anastase-Marie de., *Lughat al-Arab* (Najaf, 1911), vol 1, p. 142.
39. Nakash, Yitzhak., *The Shi'is of Iraq* (Oxford, 1995), p. 24.
40. Mahallati: *Maathir Al-Kubara Fi Tarikh Samarra*, vol 2, p. 63.
41. Saint-Elie: *Lughat al-Arab*, vol 1, p. 142.
42. Arab, Muhammad Mahmud., *Al-Saraa Fi Ahwal Samarra.* (London, 2006), p. 23.
43. Saint-Elie: *Lughat al-Arab*, vol 1, p. 140.
44. Series of interviews with Sayed Salih Dhul Ri'asatain, Damascus, Summer 2008.

CHAPTER 2

THE SHRINE IN ITS HISTORICAL CONTEXT

Alastair Northedge

The shrine of the tenth and eleventh Shiʿi Imams at Samarra was built over the tombs where they were buried, after having been brought to the city by the tenth Abbasid caliph, al-Mutawakkil (d. 246/861). Although the site of their tombs has long been known and developed from the tenth century onwards, it is only recently that it has been possible to work out how the shrine developed. My chapter discusses the historical and archaeological context of the shrine's construction in the Abbasid capital of *Surra Man Raʾa*. I will specifically present the architectural history of the tombs, up to the present-day reconstruction of the damaged buildings under the control of the United Nations Educational, Scientific and Cultural Organisation (UNESCO). Considering the archaeological aspects of this chapter, I have purposefully decided to take an illustrative approach to the piece to provide the reader with a sense of how the shrine has developed. I will conclude by commenting on the modernisation of the shrine.

The city of Samarra (Figure 1)

Samarra was not an important city in antiquity. The Assyrian chronicles speak of a city of *Surmarrate* in the first millennium BCE but it is

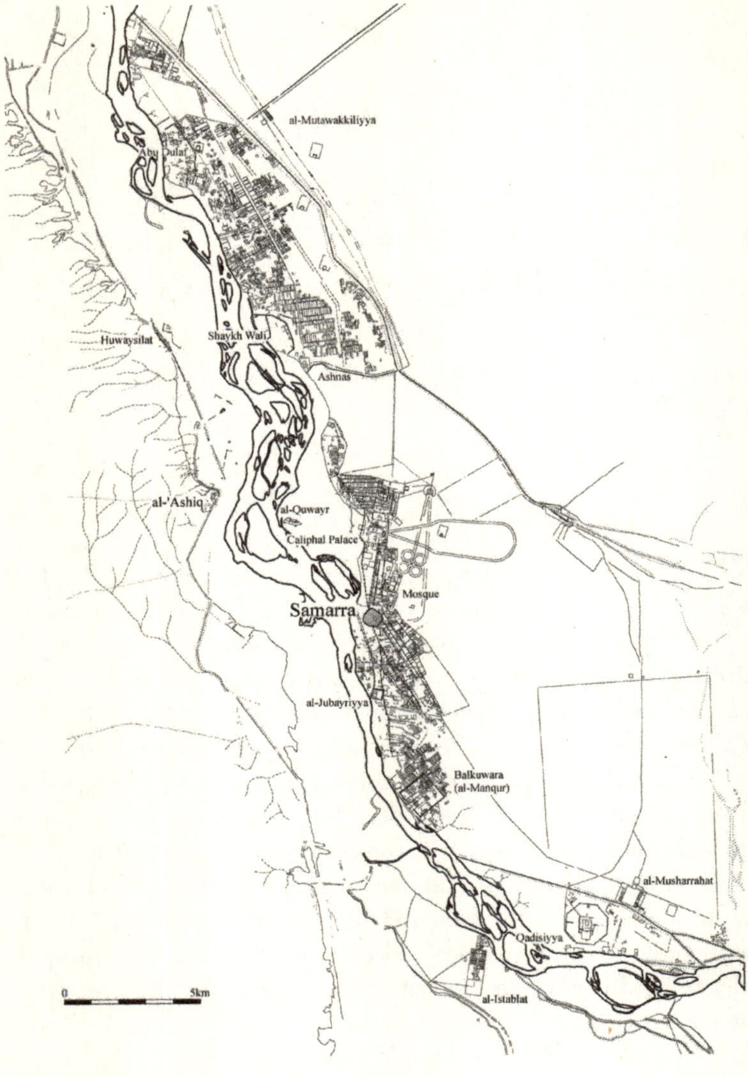

Figure 1 Archaeological site of Samarra (Samarra Archaeological Survey)

not certain where it was located. The archaeological site which might correspond to this city is however not located at Samarra itself but opposite on the west bank of the Tigris. The name of Samarra appears again in the fourth century in the account of the war of the Roman emperor, Julian the Apostate. In this account, a fortress with the name of *Sumere* appears where he was killed.

The region became important when the Sassanid king, Khusraw Anushirvan (d. 45 B.H/578), dug the canal called *al-Qatul al-Kisrawi* and intended to irrigate the land behind Baghdad. At this time, either Khusraw himself or his successor, Khusraw Parviz, (d. 6/628), built a palace at the entrance to the canal, together with a large hunting enclosure. Samarra was appreciated as good land for hunting, as it has remained to this day. One member of the royal family of Abu Dhabi has recounted to me his adventures hunting at Samarra.

After the advent of Islam, the Abbasid caliphs also thought of Samarra. Harun al-Rashid (d. 193/809), the fifth Abbasid caliph, began to build a palace-city called *al-Mubarak* to the south of Samarra but abandoned it unfinished in 180/796. Forty years later, his son, Abu Ishaq al-Muʿtasim, was faced with a political problem of rejection of his Turkish soldiers by the people of Baghdad and desired to find a new imperial city. After searching for two years, he finally settled in 221/836 on Samarra, which he renamed as *Surra Man Raʿa*. The choice seems to have been made on the basis of a good site for hunting but it was not an ideal site for a large imperial city as water was lacking and there was little agriculture in the region. Nevertheless, it grew over the reigns of eight caliphs until 279/891 until it reached a length of nearly 45 kilometres along the banks of the Tigris and covered a built-up area of 58 square kilometres, comparable with a modern city.

Most of the city was composed of the cantonments of the army, which included Arab, Iranian, and Central Asian soldiers, but also of the new city of the caliph, al-Mutawakkil, called *al-Mutawakkiliyya* (245–247/859–861). At the centre of the city, there were the markets and the first mosque, now covered by the modern city and seven avenues leading to the south, recounted in a classic description by the contemporary Abbasid geographer, al-Yaʿqubi (Figures 2 and 3). The caliph, al-Mutawakkil, added the famous congregational mosque of

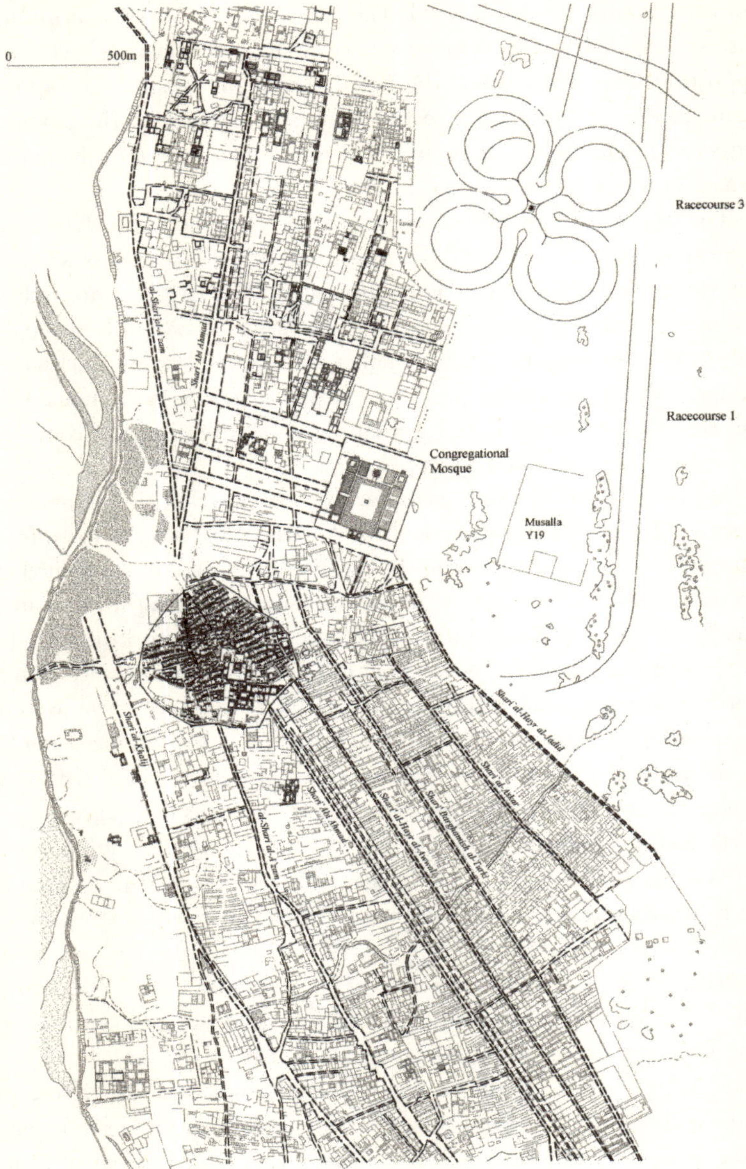

Figure 2 Askar al-Mu'tasim, the central city (Samarra Archaeological Survey)

Figure 3 The centre of the Abbasid city, with the modern city located over the markets, as in 1953

the Malwiya, built in 233–235/849–852. This mosque, with its spiral minaret, survived until the end of the eleventh century and remains today a major monument of Samarra. This older centre of the city was called *Askar al-Mu'tasim* and so people were called al-Askari, including the eleventh Imam himself.

Nevertheless, as Samarra was not a good site for a grand city, it was gradually abandoned and the population moved back to Baghdad and elsewhere, when the politics changed. Al-Mu'tadid, the sixteenth

Abbasid caliph, made the change definitive in 279/892. The houses were abandoned, the city shrank back to the core that exists today over the markets, leaving a trace that is ideal for the archaeologists to rediscover. The medieval city was of about the same dimensions as today but it was not fortified. It shrank further in the Ottoman period. The fortifications of the city which were demolished from 1936 onwards were not, however, built until 1258/1842, which resulted from a charitable donation. The donor was the Shi'i king of Oudh, Amjad Ali Shah (d. 1263/1847).[1] The town was fortified with four gates and nineteen half-round solid towers. The bricks were recovered from Abbasid buildings, notably from al-Quwayr, identified as the palace of al-Haruni.

The Imams at Samarra and their houses

Abu al-Hasan Ali b. Muhammad, the tenth Shi'i Imam, known as *al-Hadi* (the guide), was born in Madinah in 214/829. He was brought to Samarra during 233–234/848–9 at the age of twenty, by the order of al-Mutawakkil, after suspicions of sedition, to live under surveillance at the court. He was accompanied by his family, including his sons. The Imam was closely watched but left to live a peaceful life. He was known for his piety and his modesty. He died in 254/868 after 21 years in Samarra. He was succeeded by his son, al-Hasan b. Ali al-Askari, the eleventh Shi'i Imam. Al-Hasan b. Ali had been born already in Madinah in 230 or 232/844 or 847 and thus was either 22 or 24 years old. He was persecuted more than his father and spent some time in prison under al-Mu'tamid (d.279/892), the fifteenth Abbasid caliph. He survived another six years, dying in 260/873–4 after an illness. His son, Muhammad al-Qa'im, was born in 255 or 258/869 or 872 and was only young when he went into occultation, shortly after the death of his father.

According to the texts, the Imams' house was established in the area of the markets on the avenue of Shari' Abi Ahmad, close to the old mosque of al-Mu'tasim. There was also a small mosque adjacent to the house where the Imams used to pray (figure 4). When the Imams died, they were buried under the floor of the house or in the courtyard:

> In this year 254/868 died Ali b. Muhammad b. Ali b. Musa al-Rida on Monday four days remaining of Jumada al-Akhira,

and Abu Ahmad b. al-Mutawakkil prayed over him, in the avenue attributed to Abu Ahmad, and he was buried in his house.[2]

The Serdab al-Mahdi commemorates the occultation of al-Qa'im. Of course, nothing of this house is preserved today but we can deduce some conclusions about it. Shari' Abi Ahmad was one of the seven avenues of the central city, as described by al-Ya'qubi. The text of al-Ya'qubi's *Kitab al-Buldan* speaks of Samarra at a time when he visited it, probably around 245/860. These seven avenues developed after the initial foundation, the plan of which was based on a single avenue which ran the length of the site from the *dar al-khilafa* (palace of the caliph) to the southern limits of the city, passing by the markets and the early mosque of al-Mu'tasim. The avenue was 80 metres wide and 7 kilometres long with a single bend. At a later date, over nearly all of its length, the avenue was reduced in width to 18 metres; the space gained being used for new houses. In fact, analysis of the text of al-Ya'qubi shows that what is called by al-Ya'qubi as 'Shari' Abi Ahmad' is to be identified with this first avenue.[3]

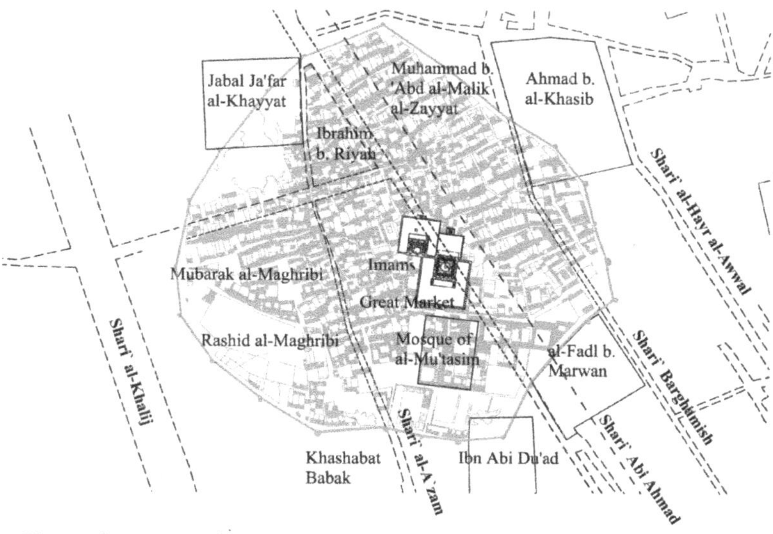

Figure 4 Location of the house of the Imams in the centre of the city (Samarra Archaeological Survey)

If we overlay the street pattern of the Abbasid city over the plan of the modern city (figure 4), we can see that the sites of the tombs are indeed located on the alignment of the avenue identified as Shari' Abi Ahmad, on its west side. Another way to derive information about the house is to note that the tombs of the Imams and the point where Muhammad al-Mahdi disappeared were certainly located in the same house. The distance between the two domes is 56.08 metres and thus we can say that the house was of a substantial size and probably oriented with its long dimensions along the avenue with minimum dimensions of 56 metres long and 20 metres wide. However, it was not among the largest houses in Samarra.

In fact, we can only judge what the house might have looked like by comparing the approximately fifty Abbasid houses excavated by the German Samarra Expedition in 1911–13 and by the Iraq Directorate of Antiquities, now the State Board of Antiquities and Heritage since 1936.[4] The houses in Abbasid Samarra were single-storey, built of sun-dried coursed earth or occasionally fired brick with gypsum plastering and flat wooden roofs. They are best known for the use of carved stucco revetments, in three styles – the Vine-leaf style, the Cross-hatched style and the Bevelled style.[5] The common form of the reception room is a T-shaped *iwan*, that is, an open-fronted room with a portico across the front (figure 5). Apart from the main courtyard and reception room, there are commonly secondary apartments, which one can imagine were allotted to different members of the family. One example, Bayt al-Zakharif, excavated in 1965, measuring 70 x 67 metres, corresponds to the minimum dimensions of the house of the Imams (figure 6). Another, house no. 4, excavated in 1936, is somewhat larger – 118 x 60 metres but is close in date, being built around 237/852 (figure 7).[6] House no. 4 also illustrates well the typical plan – developing at this time – of a front courtyard at the entrance with a reception room, in this case octagonal and behind it a number of apartments.

The construction of the shrine (Figures 8 and 9)

The history of the shrine is treated by the local historian, Yunus al-Shaykh Ibrahim al-Samarra'i, in his work, *Maraqid al-A'imma*

Figure 5 A comparable Abbasid house – House no. 5, excavated in 1983 (State Board of Antiquities and Heritage)

wal-Awliya fi Samarra.[7] The major source is a nineteenth-century verse composition, al-Shaykh Muhammad al-Samawi, *Washa'ij al-Sara' fi Sha'n Samarra*. The manuscript of this verse composition appears to be conserved in the library of the shrine.[8] Its sources for the history of the complex would appear to be the internal tradition of the institution.

The period from the death of the Imams to the final decline of the Abbasid capital city at the end of the ninth century remains little known. All we know is that the city rapidly shrank to around the market area, similar to the city of the early twentieth century, with an additional extension to the north around the congregational mosque of al-Mutawakkil, which continued to be prayed in into the eleventh century, possibly as late as 485/1092.

Circa 378/988, Ibn Hawqal described the city:

> And the city of Surra Man Ra'a in our time is shrunken (*mukhtalla*) and its districts and estates abandoned, and the people of every quarter of it have collected in a place where they have a congregational

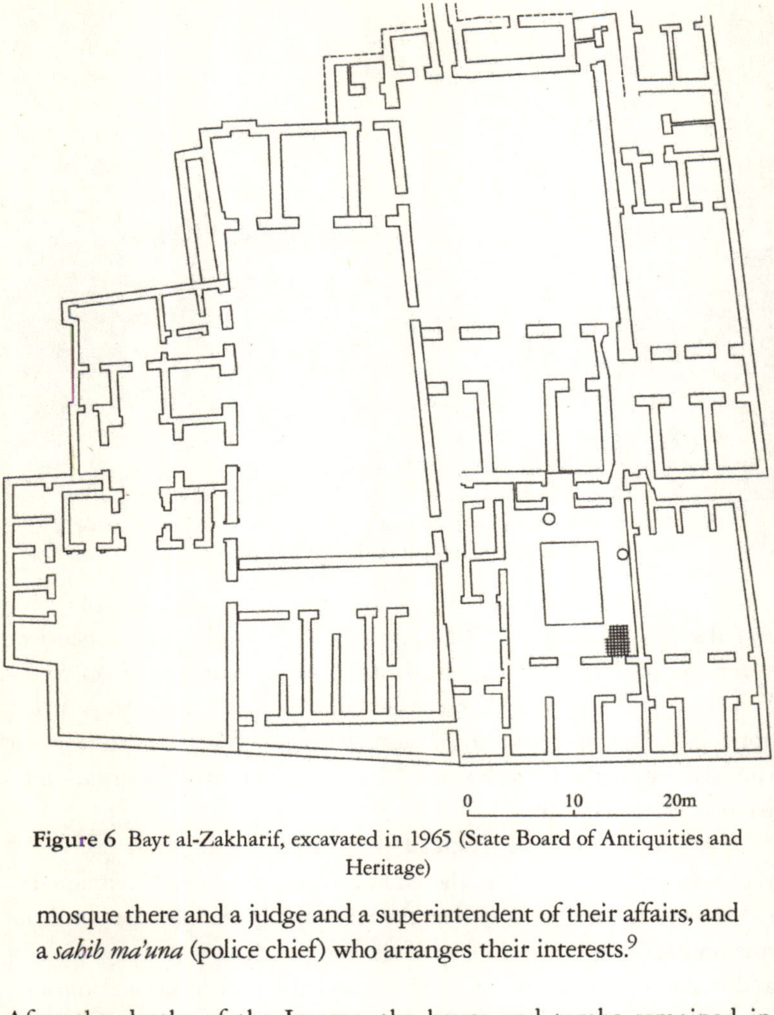

Figure 6 Bayt al-Zakharif, excavated in 1965 (State Board of Antiquities and Heritage)

mosque there and a judge and a superintendent of their affairs, and a *sahib ma'una* (police chief) who arranges their interests.[9]

After the deaths of the Imams, the house and tombs remained in their original state until 328/939–40. However, around 298/902, the tombs were plastered and a window opening was made in the wall of the house through which people could pay their respects to the graves. In addition to the Imams, Yahya and Husayn, the brothers of Ali b. Muhammad al-Hadi, were buried there, together with Hakima, the sister of Ali al-Hadi and Narjis, the wife of al-Hasan al-Askari.

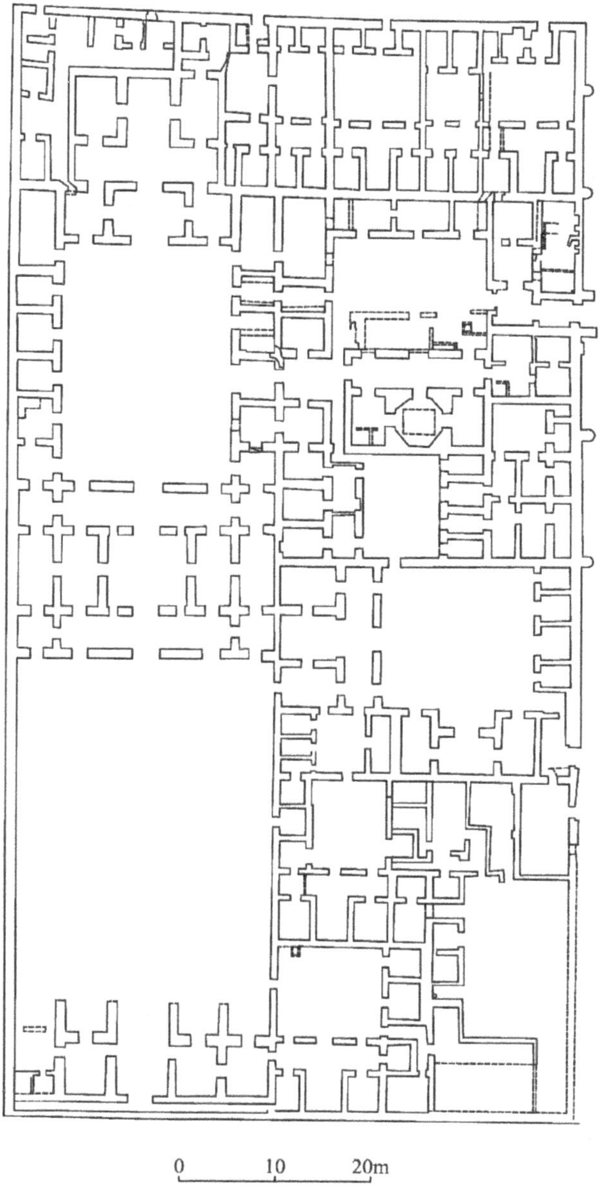

Figure 7 House no. 4, excavated in 1936 (State Board of Antiquities and Heritage)

Figure 8 Air-view of the Shrine in 1937 (University College London)

The shrine was first developed in 333/944–5 by the Hamdanid Nasir al-Dawla who built an enclosure wall for the complex and adorned the tombs with curtains. He also built houses around the shrine; one presumes for the scholars and servants. Nasir al-Dawla Hasan b. Abdallah was the Hamdanid *amir* of Mosul, which he had gained around 318/930 and in the confusion after the reign of the caliph al-Radi, moved south to occupy Baghdad in 330/942 but was pushed back north to Mosul by the arrival of the Buyid Mu'izz al-Dawla in Baghdad in 334/946.

Of course, both the Arab tribal Hamdanid and the Iranian Buyid were Shi'a and could be expected to develop the shrine. The principal builders of the shrine were in fact the Buyids. Mu'izz al-Dawla Ahmad b. Buya in 337/948–9 arranged salaries for the personnel and first built the dome over the tombs. He also first built the *sanduq* (box) from teak. In 368/978–9, Adud al-Dawla repaired the *rawda* (sanctuary)[10] with teakwood, strengthened the enclosure wall and added *arwiqa* (porticoes). It is evident that in these two phases, the shrine first took the form it has today although the present-day buildings are later.

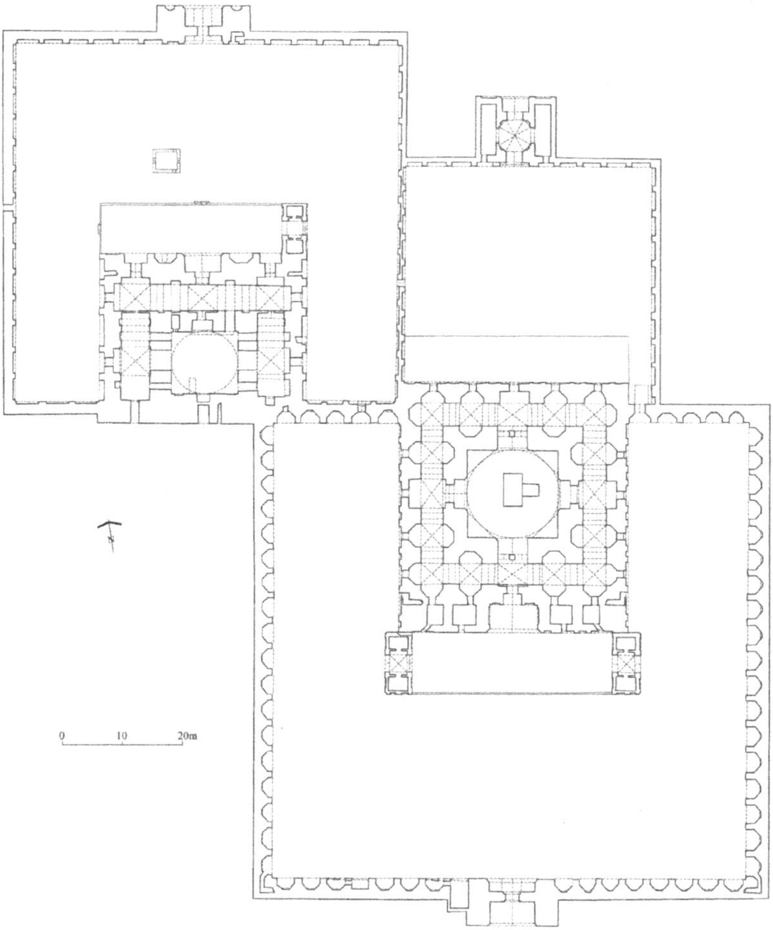

Figure 9 Plan of the shrine in the early twentieth century (State Board of Antiquities and Heritage)

The *ziyarah* also developed in the fourth/tenth century. According to Ibn Qawluwayh (d. 356/966–7) in *Kamil al-Ziyarah*:

Visit to Abu al-Hasan Ali b. Muhammad al-Hadi and Abu Muhammad Husayn b. Ali al-Askari, *alayhima al-salam* (peace be upon them) at Surra Man Ra'a. It is related from one of them that he said if you want to visit Abu al-Hasan the third Ali b.

Muhammad al-Jawad and Abu Muhammad al-Hasan al-Askari, *alayhima al-salam* (peace be upon them) you say after the ablution that I have come to their tombs, and otherwise may he die in peace, from by the gate which is on the avenue, the grill .... Pray two *rak'as* at their tombs, and if you enter the mosque and pray, you may call upon God for what you desire – He is Close and Answering – and this mosque is at the side of the Residence, and in it the two used to pray.[11]

The development of the shrine

Seventy-five years later, in 445/1053–4, the Amir Arslan al-Basasiri, originally a Turkish slave, came to Samarra. He was a general in the last years of the Buyids and fought the advance of the Saljuqs in Baghdad, intriguing and taking power in Iraq until finally killed in 451/1060. He may have been Shi'i himself but he certainly allied with the Shi'i tribal leaders, Dubays, of the Mazyadids of Hilla and Quraysh, of the Uqaylids of Mosul. At the climax, in 450/1058–9, when al-Basasiri retook Baghdad, the *khutba* (sermon) was recited in the name of the Fatimids there for nearly a year. Five years earlier in 445/1053, he had ordered a new building for the tombs at Samarra and a new *sanduq* with golden pomegranates on it.[12] However, fifty years later in 495/1101–2, it was the Sunni Saljuq Sultan, Berkyaruq b. Malikshah, who renewed the gates, repaired the dome, *arwiqa* (porticoes, pl. of *riwaq*) and courtyard.

Intervention by the Abbasid caliphs themselves came with the revival of their independence. In 606/1209–10, al-Nasir li-Din Allah undertook repair of the dome of *al-Ghayba* and the minarets. The inscription is still preserved in the Serdab al-Mahdi underneath the dome of *al-Ghayba.* It was only thirty years later in 640/1242–3 that there was a fire in the shrine and it had to be restored by the thirty-sixth Abbasid caliph, al-Mustansir (d. 640/1242) with a new wooden *sanduq:*

In the year 640, fire fell into the shrine of Surra Man Ra'a ... in the tombs of Ali al-Hadi and al-Hasan al-Askari. And so the Caliph al-Mustansir billah proceeded to the repair of the holy shrine and the noble tombs, and their restoration to their finest state.[13]

The shrine survived the Mongol invasions without problem, although there was a considerable economic decline in the region of Samarra. The majority of the smaller towns and villages around Samarra were abandoned following the Mongol invasion of Iraq in 656/1258.[14] However, this problem does not seem to have touched the shrine in Samarra.

It was a century later in 750/1349–50 that Hasan-i Buzurg, the founder and most famous of the Jalayirids, one of the successor dynasties to the Mongols, ordered work on the shrine. Hasan-i Buzurg had been governor of Rum (Anatolia) under the last Il-Khan, Abu Sa'id. The Jalayirids were close to the Shi'a. Hasan decorated the tomb and restored the dome and minarets. He also strengthened the terrace in front of the shrine *(al-bahw)*. Subsequently, it was always Shi'i powers who contributed to the development of the shrine until the end of the nineteenth century.

With the coming to power of the Shi'a in Iran under the Safavids, Iran became an important player. Even the first Safavid Shah Isma'il supplied two new boxes for the tombs in 914/1508–9. However, the first major work was by Shah Tahmasp in 930/1523–4 when the dome and *arwiqa* were rebuilt and the tombs decorated. A century later, Shah Abbas rebuilt the tomb of Ali al-Hadi and repaired the dome and *sahn* (courtyard) in 1033/1623–4. However, it was at the end of the 17th century in 1106/1694 that the sanctuary caught fire again. A lamp set fire to furnishings and then the wood of the boxes and doors. The last Safavid, Shah Husayn (d. 1134/1722), ordered the manufacture of four ornamented wooden boxes and a steel cage to go around the cenotaphs. He also paved the floors with marble.

A century later, in 1200/1785–6, a further major campaign of work was carried out by Ahmad b. Murtada Quli Khan al-Dunbuli, governor of Azerbaijan. He was a Shi'i Kurd, from the Dunbuli tribe.[15] He rebuilt the walls of the *sahn* and the staircase down into the Serdab al-Mahdi. In addition, he added a *khan*, a bathhouse and a new mosque in the city. His son Husayn covered the dome of *al-Ghayba* with tiles in 1225/1810. The constructions of Ahmad Quli Khan al-Dunbuli in the town were probably intended to provide for increasing numbers of pilgrims to Samarra. Further improvements for pilgrims took place in the second quarter of the nineteenth century. The fortifications of the city were built around 1258/1842, which was the result of a charitable donation by the Shi'i king of Oudh, Amjad Ali Shah (d. 1263/1847). A house today in Samarra is still known as *bayt al-raja* (the house of hope). In addition, *khans* were built at al-Sa'yawiya, south-east of Samarra and Balad, to provide overnight halts for pilgrims coming from Baghdad. Owing to trouble with the tribes at Harba, north of Dujayl, pilgrims crossed to the east bank of the Tigris at Balad and continued their journey on the east bank.

Thirty years later, in 1285/1868–9, the Qajars of Iran intervened. Nasir al-Din Shah repaved the *sahn*, *arwiqa* and *rawda*, replacing the steel cage of the cenotaph with a silver one with a golden top. Furthermore, he covered the dome and minarets with 72,000 gold-plated bronze tiles. He also introduced mirror mosaic for decorating the walls and ceilings. When Muhammad Hasan al-Shirazi moved from Najaf to Samarra, he also added to the complex. In 1295/1878, he supported the construction of the clock tower over the Bab al-Qibla (South Gate), equipped with a clock bought for 700 *tomans*. Finally, to receive the increasing numbers of scholars and students, a *madrasa* (religious school) was built, together with houses, baths and markets.

Modernisation of the shrine

With the beginning of the twentieth century, modernisation began to take place. In 1905 piped water was installed and in 1924–25, electricity was brought in. In 1980, the Ministry of Religious Affairs installed central heating and air conditioning. On the other hand, there was also a process of elaboration. In 1920–21, Muhammad Taqi al-Tehrani carried out extensive decorative work. This consisted of curtains, a silver door to replace the wooden door of the Serdab at the expense of King Faisal I, marble steps to the Serdab, carpets for the *rawda* at a cost of 2,000 dinars, a silver gate for arcades at a cost of 13,000 rupees, silver gates for the sanctuary and construction of gates around the *riwaq*.

Figure 10 Vertical view of the shrine in 1924

Figure 11 Helicopter view of the shrine in 2003

In 1941, a new grille was placed around the cenotaph, brought from the shrine of Husayn (d. 61/680), the third Shi'i Imam, at Karbala. In 1962–3, new gold boxes above tombs, to replace the wooden ones and three gold gates covered with glass were constructed, at the expense of charitable persons in Iraq, Kuwait and Iran. In 1979, a new silver cage decorated with pieces of gold was placed around the cenotaph. The south door of the *riwaq* was replaced with a new golden door, both manufactured in Iran.

However, there were also major additions in the twentieth century (Figures 10 and 11). The most important was the addition of a *tarma* (a pillared veranda, first found in Safavid Iran) on the main south façade in 1948–9, paid for by Hajj Abd al-Wahid Sukkar at a cost of 12,000 dinars. In 1960–1, a *tarma* was also added on the north side of the *Ghaybat al-Mahdi* (the place where al-Mahdi is said to have gone into occultation). The *sahn* around the tombs was also extended. Its original form can be seen in Figures 10 and 11. Probably in 1966, it was extended for a first time to the north. Then between 1980 and 1990, it was again extended to make a single courtyard surrounding the two shrines and a new street built around the rear. Then came the invasion of Iraq in 2003 and on 22 February 2006, the main dome was blown up.

Notes

1. Al-Samarra'i, Yunis al-Shaykh Ibraham.,*Ta'rikh Madinat Samarra*, (Baghdad, 1968), vol 3, p. 164. Oudh is the common English spelling of Awadh.
2. Al-Tabari, Muhammad b. Jarir., *Ta'rikh al-Rusul wal-Muluk*, ed. de Goeje et al., (Leiden, 1879–1901), vol 3, p. 1697.
3. Northedge, Alastair., *The Historical Topography of Samarra, Samarra Studies I* (Oxford, 2005), pp. 102–4.
4. For a complete catalogue of excavated houses, see Northedge, A., and Kennet, D., *Archaeological Atlas of Samarra, Samarra Studies* II, British Institute for Studies of Iraq/Oxbow Books (in press).
5. See Herzfeld, Ernst., *Die Ausgrabungen von Samarra I, Der Wandschmuck der Bauten von Samarra und seine Ornamentik* (Berlin, 1923).
6. See Directorate-General of Antiquities., *Hafriyyat Samarra 1936–1939*, 2 vols (Baghdad, 1940).
7. Samarra'i took his material from Dhabih Allah Al-Mahallati's book, *Ma'athir al-kubara' fi ta'rikh Samarra'*, 3 vols., (Najaf, 1931).
8. The manuscript has not been seen by this author.
9. Ibn Hawqal, Abu al-Qasim al-Nasibi., *Kitab surat al-ard*, ed. J. H. Kramers, BGA 2, (Leiden 1938–9). Fr. Tr. J. H. Kramers and G. Wiet, *Configuration de la Terre*, 2 vols. (Paris, 1964), pp. 243–4.
10. *Al-rawda* strictly means 'garden'. It was first applied to the enclosed space around the Prophet's tomb in Madinah, and was later applied to other mausolea (EI^2, s.v. masdjid).
11. Ibn Qawlawayh, Abu al-Qasim Ja'far b. Muhammad., *Kamil al-Ziyarah*. ed. Abd Husayn al-Amini al-Tabrizi (Najaf, 1356/1937), ch. 103.
12. There had already been a fire in 407/1017 but the damage was light.
13. See Ibn al-Futi, Abdu al-Razaq ibn Ahmad al-Shaybani., *al-Hawadith al-Jamiah wa al-Tajarib al-Nafiah fi al-Miah al-Sabiah* (Baghdad, 1932).
14. Northedge, Alastair., *The Historical Topography of Samarra, Samarra Studies I*, (Oxford, 2005), pp. 43–62.
15. Glasse, Cyril. *Encyclopaedia of Islam*, 2nd Edition, (Leiden ,1954–2003), EI^2, sv. Kurds.

CHAPTER 3

REBUILDING AL-ASKARIYYAIN SHRINE

Usam Ghaidan

Every so often in human history there comes a period of such supreme brilliance one can only ponder and admire. One such time was about 3,000 BCE when humanity first achieved civilisation and developed the technology of irrigation. This happened in the city of Uruk on an arm of the Euphrates in southern Iraq. There an unknown man or woman invented writing, forever liberating the language from the speaker and setting into motion an historical process which has continued ever since.

Four thousand years had to pass before a period with comparable energy came. That was around the middle of the second/ninth century in the newly founded city of Samarra on the eastern bank of the River Tigris. Its construction began in 221/836. Thanks to the wealth and stability of the Abbasids and the confidence necessary to push through projects, Samarra grew very quickly to become what may be termed the first world city in history.

In every branch of life – philosophy, technology, music, medicine, mathematics, art and architecture – there was an outpouring of energy. A cash-based economy created during the early Islamic world meant a massive amount of coinage was put into circulation leading to urbanisation and revitalisation of commercial life. This attracted scientists, scholars and craftsmen from the rest of the Muslim world as well as from the towns and cities of Byzantium and Persia.

A hybrid culture began to take shape. This took the form of a nominally Arabic but diverse and rich merger with the literacy and opulence of Persia and Byzantium, along with echoes of Greece and Rome. The cross-fertilisation resulting from the interaction amongst the varying cultural and social traditions proved propitious to artistic and architectural development. The caliphs, scholars, philosophers and *imams* (religious leaders) of Samarra were all larger than life and contributed to the cultural growth of the city.

This Chapter traces the historical and architectural origin of al-Askariyyain shrine in the ninth century Abbasid capital and describes its design features as a significant example of Islamic tomb design. It also discusses its importance as an economic resource for the people of Samarra, heritage monument for the people of Iraq and a pilgrim destination for Muslims hailing from all parts of the world. The second part of my Chapter focuses on the nature of the two attacks al-Askariyyain shrine suffered in 2006 and 2007.

As a conservation architect, my approach to this Chapter is descriptive and illustrative to give the reader a feel of how the shrine was built as well as its current status. Therefore, to differentiate this Chapter from other Chapters dealing with the shrine's heritage, I would like to highlight the current reconstruction work which is taking place under the direction of the UNESCO Iraq office. My Chapter ends by outlining the importance of this reconstruction for shoring up hope and reinforcing the ongoing reconciliation efforts in Iraq.

Legacies in Samarra and their effects on the shrine

Two legacies are relevant to al-Askariyyain shrine. The first is Habshiyya, the Greek-Christian wife of caliph al-Mutawakkil (the tenth Abbasid caliph) and mother of his successor, al-Muntasir. She ordered the erection of a monumental tomb for her son, Qubbat al-Sulaibiyya, on the west bank of the Tigris opposite the great mosque with the spiral minaret.

The building consists of two concentric octagons; the outer has pointed arched entrances and the inner is covered by a dome, 6 metres in diameter and 9.5 metres high, resting on a drum formed by 8 arches. The building was restored by the Iraqi State Board of Antiquities and Heritage in the 1970s. As far as we know, this was the earliest monumental tomb in the history of Islam (Figure 1).

All the caliphs before al-Muntasir followed the funerary rites handed down to them from the time of the Prophet Muhammad, namely to be buried in simple graves. Al-Muntasir was the first to have a purpose-built mausoleum. Incredibly this break with tradition was vindicated by the spread of domed shrines throughout the Islamic world. Less than two centuries after its erection, the monumental tomb became a building type in its own right, as important as the mosque and the palace. From the fourth/eleventh century onwards, the construction of shrines over the graves of important and holy individuals became a standard practice throughout the lands of Islam.

The second person whose legacy is intertwined with that of the Samarra shrine is Ali al-Hadi, the tenth of the Shi'i *Ithna-Ashari*

Figure 1 Qubbat al-Sulaibiyya: The first monumental mausoleum in Islam, built for the Abbasid caliph al-Muntasir

(Twelver) Imams. In 236/851, he and his son were forcibly evicted by al-Mutawakkil from their home in Madinah where he had dedicated himself to religious teaching. They were brought to Samarra to be under the watch of the caliph's men. After his death in 254/868, al-Hadi was buried in the courtyard of his house. The *Imamah* (religious leadership) passed to his son, the eleventh Imam, al-Hasan al-Askari, who was buried next to his father when he died in 260/874. The *Imamah* then fell to his five-year old son, Muhammad al-Mahdi, who went into *ghayba* (occultation) for his own safety in the same year. Near the tombs of the two Imams is the basement of *al-Ghaybah* from which it is believed that he disappeared and will return to bring justice to the world. The tombs and basement began to attract religious visitors seeking the *shafa'a* (intercession) of the holy men. The influx of pilgrims ensured the survival of the neighbourhood around the house after Samarra was deserted in 278/892 when caliph al-Mu'tadid (the sixteenth Abbasid caliph) moved the capital to Baghdad in that same year.

The house and tomb remained in their original state until 332/944 when the Hamdanid Nasir al-Dawla enclosed the tombs with a wall and built houses around the shrine. This tells us that the shrine had now become an established pilgrimage destination. By the time the Buyid leader, Mu'izz al-Dawla, embarked on his expansion project in 336/948, the shrine had assumed cult status; pilgrims had got into the habit of taking handfuls of soil from the floor of the *sahn* (courtyard), which they considered to be holy because the Imams had sometimes used it for the purpose of *tayammum* (dry ablution). This had created depressions in the floor of the *sahn* which the builders had to refill with new soil. The dome which Mu'izz al-Dawla built was of mud bricks; 74 years later, another Buyid leader, al-Amir Arsalan al-Bassasiri, replaced it with one built of baked bricks. In 605/1209, during the reign of the Abbasid caliph, Nasir li-din Allah, a mosque was added and the complex took the form it had, before it was blown up in 2006.

The Hamdanis and Buyids were of course Shi'i dynasties but the Sunni dynasties were just as involved in the reconstruction of the shrines: the Seljuk ruler Berkiarook b. Malikshah renewed the gates and repaired the dome, *riwaq* (portico) and *sahn* in 499/1106.

Figure 2 The view of al-Askariyyain shrine from the south of the city

The shrine is a lofty, square masonry structure measuring 42.21 metres x 36.72 metres; its thick walls are built of *farshi* (square-shaped baked bricks). The central tombs' *haram* (sanctuary) was surmounted by two domes; the outer one was onion-shaped. In 1286/1868-9, it was covered with 72,000 gold-plated bronze panels by the Qajari sultan, Nasir al-Din Shah (Figure 2).

Attached to the south facade is the main entrance veranda which has a high central portion flanked by low wings on the sides (Figure 3). The veranda leads to the shrine through a *pishtaq* (central arched portal) 5 meters deep and 12 metres high. Left and right of the veranda, two slender minarets rise about 35 metres from cylindrical bases. The minarets were built in 606/1210. In 1303/1886, the same Qajari sultan Nasir al-Din Shah had them clad in gold-plated bronze panels.

Passing through the portal, one enters the *riwaq* which runs around the central sanctuary. Its floor is paved in white marble and its walls are decorated with mirror mosaic. The external surfaces of the *riwaq* walls are clad in marble to a height of 1.9 metres, above which are decorative glazed tiles.

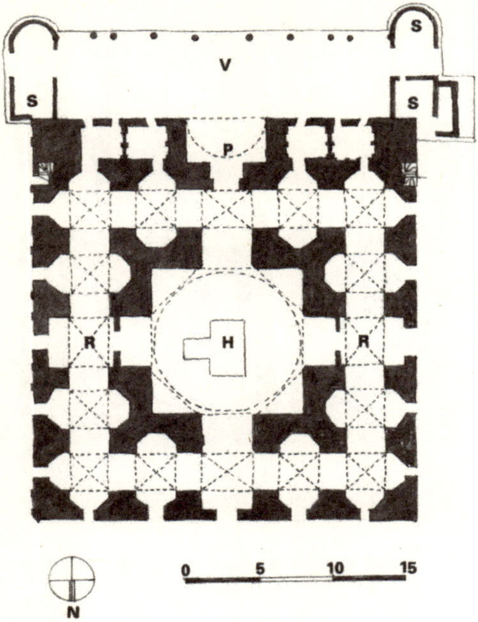

Figure 3 A plan of al-Askariyyain shrine

There are four tombs in the *haram* belonging to the two Imams, the wife of the eleventh and sister of the tenth. On each of the tombs is a carved wooden box; one of them is dated 502/1109 and carries the name of the Safavid sultan, Shah Husayn. The area of the *haram* is 15 metres to a side and is surrounded by 4 metre thick walls which support the domes above; their lower parts are finished in marble and the top parts are clad in glittering mirror mosaic, as is the inside surface of the inner dome. The mirrors are cut into polygonal, triangular and star shapes; the light reflected from them makes a stunning visual and psychological impact, symbolic of the light with which God illuminates the heavens in the Qur'an in 24:35 and 41:12.[1]

Above the *haram* is a double-shell dome, the largest of all the Shi'i shrines in Iraq; it has an external diameter of 22.43 metres and internal diameter of 14.44 metres. The apex of the outer shell is 32 metres

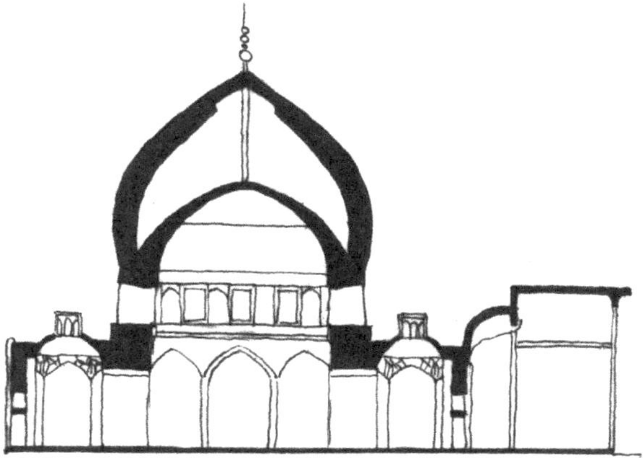

Figure 4 An illustration showing the double dome of al-Askariyyain shrine

above the ground floor; that of the inner one is 23 metres high. The domes sit on a drum 5 metres high pierced by 12 windows bridged by 4-centre (onion-shaped) arches (Figure 4).

The explosions

Al-Askariyyain Shrine was the target of two explosions. The first, which took place in the morning of Wednesday 22 February 2006, demolished the dome (Figure 5). Some of the debris from the outer dome fell on the roof of the *arwiqa* and destroyed it. Large pieces of the inner dome, some about 20m^3 weighing over 30 tons, fell inside the *haram* destroying the grilled cage around the cenotaph and created depressions in the floor below it and around it. The gold-plated panels cladding the dome and minarets were dispersed over an area of one kilometre radius. Explosives were also placed at the entrance of *al-Ghaybah* basement[2] and inside it; they damaged the ceilings, walls and destroyed the entrance veranda. The second explosion which took place on Wednesday 13 June 2007 demolished the two minarets (Figure 6). The debris from one of them fell on the western veranda and from the other on the eastern wall, damaging both of them.

Figure 5 The demolished dome of the shrine after the first explosion which occurred on Wednesday 22nd February 2006

Figure 6 The demolished minaret of the shrine after the second explosion which occurred on Wednesday 13th June 2007

Experts have identified the explosives used as Composition 4 or C-4. This is a very high velocity explosive, which is nearly one and a half times as potent as trinitrotoluene or TNT. It is supplied in bulk in drums, in a slightly powdery form. Upon manipulation, the material immediately solidifies into a plasticised rubbery mass which may be kneaded and pressed into any shape. Its shelf life is more than 10 years. The explosives were placed inside the dome space, which is an unventilated enclosure with no possibility for the gases to escape to relieve the pressure in order to cause maximum damage. When detonated, C-4 creates a chemical explosion involving the rapid oxidation of fuel elements (carbon and hydrogen atoms) forming part of the explosive compound. The compound decomposes violently with the evolution of heat and the production of gas. The rapid expansion of the gas creates blast waves in the air reaching speeds of between 1,500 and 9,000 metres per second and pressures from 100–300 kilobars at a temperature of about 3,000–4,000°C forcing the surrounding air out of the volume it occupies. The domes were built of bricks and gypsum mortar, not strong enough to resist dynamic loads of this magnitude. As a result, the entire external dome and more than half the inner dome were blown away, falling on the other parts of the structure and damaging them.

The attacks set off waves of sectarian killings that claimed tens of thousands of lives in all parts of Iraq. The Iraqi government turned to UNESCO, in its capacity as the United Nations' heritage agency, to organise the task of reconstructing the shrine. This was seen as a pivotal step towards fixing the damage caused by the slaughter that pushed the country to the brink of civil war.

A memorandum of understanding was signed between the Iraq government and UNESCO whereby the latter was to formulate a project for rebuilding the shrine. In September 2007, one of the elders of the town of Samarra was appointed as a UNESCO consultant and charged with the task of preparing the site for the rebuilding operations. He put together a security team to guard the site and recruited local workers to clear the debris from the courtyards and building. By April 2008, almost all debris from inside the building and the surrounding courts was moved outside the site. The heap measured approximately 18,000 m^3 and weighed more than 20,000 tons, about a third of the weight of the Empire State Building in New York.

Accommodation for the personnel and workers who were soon to be employed on the site was prepared. This meant turning one of the existing rooms into a kitchen, erecting six caravans, providing 27 tons of air-conditioning, five water coolers, office furniture, rehabilitating existing toilets, showers and drains, providing running cold and hot water, floodlights, generator and working tools. By the beginning of February 2009, the shrine building had become a secure and self-contained work camp.

During February and March 2009, six visits by international consultants were arranged by UNESCO. They directed the debris-clearing work and put in place a system for identifying and sorting valuable items contained in the rubble and storing them for future reuse or display. They took samples of building materials for analysis abroad and presented reports containing an assessment of the state of the building after the explosions and a preliminary appraisal of the standing structure.

In April 2006, I went to the site as project supervisor. My job was to represent UNESCO on the site and in meetings with the local authorities and town's civil society. I was also to ensure that the reconstruction work which followed acknowledged international guidelines for dealing with heritage buildings. I worked together with a team of young architects, engineers and surveyors from the Iraqi government who came to survey the standing remains of the building and, by reference to old documents and photographs, produce plans, sections and elevations of the structure as it was before the attacks of February 2006 and June 2007. Fortunately, there was enough in the standing remains to enable producing accurate drawings of the arches, domes and vaults all of which were of the four-centre type. These were used to prepare steel moulds to aid in the rebuilding of the *riwaq* roof (Figure 7).

Figure 7 Rebuilding the domed roof of the shrine

The drawings were later handed over to the consultant who was appointed by UNESCO to prepare the working drawings for the reconstruction. The contract of implementation was given to a committee formed by the office of the Prime Minister. The consultant and contractor were required by the terms of the UNESCO contract to stick to the same materials and work methods of the original structure. Where modern materials had to be employed for whatever reason they had to be used in a manner that did not compromise the traditional look of the structure. This was the case with rebuilding the new domes. Here steel girders were used as structural members hidden behind brick walls externally and internally (Figure 8).

From the outset, close contact was maintained with Samarra's civil society. Town elders were briefed regularly on the progress of work and other aspects of the project. During the first three months of site preparation, the project provided employment for hundreds of local men. Later these were joined by young men from other parts of Iraq. Working together on one site and seeing the result of their joint effort was the best recipe for achieving national reconciliation. The rebuilding began in May 2008. For ordinary Iraqis, there was

Figure 8 The design for the new dome

only one way to mark the occasion: visit the shrine by the hundreds impelled by a desire to replace the hate which the terrorists came to sow in Samarra with hope in the future of their country. Indeed, it is hope that will eventually triumph and dissolve the terrorists' evil energy into oblivion.

The continued importance and future of the shrine

The shrine is located in the centre of the town, which covers an area of about 40 hectares containing around 2,000 residences (Figure 9). The majority of the population has relied for its livelihood on income accrued directly from religious tourism. On a normal day, Samarra could expect about 1,000 pilgrims; the number rose to 3,000 on Fridays and increased on special religious days. It is clear that the shrine not only provides material sustenance to the people of Samarra but also expresses and nurtures the spiritual life of large communities of believers in Iraq and outside it. It plays a cultural role in the formation

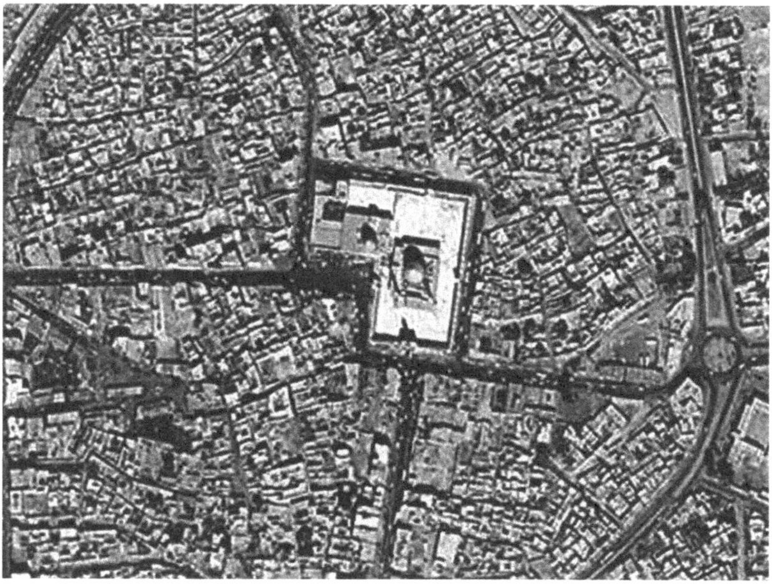

Figure 9 A satellite view of the town around al-Askariyyain shrine

of individual and communal identities for hundreds of thousands, if not millions of people.

The design of the shrine is the culmination of a process that began with Qubbat al-Sulaibiyya in Samarra at the end of the second/ninth century and reached its zenith under the Buyids at the beginning of the fourth/eleventh century when its plan took its final form. The central chamber and surrounding vestibules concentrating their axes on the single central focal point, the tomb, echo the centralisation of God in the universe and represent the highest expression of the spiritual life of Muslims.

One of the ghastly lessons to be drawn from the destruction of the shrine is the fragility of culture in times of civil unrest. The iconic nature

Figure 10 An entrance in the shrine is destroyed by the bombings

Figure 11 Builders clearing up the rubble of the shrine

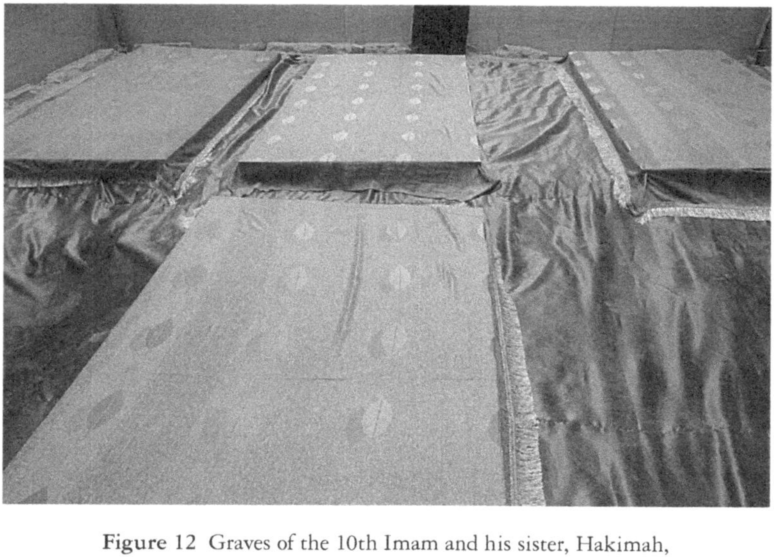

Figure 12 Graves of the 10th Imam and his sister, Hakimah, and 11th Imam and his wife, Narjis

Figure 13 Damaged mausoleum containing the graves of the 10th Imam and his sister, Hakimah, and 11th Imam and his wife, Narjis

Figure 14 View of the damaged shrine

of heritage buildings makes them preferred targets for professional terrorist groups. The rebuilding project is seen as a statement against terror and the involvement of UNESCO supported by the European community is proof that the world today has a far more effective system for protection of important monuments and sites than it used to have. UNESCO, ICCROM[3], ICOMOS[4] together with many other specialised international organisations now list monuments, monitor threats and help sustain sites more comprehensively than in the past. The opposition to the willed destruction of heritage is growing and it is organised.

Notes

1. 'Allah is the light of the heavens and the earth; a likeness of His light is as a niche in which is a lamp, the lamp is in a glass, (and) the glass is as it were a brightly shining star, lit from a blessed olive-tree, neither eastern nor western, the oil whereof almost gives light though fire touch it not – light upon light – Allah guides to His light whom He pleases, and Allah sets forth parables for men, and Allah is cognizant of all things' (24:35) and 'So He ordained them seven heavens in two periods, and revealed in every heaven its affair; and We adorned the lower heaven with brilliant stars and (made it) to guard; that is the decree of the Mighty, the Knowing' (41:12).
2. The place where the 12th Imam, Muhammad al-Mahdi, is said to have gone into occultation.
3. The International Centre for the Study of the Preservation and Restoration of Cultural Property.
4. The International Council on Monuments and Sites.

PART II

THE LIFE AND LEGACY OF RELIGIOUS AND SCHOLARLY FIGURES IN SAMARRA'S HISTORY

CHAPTER 4

THE POLITICAL TURMOIL FACING IMAM ALI AL-HADI AND IMAM HASAN AL-ASKARI

Sayyid Qamar Abbas

Ali al-Hadi and Hasan al-Askari, the tenth and eleventh Shi'i Imams, are known as al-Askariyyain (dwellers in the camp) because they were garrisoned for most of their life in Samarra. They were put under house arrest, spied upon and carefully monitored by the Abbasid caliphs. My aim in this Chapter is to examine the life of both Imams but in particular the political difficulties which they found themselves in. This involves analysing the kind of threats they faced in their lives, the strife within the Abbasid government at the time and the way they guided the Shi'a under these circumstances.

An insight into the history of Shi'i *Imamah* (leadership)

Samarra has a great affiliation for Shi'i Muslims because Ali al-Hadi and Hasan al-Askari, who are buried there, represent the continuing line of *Imamah* since Prophet Muhammad. Samarra also contains the last known residence of Muhammad al-Mahdi, the twelfth and concealed Shi'i Imam. In Shi'i theology, al-Mahdi is hidden by Allah for his safety and he has lived in hiding since. Al-Mahdi is expected to bring peace and justice to humanity at a time when it would be filled with injustice and strife. In order to appreciate the significance of the status of Ali al-Hadi and Hasan al-Askari as Imams, a brief discussion on the history of the Shi'i *Imamah* is necessary.

Shi'i Muslims believe Prophet Muhammad chose his successor after his farewell *hajj* (pilgrimage). It is reported he said, 'I have left among you two weighty matters which if you cling to them, you shall not be led into error after me. One of them is greater than the other. The book of Allah, which is a rope stretched from heaven to earth and my progeny, the people of my house. These two shall not part ways until they return to the pool (of paradise).'[1] The Shi'i believe this statement was for the family of his daughter, Fatimah. In particular, Fatimah's husband, Ali b. Abi Talib, was explicitly designated as the Prophet's successor and first Imam by the Prophet himself at a place known as *Ghadir al-Khumm* (the Pond of Khumm); though the Shi'i refer to many narrations before this event which show the Prophet indicating Ali as his successor.

According to the Shi'i, however, Ali's right to succession was usurped soon after Prophet Muhammad's demise when a minority of the Prophet's companions chose Abu Bakr as the next caliph at the *Saqifah* (portico) of Banu Sa'ida. There both groups of immigrants and Madinans laid claims to the Prophet's successorship. Although Ali had acquired the status of the Prophet's confidante, it was pointed out at saqifah as well as later on by Umar b. Khattab that 'the people did not like having prophethood and caliphate joined together in your (the clan of Hashim) house.'[2] There was a faint discussion about Ali's claim to succession but that was soon to be put away.[3]

After the death of the Prophet, the Muslim community saw three eras of caliphs which were not from the Prophet's family. This caused huge discontentment amongst Muslims towards the end of era of the third caliph, Uthman b. Affan. His appointed governors were mostly from his clan of Banu Umayyah, which had been a staunch opposition to Prophet Muhammad and Ali. These governors were involved in corruption, immorality and nepotism.[4] After Uthman was assassinated, Ali was selected as the fourth caliph, but by then corrupt governors had taken refuge in Damascus, which was ruled by the Umayyad family. After Ali was martyred, his son Hasan was expected to continue the line of *Imamah*. However, Mu'awiyah disputed this and upon a peace treaty which Hasan agreed to in order to prevent bloodshed amongst supporters from each side, Mu'awiyah became the first Umayyad caliph. Importantly, the treaty emphasised that the caliphate should be returned to Husayn, Hasan's brother, after Mu'awiyah's reign. Considering that a treaty was agreed upon, the expectation of the Shi'a that their next caliph would be Husayn was firmly present. However, this expectation was not met when Mu'awiyah broke the terms of the treaty by nominating his son, Yazid, as the next caliph.

Though the Shi'a cite *Ghadir al-Khumm* as well as the broken treaty by Mu'awiyah as principal events which gave them a distinct identity as followers of Ali b. Abi Talib, it was the battle of Karbala in 61/680 which gave the Shi'a greater impetus and implanted this usurpation deeply into their hearts. The battle of Karbala was significant because Ali b. Abi Talib's son, Husayn, was brutally martyred along with his family (including children) at the hands of Yazid b. Mu'awiyah.[5] Husayn refused to give allegiance to Yazid because he was a corrupt and immoral man.[6] Yazid eventually ordered his large army to kill Husayn, his family and small band of companions. The tragedy continues to remain in the hearts of the Shi'a today precisely because it was such an overt disruption of the Shi'i *Imamah*. Even Husayn's son and the fourth Shi'i Imam, Zayn al-Abidin (who was ill during the battle of Karbala) was put in chains and not allowed to express his *Imamah*. According to the Shi'a, the sequence and importance of *Imamah* has also been stated by Imams after Husayn such as the sixth Shi'i Imam, Ja'far al-Sadiq, who said, 'after the Prophet, Ali was the leader, then Hasan, then Husayn, then Ali, son of Husayn, then Muhammad, son of Ali was the leader. Whoever refuted them will refute the knowledge of God and knowledge of the Prophet.'[7]

The martyrdom of Husayn and the death of Zayn al-Abidin saw Zayn al-Abidin's son, Muhammad al-Baqir, take the mantle as the fifth Imam on 94/712. During this time, there was greater freedom to guide and teach the Shi'a with numerous students studying under al-Baqir. Al-Mufid reports that al-Baqir had

> outstanding merit in traditional knowledge, asceticism and leadership. He was the most renowned of them, the one among them who was most esteemed by both non-Shi'a and Shi'a , and the most able of them ... the surviving Companions (of the Prophet), the leading members of the next generation and the leaders of the Muslim jurists reported the principal features of religion on his authority.[8]

Al-Baqir was, however, poisoned and his son, Ja'far al-Sadiq continued to lead the Shi'a as the sixth Imam. He also had some freedom to express his leadership through his knowledge and established institutes of learning, teaching students like the scientist, Jabir b. Hayyan (Geber) and scholars like Abu Hanifa and Malik b.Anas. He was poisoned on caliph al-Mansur's instructions in 147/765.[9]

After Ja'far al-Sadiq, his son, Musa al-Kadhim, became the seventh Imam but he was imprisoned for a long period by the fifth Abbasid caliph, Harun al-Rashid and finally poisoned on 183/799. Al-Kadhim's son and grandson, Ali al-Ridha (the eighth Imam) and Muhammad al-Taqi (the ninth Imam) were given positions by caliph al-Ma'mun but he always felt threatened by their presence and influence on the Muslim community. Although al-Ridha is reputed to have saved al-Ma'mun's caliphate from times of rebellion[10], al-Ma'mun sent instructions to his close aides to kill al-Ridha, which occurred in 202/818. Al-Ridha's son, Muhammad al-Taqi, became the Imam at just eight years of age but did not live long. In 219/835, on the instructions of the Abbasid caliph al-Mu'tasim, al-Taqi was poisoned at the age of 25 years by his wife, Umm al-Fazal (who was also caliph al-Mu'tasim's sister). According to the Shi'a, Umm al-Fazal was married to al-Taqi for political reasons to keep the Shi'a calm during the caliphate of al-Mu'tasim.[11] The death of al-Taqi saw his son, Ali al-Hadi, assume the mantle of Imam.

From the above, we find that the line of *Imamah* is extremely important for the Shi'a because it signifies a continuation of Divine leadership, initiated by the Prophet's appointment of Ali b. Abi Talib as his successor. The fact that Ali al-Hadi assumed the position of Imam after a continuing string of usurpation by the Umayyad and Abbasid dynasties exemplifies the heavy burden on his shoulders to guide the Muslim community. It also showed that the oppression against himself and his family was unrelenting, which immediately restricted how he could demonstrate his knowledge and moral leadership. I now turn to his life.

Ali al-Hadi's early life and the political situation of the Abbasid caliphate

Like all other Imams, al-Hadi was also born in Madinah. Another narration states that there was a small village near Madinah called 'Sarayya' where he was born.[12] His actual name was Ali. His mother was called Sumanah, also known as Umm al-Walad or Umm al-Fazal. She was from the offspring of Ali b. Abi Talib's close companion, Ammar b. Yasir. The birthplace of al-Hadi points to an interesting trend; all the Shi'i Imams were born in the Hijaz. Ali b. Abi Talib was born in Makkah whereas the ten Imams after him were born in or around Madinah. This demonstrates the level of loyalty the Prophet's descendants had with the Prophet's burial place of Madinah and the importance they gave in preserving the Shi'i faith in the nucleus city of the Muslim state. Al-Hadi's date of birth is documented as 15th Dhu al-Hijjah 212/5th March 828,[13] though some historians have given his date of birth as 5th Rajab 214/7th September 829.[14] Although his name was Ali he was called by his titles (as per Arab tradition). His most famous titles are *al-Naqi* (the pure), *al-Hadi* (the guide), *al-Qayam* (the one who rises), *al-Faqih* (the jurist), *al-Amin* (the trustworthy) and *al-Tayyab* (the pure). He was also known as *Abu al-Hasan al-Thalith* (father of Hasan, the third).[15]

Al-Hadi was born during the reign of al-Ma'mun. Al-Ma'mun died in 217/833 after he got food poisoning whilst eating dates and river water. He was buried in Tarsus in current south central Turkey[16] and was succeeded by his half-brother, Abu Ishaq al-Mu'tasim. Al-Mu'tasim summoned al-Hadi's father, Muhammad al-Taqi, to Baghdad in 219/835 for the second time. In al-Taqi's previous trip to Baghdad, he got married to al-Ma'mun's daughter, Umm al-Fazal and narrations say that after her marriage, she moved to Madinah. However, she never liked living there and wrote to her father complaining about al-Taqi. Al-Ma'mun did not pay any attention to her grievances but after al-Ma'mun's death, al-Mu'tasim, who had vocally opposed this marriage, summoned them back to Baghdad where al-Taqi was imprisoned and then poisoned in 219/835.[17] Ali al-Hadi was only eight years old when he became an orphan in Madinah. Al-Hadi's age and distance from Baghdad lessened the political worries of al-Mu'tasim in watching al-Hadi's influence on the Muslim communities in Arabia. However, al-Mu'tasim did keep an eye on al-Hadi by appointing the scholar, Ubaydullah Junaydi, as his teacher. The aim was to brainwash the young al-Hadi and to monitor his movements. Interestingly, however, it is reported that Ubaydullah Junaydi was unable to teach al-Hadi anything since he was extremely knowledgeable, despite his young age.[18]

During al-Mu'tasim's tenure as caliph, al-Hadi witnessed scattered uprisings all over the kingdom. Al-Mu'tasim crushed the Khurramiyyah revolt in Iran in 217/833 as well those in surrounding areas such as the revolts of Muhammad b. Qasim Alavi in Taloqan (current Northern Afghanistan) and of Babak Khorramdin in Azerbaijan. The uprisings showed the discontentment of communities under al-Mu'tasim's reign. For the Shi'a, however, al-Mu'tasim's preoccupation with these uprisings gave breathing space to al-Hadi. During this time, al-Hadi managed to develop a close circle of friends and followers. For example, Aslam b. Mahraz Abu al-Ghaus used to recite poetry in al-Hadi's praise, Ali b. Ja'far Hamadani was delegated by al-Hadi to gather *khums* (one-fifth charity tax) and ibn Band and ibn Asim were killed by the Abbasids for their favours to al-Hadi in Baghdad.[19] This demonstrated the loyalty which al-Hadi inspired in his followers.

Al-Hadi was also able to teach students from a variety of backgrounds in their own languages including Persians, Slavs, Indians and Nabataeans. His knowledge went beyond legal and scientific areas and he is attributed to foreknowing future events such as storms and deaths. Al-Hadi's students included jurists like Sahl b. Ya'qub Abu Nawas, Ahmad b. Hamza Alyasa, Saleh b. Muhammad Hamadani, Muhammad b. Jazak al-Jamal, Ja'far b. Suhayl Sayqal, Dawud b. Zayd, Abu Sulayman Zankan, Husayn b. Muhammad Madayni, Bashar b. Bashar Nishapuri Shazani, Saleem b. Ja'far Muzuri, Ali b. Mahzyar, Abu al-Hashim Jafri, Ali b. Ja'far Hamadani, Ayyub b. Nuh, Abu Muhammad Basri, Muhammad b. Faraj, Saleh b. Said and many others.

In 836, however, there was another threat to al-Mu'tasim's caliphate by the *ghilman*. The *ghilman* were initially slaves, mainly of Turkish origin, captured by the Abbasids. The *ghilman* soon formed larger armies and brought many episodes of unrest to Baghdad. Fearing this, al-Mu'tasim decided to move his capital to the northern town of Samarra. By the time the capital had moved to Samarra, al-Hadi had endured the tenures of al-Ma'mun (813–833) and al-Mu'tasim (833–842). As we shall see, he would have to endure the further reigns of al-Wathiq (841–847) and al-Mutwakkil (847–861). Al-Hadi's existence in Madinah was one of restriction, pressure and increasing strife. The relative freedom he had only allowed him to express his knowledge to loyal groups around him. Other than that, he was generally kept under a watchful eye by the caliphs. This continued in Samarra.

Samarra and al-Hadi's travel to Iraq

Before al-Mu'tasim's death in 227/842, he tried to develop Samarra by extending the area of his palace and building residences and camps for the army generals. This development was continued by al-Wathiq, al-Mu'tasim's son and successor. Al-Wathiq had a short tenure before dying of high fever but had an interest in promoting culture and literature.[20] Al-Wathiq extended the garrison called *Askar al-Mu'tasim* into a real city.[21] Al-Wathiq's death in 847, however, saw his brother Ja'far al-Mutawakkil assume the position of caliph.

Al-Mutawakkil's reign was more turbulent than his predecessors. As soon as he came to power, he succeeded in arresting and killing the Prime Minister, Muhammad b. Abd al-Malik and went on to crush the growing number of rebellions against his rule. His cruelty to al-Hadi and the Shi'a was no exception. He desecrated the graves of Husayn b. Ali and his companions and made sure the river water ran over the graves in order to conceal them.[22] He specifically turned his attention to al-Hadi and summoned him to Samarra from Madinah. Al-Hadi became a cause for concern to al-Mutawakkil because the governor of Madinah, Abdullah b. Muhammad, wrote various letters to al-Mutawakkil complaining about al-Hadi's increasing influence on the Muslim community. In learning about this exchange, al-Hadi wrote a letter to al-Mutawakkil to explain his position. Finally, al-Mutawakkil decided to summon al-Hadi to Samarra.[23]

Al-Hadi arrived in Samarra in 233/848 with his wife, Hadithah and young son, Hasan Al-Askari, who was 4 years old at the time.[24] However, upon al-Hadi's arrival, al-Mutawakkil put him under house arrest in an extremely impoverished area called Khan al-Sa'alik. Despite al-Hadi's house arrest, he was increasingly surrounded by the Shi'a and non-Shi'a who had an abiding affection for the *Ahl al-Bayt* (family of the Prophet's household).

Al-Hadi's arrival in Samarra also coincided with the uprising of Yahya b. Umar ibn Husayn, who was to be declared a Zaydi Imam by his followers.[25] Yahya b. Umar was arrested in 235/850 and was brought to Baghdad where he was flogged 18 lashes by one of al-Mutawakkil's ministers, Umar b. Faraj al-Rukhkhaj al-Sijistani.[26] Despite these uprisings and the turbulent actions of al-Mutawakkil, al-Hadi continued to make an intellectual impression in Samarra. He was famous for interpreting verses of the Qur'an which people did not understand. For example, on one occasion, al-Mutawakkil fell ill and he promised to Allah that upon his recovery, he would pay *al-mal al-kathir* (abundant wealth) in the name of Allah. When he recovered, he asked his aides and jurors how much abundant wealth is. No two jurors of that time could agree. One of al-Mutawakkil's doormen, Hasan, volunteered to ask al-Hadi about this issue and al-Mutawakkil agreed. Al-Hadi came up with the answer of 80 dirham. When al-Mutawakkil asked how he obtained that figure, al-Hadi quoted from the Qur'an that Allah has assisted the Prophet by *kathir* (abundance). He continued to show that in the Qur'an the amount of times Allah had assisted the Prophet was 80.[27] Al-Hadi also contributed in theological debates. Perhaps one of the most famous debates amongst Muslim theologians is whether a human is predestined or free to perform actions. Al-Hadi viewed that a human being's actions lies between the two states. He is free to act but does not have the power to control the final consequences of his actions.[28]

Despite the above, al-Mutawakkil did not have much respect for knowledge. Instead, he was worried about maintaining his authority as caliph. He ordered his soldiers to search the house of al-Hadi and on one occasion, he arrested al-Hadi in the middle of the night when he was peacefully reciting Qur'an. The soldiers brought him to al-Mutawakkil, who at that time was drinking alcohol and reported that they did not find any evidence of hostility at al-Hadi's house. On hearing this, al-Mutawakkil offered al-Hadi wine but he refused and poetically replied,

> Even people who live on top of mountains and protect themselves cannot escape death. From the heights of honour, it brings them to earth and carries them to their graves. Later a voice from the skies asked, 'Where are your throne and crowns? Where are your decorated robes? Where are those who had ornamented tents erected for them wherever they went?' The graves will reply: 'In this world, they all ate for all their lives but now they are the morsel for small insects. Their bodies are being trampled upon by small insects of graves.'[29]

This reply brought tears to al-Mutawakkil and he asked for al-Hadi to be taken back to his house.

Al-Hadi's final days in Samarra during the turmoil of the Abbasid caliphate

Despite al-Mutawakkil being aware of al-Hadi's piety, he continued to show animosity towards al-Hadi's family lineage and his followers. He took away the wealth and properties of those who showed affection to al-Hadi and used to employ a jester in his court to ridicule Ali b. Abi Talib.[30] Al-Mutawakkil also used to use foul language towards the Prophet's daughter and Ali's wife, Fatimah, who Muslims (and the Shi'a in particular) hold as the most pious lady of the universe.[31]

Al-Mutawakkil's most infamous act was his desecration of Ali and Husayn's graves. He initially ruled that whoever visited Husayn's grave should have their hands chopped off and after that, if they should repeat the act, they should be killed.[32] When people did not accept this, he ordered the grave's domes to be destroyed and ordered that river water run over it to 'cultivate' the land. Interestingly, as the water began to reach Husayn's grave, it surrounded the grave rather than covering it. As a result, a small island formed with Husayn's grave positioned in the middle and lower to the ground. The lower place on the ground is known is *hayar* in Arabic and it has been known by that name ever since. A poet wrote the following verses on the desecration of Husayn's graves, 'The Banu Abbas look so anguished about the fact that they did not kill Husayn, therefore, to compensate, they have attacked the bare bones of Husayn.'[33]

Al-Mutawakkil attacked and desecrated Karbala four times due to his anger towards Husayn and his family. The last attempt was in 246/861. It was coupled with al-Mutawakkil's murder of his Turkish commander-in-chief. This caused great unrest amongst al-Mutawakkil's own family and entourage to the point where his own son, al-Muntasir, a Shi'a, turned against him and co-ordinated with Turkish slaves to organise his father's murder. Al-Mutawakkil was killed by a Turkish soldier on eleventh December 246/861.[34]

Turkish slaves helped al-Muntasir to acquire the caliphate and then forced his brothers to abdicate their right to inherit. However, Al-Muntasir died suddenly within a year. Since he died without an heir, Turkish slaves held a council and elected al-Musta'in, another grandson of al-Mu'tasim, as the next caliph. Al-Musta'in's rule was marked by great confusion. He was dependent on Turkish slaves in Samarra to hold his power. These were the years that al-Hadi was fairly at liberty to establish his group of students and companions, who I discussed earlier in this Chapter. Al-Musta'in fought certain battles with Turkish slaves alongside him but by 251/865, he was at odds with them. After a quarrel, they lobbied to get al-Musta'in's cousin, al-Mu'tazz, in power. Al-Musta'in was held in Baghdad and later beheaded in 252/866.

As al-Mu'tazz took power, he turned his wrath again towards al-Hadi and his followers. Al-Hadi remained in house arrest in Samarra but after being the leader for Shi'a Muslims for approximately 34 years, al-Mu'tazz ordered al-Hadi to be poisoned. Al-Hadi died on 4th Rajab 254/27th June 868 in the same house where he lived. His 22 year old son, Hasan al-Askari, led the funeral prayers and buried him. It is further narrated that al-Askari was all alone at his father's funeral[35] and could not hold his grief, tearing his shirt apart in distress.[36] Al-Hadi was survived by five children. The oldest one was Hasan who took over the burden of leadership from his father.

At first sight, the political turmoil of the Abbasids did not allow al-Hadi room to express his leadership in any tangible way. However, on closer inspection, al-Hadi used *taqiyyah* (concealing one's faith in the face of persecution) in order to preserve and advance the Shi'i faith. *Taqiyyah* specifically refers to a dispensation allowing believers to hide their faith when under threat, persecution or compulsion.[37] His continued efforts in teaching students and maintaining contact with his followers ensured the survival of the Shi'i faith and in his absence, continued propagation of it. The task of continuing this development was now upon Hasan al-Askari.

Hasan al-Askari's early years and the tenures of the Abbasid caliphs

Al-Askari was born in Madinah on 8th Rabi' al-thani 232 AH/1st December 846.[38] His mother's name was Haditha, although other names have been mentioned in history such as Susan or Salil.[39] In his life, he acquired various titles which include *al-Zaki* (the pious), *al-Samit* (the quiet one), *al-Rafiq* (the friend), *al-Siraj* (the light) and *al-Shafi* (the mediator).[40] Al-Askari went on to marry a noble lady, arguably a princess, named Narjis. She bore him a child called Muhammad. According to Shi'i belief, Muhammad is the twelfth and last Imam, who lives in occultation at this moment and is known as *al-Mahdi* (the guide).

Al-Askari moved to Samarra at the tender age of four with his parents. He had great wisdom from his childhood. It is narrated that on one occasion, a companion of al-Hadi saw several children playing in the street with the exception of a young boy who had tears flowing down his cheeks. The companion felt sad and offered to buy toys for the boy. The young boy replied, 'We are not created to play games. We are created for knowledge and contemplation'. The companion asked how he arrived at such a conclusion. 'The child replied, 'The Qur'an guides us towards it. Have you not read in Qur'an, where Allah says,

"Do you think that I have only created you for play and are you not going to return to me?" 'The companion asked, 'Then why were you crying?' The child replied, 'I have watched my mother light a fire; she uses the little twigs to get the big pieces of wood to burn; I fear that on the Day of Judgement, Allah too will use little ones to light the big ones.'[41] Although it is clear in Islam that children are not responsible for their actions until they reach the age of puberty, al-Askari's thoughts reflected his contemplative and God-fearing personality.

Al-Askari was nominated to be the successor by his father, al-Hadi. Al-Hadi explicitly informed this nomination to his companions and stated that 'the one who will be my successor will be the one who will recite my funeral prayers.' When the day arrived, it was none other than al-Askari.[42] Al-Askari lived during the days of al-Wathiq (842–7), al-Mutawakkil (847–61), al-Muntasir (861–2), al-Musta'in (862–6), al-Mu'tazz (866–9), al-Muhtadi (869–70) and al-Mu'tamid (870–92). Although his own leadership started during the reign of al-Mu'tazz, al-Askari lived at a time of great turmoil within the Abbasid caliphate. He was constantly surrounded by brutality, fear and rebellions. I will briefly explain the political circumstances in which he lived.

Al-Mu'tazz was a cruel and power-hungry ruler. He killed his cousin and caliph al-Musta'in, his brother al-Mu'iyyad and his other brother, Abu Ahmad, who had fought to bring al-Mu'tazz into power. Abu Ahmad was imprisoned and finally killed by being frozen in a bed of ice.[43] However, al-Mu'tazz's own brutality brought about his downfall when at the young age of 24 he was overpowered by two rebels in his own courtroom and was starved to death in heat. During this time, al-Askari had little freedom to guide the Shi'i community and this restriction continued during the reign of al-Muhtadi and al-Mu'tamid. Al-Muhtadi was the son of al-Wathiq and in contrast to al-Mu'tazz, he chose not to play into the hands of the Turkish slaves who were now effectively kingmakers in the government. Despite al-Muhtadi's firmness, he was brought to an abrupt end by the Turkish slaves.[44]

Al-Mu'tamid continued the Abbasid reign. He was a brother to al-Muntasir and al-Mu'tazz and cousin to al-Muhtadi. Initially he was a prisoner during the tenure of al-Muhtadi but was freed by the Turkish slaves and made caliph. On coming to power, he immediately had to deal with the revolt of Ali b. Muhammad near Basra which is famously known as the 'Zanj rebellion.'[45] Ali b. Muhammad declared himself as a Shi'a and started collecting taxes for al-Askari in Bahrain. He fought many battles against the Abbasids but as he posed an increasing threat to the caliphate, al-Mu'tamid sought help from his brother, al-Muwaffaq. Al-Muwaffaq crushed Ali b. Muhammad's rebellion brutally and that effectively gained him the status of regent to caliph. Although al-Mu'tamid still held the position of caliph, in reality it was al-Muwaffaq who ran the government.

During these tenures, al-Askari was under close surveillance and with so much political instability around him, he could not provide open leadership. Interestingly, however, he used teaching, scholarly pursuits and his representatives to increase the knowledge and moral growth of the Muslim community. This increased al-Askari's followers and ensured the survival of the Shi'i community and its principles.

Al-Askari's leadership in Samarra

Perhaps the most notable aspect of al-Askari's tenure as Imam was that he attracted thousands of companions and students in Samarra. He would often gather his companions and train them to preach to the surrounding community. Furthermore, he would teach several disciplines ranging from Qur'anic exegesis and jurisprudence to history and theology. He also wrote a commentary on the Qur'an.[46] It was through this scholarly leadership that many jurisprudential principles were laid, Shi'i scholars emerged and religious principles by which the Shi'a could live by were cemented. He famously narrated that a Shi'i believer should have the following signs: being able to offer 51 prayers in a day (as opposed to just the obligatory 17 prayers), prostrating on the dust of Karbala, having a ring on one's right hand, reciting *bismillah* (in the name of God) loudly in prayers and offering salutations or visiting Imam Husayn on the 40th day of his martyrdom, which is 20th Safar in the Islamic calendar.[47]

Al-Askari's companion, Ahmed b. Ishaq al-Qummi, narrates that he established 9th Rabi al-Awwal as the final day of mourning for the Shi'a. Historically, the Shi'a commemorate the martyrdom of Husayn and his companions on the plains of Karbala during Muharram and Safar, the first and second Islamic months. Al-Askari also established the institution of imitation (*taqlid*) amongst Shi'as by encouraging them to follow learned and pious scholars. He said that 'if there is anyone among the learned who is in control over his own self, protects his religion, suppresses his evil desires and is obedient to the commands of his Master, then the people should follow him.'[48]

Al-Askari's knowledge and popularity also spread outside of Iraq. The famous Turkish chief minister to the Abbasid court, Ahmad b. Abdullah b. Khaqan, is reported to have said, 'I have not come across anyone from Banu Hashim's family in Samarra, who is more pious, virtuous and chaste than Hasan al-Askari. If the caliphate goes out of the Abbasid's family then no one except Hasan al-Askari will be capable and fit for it. One day I was present with my father when Hasan al-Askari arrived there, although he was the enemy of the Ahl al-Bayt, yet he got up from his place, kissed his hand and made him seated upon his own place and sat before him like a pupil in front of a teacher.'[49]

The last days of Hasan al-Askari

Al-Mu'tamid and al-Muwaffaq were incensed at the growing popularity of al-Askari and decided to imprison him in 256/870. Although al-Askari was freed later that year, he was put under house arrest. Al-Mu'tamid continued to worry about the loyalty the Shi'a showed for al-Askari and once again decided to put him in prison in 257/871. This time, al-Askari was kept in a dungeon with little food and threatened by beasts.[50] During these years, he experienced harsh living conditions and constant supervision. This continued until his death in 260/874. It is reported al-Askari told his servant, Abu al-Adyan (who was about to travel to Madinah), that upon his return, he would hear the sound of wailing from al-Askari's house in Samarra. Indeed, this is what happened when Abu al-Adyan returned to the house. He found out that al-Askari was poisoned on the instructions of Mu'tamid and eventually died on 8th Rabi al-Awwal 260/1st January 874.

Al-Askari's brother, Ja'far, wanted to lead the funeral prayers but as he stood there, a child of barely four years of age appeared. This child was Muhammad al-Mahdi, the promised successor after al-Askari. He told his uncle Ja'far to step aside as only an Imam can lead the funeral prayers of another Imam. After al-Mahdi led the prayers, he walked towards the Sardab, a place near al-Askari's house. Al-Mu'tamid's horsemen waited for him in order to kill him but he never showed.[51] Though al-Mu'tamid's men tried to find him, they failed to do so. According to the Shi'a, al-Mahdi has been in occultation ever since.

Al-Askari's death serves to underscore the oppression which he faced, just like his father al-Hadi. However, during his restricted existence, al-Askari managed to lay firm guiding principles for the Shi'i community. Perhaps the most immediate principle that comes to mind was the importance of practising *taqiyyah*, a legacy left by al-Hadi. The Shi'a were a minority and disliked by the Abbasid caliphate. In this situation, al-Askari felt the best way to preserve the Shi'a faith as well as propagate it was not to give any excuses to the Abbasid government to abruptly interrupt his scholarship, teachings and preaching. Al-Askari's own followers such as Abu Hashim Ja'fari also suffered as a result of their firm loyalty towards him. As a result, al-Askari had to write letters to avoid physical contact with his followers but still offer some form of guidance to the masses.[52]

Secondly, al-Askari managed to support the Shi'a economically. According to Shi'i doctrine, an Imam is entitled to a share from the charity tax imposed upon every Shi'a. The Imam can then spend that share according to his discretion – mainly to propagate the religion by various means. This is called *khums* (one-fifth charity tax). Al-Askari appointed representatives to collect such taxes. For example, his companion Uthman b. Said used to sell *ghee* (a form of butter). He used to collect *khums* from people and then distribute it amongst the needy followers by hiding money in the containers of *ghee*.[53]

Al-Askari trained four deputies in order to keep contact with the Shi'i community. During the period 260/874–329/941, they would collect taxes for distribution amongst the needy, preach to the masses and prepare them for the foretold occultation of al-Askari's son, al-Mahdi. These deputies were Uthman b. Said al-Asadi, Abu Ja'far Muhammad b. Uthman, Abu al-Qasim Husayn b. Ruh al-Nawbakhti and Abu al-Hasan Ali b. Muhammad al-Samarri.[54] Although Prophet Muhammad and the Imams after him talked about the occultation and coming of al-Mahdi, preparing the Shi'a for the actual event was a huge responsibility. Not having a physically present Imam to guide the community would be a massive transformation for the community and this required an understanding that people now had to use the intellectual tools which al-Askari and those before him had left to retain and advance their faith. This is precisely why al-Askari entrusted this responsibility to four of his closest aides and when al-Mahdi was born, he made sure that his existence was known before he went into the major occultation. The prime example of this was after al-Askari's death where al-Mahdi led the funeral prayers thereby making himself known as the next leader of the Shi'a.

Al-Hadi's and al-Askari's legacies for the Shi'a

Considering that al-Hadi and al-Askari faced similar difficulties (restriction and house arrest), the legacies they left for the Shi'a point to one major theme: consolidation and survival of faith. At a time when the Abbasid caliphate was in internal and external turmoil, al-Hadi's and al-Askari's lives were in danger if they were seen to be a direct threat to the government. What is interesting is the way in which both Imams managed to guide the Shi'a community but at the same time, not give any outright legitimacy to the Abbasid caliphs. With the exception of Husayn who was forced under extreme and bloody circumstances to physically defend the principles of Islam (and morality itself), al-Hadi and al-Askari emphasised scholarship and preaching. These are primary tools which *hawzas* (Shi'i religious seminaries) and Shi'i communities worldwide use in order to educate their believers and sustain the progress of Shi'i institutions. This peaceful, intelligent and gradual manner of developing Shi'i believers, who are still a minority in many places, is a testament to the efforts of al-Hadi and al-Askari.

Secondly, both Imams never gave up their claim of *Imamah*. As I described earlier, *Imamah* is a fundamental concept in Shi'i theology and represents a continuing form of Prophetic leadership. Despite being oppressed, they continued to play the role of spiritual and educational guides who were also concerned about the welfare of their community. This showed their determination to express their authority as Imams, despite the physical threats which they faced on their lives. To this day, the Shi'a continue to hold *Imamah* as a central principle in their faith. Whenever any Imam's birthday is celebrated or death is commemorated, it is a huge event in the Shi'i calendar. The Shi'a gather to pay their respects for the efforts of the Imam to preserve the Shi'i faith and use their spiritual presence as a holy mediation (but not an end in itself) to obtain nearness to Allah.

Thirdly, both Imams emphasised unity amongst all Muslim communities. They did not engage in civil wars or instigate rebellions against other sects or the government itself. In fact, the Imams continued to give spiritual guidance to the Muslim community as a whole and distributed money to the poor, regardless of class or religious affiliation. Furthermore, despite being treated harshly by the Abbasid caliphate, they maintained a civil distance and even advised the calliphs when they needed guidance.[55] This showed the far-sightedness and practicality of al-Hadi and al-Askari, which today remains as a key part of the Shi'i faith in living with others and engaging in political and social affairs. The origins of these legacies were in Madinah and found their way to the garrison town of Samarra, in the midst of political and military turmoil. At the least, al-Hadi and al-Askari remain as shining beacons of hope for humanity in the promotion of peace, knowledge and civility.

Notes

1. Hanbal, Ahmad., *Al-Musnad* (Cairo, 1995), vol. 1, p. 84, 118, 119, 152 and Maja, Muhammad., *Sunan ibn Maja* (Texas, 2007), vol 1, ch: 11, p. 43, No. 116.
2. Al-Tabari, Muhammad., *Tarikh al-Tabari* (New York, 1988) , vol 1, pp. 2769–70.

3. Al-Yaqubi, Ahmad., *Tarikh al-Ya'qubi* (Beirut, 1960), vol 1, p. 137.
4. Al-Maududi, Sayyid Abu al-A'la., *Khilafat wa Mulukiyat* (Lahore, 1965), p. 60.
5. Momen, Moojan. *The Lives of the Imams and Early Divisions among the Shi'is: An Introduction to Shi'i Islam* (London, 1985), p. 92.
6. Ibn Kathir, Ismail. *Al-Bidayah wa al-Nihayah*, (Beirut, 1993), vol 8, p. 222.
7. Al-Kulayni, Muhammad. *Al-Kafi*. (Tehran, 1978), vol 3, ch:7, hadith no.1.
8. Al-Mufid, Muhammad. *Kitab Al-Irshad – the Book of Guidance* (London, 1981), p. 393.
9. Al-Bihbahani, Wahid. *Al-Dama'a Al-Sakiba fi-Ahwal Al-Nabi wal-'Ishra Al-Tahira*. (Beirut, 1989), vol 2, p. 481.
10. Ali, Sayyid Amir., *A Short History of Saracens,* (London, 1916), ch: 18.
11. Al-Mufid: *Kitab Al-Irshad,* p. 308.
12. Ibid, p. 494.
13. Al-Majlisi, Muhammad Baqir., *Bihar al-Anwar,* (Beiruit, 1983), vol 50, p. 116.
14. Shablanji, Momin., *Nur al-Absar fi Manaqib Al al-Bayt al-Nabi*, (Lahore, 1948) p149. http://www.ziyaraat.net/findbook.asp?srchwhat=All&LibroID=1122&AgregarVista=Si&page=6&Archivo=NoorulAbsarFeeManaqibAhlebaitArabic.pdf&escritor=All&tema=Masoomeen(a.s.)&idioma=All&orderby=titulo
15. Al-Tabarasi, Fadl ibn Hasan., *Alam al-Wara* (Tehran, 1973). p. 239.
16. Al-Tabari, Muhammad., *Tarikh al-Tabari* (New York, 1988) , vol 32, pp. 224–31.
17. Al-Arbili, Al-Fath., *Kashf al-Ghama*. (Beirut, 1985), vol 1, p. 12.
18. Al-Bahbahani: *Al-Dama'a al-Sakiba fi-Ahwal al-Nabi,* vol 2, p. 121.
19. Al-Majlisi: *Bihar al-Anwar,* vol 50, ch: 6.
20. Al-Tabari: *Tarikh al-Tabari*, vol .34, p. 55.
21. al-Hamawi, Ya'qut., *Kitab Mu'jam al-Buldan*. F.Wustenfield (ed), 6 vols, (Leipzig, 1866-70), p. 1228.
22. Ali; *A Short History of Saracens,* ch: 19.
23. Shablanji: *Nur al-Absar fi Manaqib Al al-Bayt al-Nabi*, p149. http://www.ziyaraat.net/findbook.asp?srchwhat=All&LibroID=1122&AgregarVista=Si&page=6&Archivo=NoorulAbsarFeeManaqibAhlebaitArabic.pdf&escritor=All&tema=Masoomeen(a.s.)&idioma=All&orderby=titulo
24. Qurashi, Baqir Shareef., *The Life of Imam Hasan al-Askari* (Qum, 2005), pp. 16–18.
25. The Zaydi sect is a Shi`i school of thought which follows Husayn b. Ali's grandson, Zayd b. Ali.
26. Tabari: *Tarikh al-Tabari*, vol 34, pp. 105–6.
27. Ashub, Ibn Shahr. *Al-Manaqib Al Abi Talib* (Najaf, 1956), vol 5, p. 116.
28. Al-Bahbahani: *Al-Dama'a al-Sakiba fi-Ahwal Al-Nabi,* vol 3, p. 134.
29. Ibid, p. 142.

30. Athir, Ali b., *Al-Kamil fi al-Tarikh* (Beirut, 1966), vol 7, p. 20.
31. Al-Majlisi: *Bihar al-Anwar,* vol 10, p. 307.
32. Al-Haythami, Hasan., *Majma al-Zawaid* (Beiruit, 1988), p. 502.
33. Al-Suyuti, Jalal al-Din. *Tareekh-al-Khulafa* (Beirut, 1993), p. 237.
34. Al-Bahbahani: *Al-Dama'a Al-Sakiba fi-Ahwal Al-Nabi,* vol 3, p. 147.
35. Al-Majlisi, Muhammad Baqir., *Jilal al-Uyun* (Lahore, 1983) , p. 292.
36. Ibid, p. 294
37. Esposito, John L., *Oxford Dictionary of Islam* (Oxford, 2003), 'Taqiyyah.'
38. Ashub, Ibn Shahr. *Al-Manaqib Al Abi Talib* (Najaf, 1956), vol 4, p. 422.
39. Qurashi: *The Life of Imam Hasan al-Askari*, pp. 16–18.
40. Ashub: *Al-Manaqib Al Abi Talib,* vol 22, p. 332.
41. Shablanji: *Nur al-Absar fi Manaqib Al al-Bayt al-Nabi*, p150. http://www.ziyaraat.net/findbook.asp?srchwhat=All&LibroID=1122&AgregarVista=Si&page=6&Archivo=NoorulAbsarFeeManaqibAhlebaitArabic.pdf&escritor=All&tema=Masoomeen(a.s.)&idioma=All&orderby=titulo
42. Ashub: *Al-Manaqib Al Abi Talib,* vol 22, p. 333
43. Hitti, Philip K., *History of the Arabs* (London, 2002), ch: 13, p. 468–70.
44. Ibid, see ch: 13.
45. Talhami, Ghada Hashem., 'The Zanj rebellion reconsidered.' *International Journal of African Historical studies* (Boston, 1977). 10(3), pp. 443–61.
46. Bharelvi, Shareef Husayn Sahab., *Athar al-Hydari* (Lucknow, 2003). Urdu translation of Arabic commentary by Imam Hasan Al-Askari.
47. Al-Bahbahani: *Al-Dama'a Al-Sakiba fi-Ahwal Al-Nabi,* vol 3, p. 172.
48. Al-Tabrasi, Ahmad., *Al-Ihtijaj.* (Najaf, 1966), vol 2, p. 263.
49. Ashub: *Al-Manaqib Al Abi Talib,* vol 22, p. 334.
50. Al-Tabarasi, Fadl ibn Hasan., *Alam al-Wara* (Tehran, 1973), p. 218.
51. Al-Majlisi, Muhammad Baqir., *Jilal al-Uyun* (Lahore, 1983) p. 292
52. Al-Mufid: *Kitab Al-Irshad,* p. 323.
53. Al-Tusi. Ja'far., *Al-Ghayba* (Qum, 1911), pp. 215–19.
54. Shustari, Nurullah., *Majalis al-Mominin* (Beirut, 1989), pp. 767–77.
55. See Adib, Adil., *A Research into the Political Lives of Infallible Leaders* (Karachi, 2000).

CHAPTER 5

THE DEVELOPMENT OF SHI'I SCHOLARSHIP BEFORE AND AFTER MIRZA SHIRAZI AND HIS INTELLECTUAL LEGACY IN SAMARRA

Sayyid Fadhil Bahrululoom

Mirza Sayyid Muhammad Hasan Husayni al-Shirazi, popularly known as 'Mirza Shirazi Buzurg' or simply as 'Mirza Shirazi', was a leading Shi'i scholar, jurist and *marja-i taqlid* (source of imitation) in Samarra, Iraq, during the nineteenth century. It is unfortunate that to date there is no biography of Mirza Shirazi in Western academia, which forms my impetus in writing this Chapter. However, most academics within the field of Middle Eastern Studies, Politics and Islamic History know who he was and in particular, his role in the Tobacco Protest 1890. It is therefore important to give some insight into the studies of Mirza Shirazi in order to examine what made him a leading scholar of his time thereby cementing himself as part of Samarra's intellectual heritage.

What is particularly interesting is that Mirza Shirazi's scholarship had a profound impact on his students who played a seminal part in the Constitutional Revolution of Iran 1905–11. Students such as al-Akhund al-Khurasani and Mirza Naini became central figures in the *mashruta* (constitutionalist) movement which aimed to pressurise the Shah to accept the rule of law. Though some comment that Mirza Shirazi was the principal factor in influencing the role of a scholar from an educationalist to a political-religious scholar, this is misleading as Mirza Shirazi was essentially an *alim* and his *fatwa* of 1891 during the Tobacco Protest was a unique political incident. However, his *fatwa* did have an increasing influence on the *ulama* after him who saw their role as religious guides beyond the realm of just scholarship.

In this Chapter, I will provide a brief history of Shi'i scholarship after the twelfth Shi'i Imam and then proceed to examine the scholarly life of Mirza Shirazi in Samarra. This involves analysing why he moved to Samarra and the role he played in the Tobacco Protest 1890, a Shi'i cleric-led revolt in Iran against a tobacco concession granted by Nasir al-Din Shah to the Western imperial power of Great Britain.

Early Shi'i scholarship

It is perhaps appropriate for me to begin with a brief explanation of the nature of Shi'i scholarship after the occultation of the twelfth Shi'i Imam, Muhammad al-Mahdi till the period of Mirza Shirazi. I aim to show the kinds of disciplines that were needed and studied, such as *ilm al-hadith* (the science of narration) and *ilm al-fiqh* (the science of jurisprudence), in order to guide the Shi'i community in Iraq and Iran, which formed the nucleus places of Shi'i learning. This would illustrate the increasing role of the *ulama* in guiding people and arriving at a position of spiritual leadership, a trend initiated by the Imams themselves when they took on the task of teaching the public directly.[1] I can then move on to consider Mirza Shirazi as originating from this realm of scholarship but gradually assuming a more social and political role within the Shi'i community in Samarra.

Shortly after the occultation of al-Mahdi, Shi'i scholars had the significant task of continuing the guidance from the twelve Imams through their *aqwal* (sayings), *afal* (actions) and *taqrir* (tacit approval). One method of doing this was the renewed effort of systematically compiling and categorising the narrations which had been passed down to them by trustworthy companions of the Prophet and Imams.

Amongst the first of those was Shaykh al-Kulayni (d. 329/941) who was the author of *al-Kafi*, one of the four canonical collections of Shi'i *hadith* books, known as *al-Kutub al-Arba'ah* (the four books). He was present during the first occultation when communication with the hidden Imam took place through his four deputies. In the same period was Abu Ja'far Muhammad b. Ali b. Babawayh al-Qummi (d. 327/939), known as Shaykh al-Saduq. The major work he compiled was *Man La Yahdhuru al-Faqih,* a seminal book containing Shi'i narrations, particularly in the realm of law.[2] These scholars represent the traditionist era. Their expertise was based upon collecting, classifying and, to some extent, looking at the reliability of Shi'i *hadith*. Shi'i scholars who were students of these teachers and post-*ghayba* scholars greatly revere them for their efforts in protecting the *hadith* of the Prophet and Twelve Imams, especially since the twelfth Imam had been hidden by the will of God into what is now known as the greater occultation.

However, after the traditionist era, scholars were forced by natural circumstances to analyse the *hadith* contextually, develop a science of interpretation and ultimately engage in *istinbat* (procedural derivation) to derive laws for the Shi'i community. This is because the traditionists were close in time to the twelfth Imam and so the narrations that were used had contextual relevance. But as time passed and later scholars had less contact with earlier scholars, there needed to be a consistent system of interpretation that would be helpful in applying the body of *hadith* correctly.[3]

As such, the discipline of *usul al-fiqh* (the science of the principles of jurisprudence) developed where the *ulama* had to use their rational methodologies to derive religious laws to guide the Shi'i followers based upon the core sources of the Qur'an, Sunnah (established practice of the Prophet and Imams), *ijma* (consensus) and *aql* (intellect). This happened during the time of Ibn Abi Akil al-Umani (d. 368/979)[4] and Ibn al-Junayd (d. 380/991)[5] where *fiqh* became a separate and primary subject in itself. Later their student Shaykh al-Mufid (d. 412/1022), who was the first supreme scholar of the Shi'i, was the primary exponent of the rationalist Baghdad school and developed *fiqh* further.[6] Al-Mufid had studied under different teachers and wrote many notable books including *Kitab al-Irshad* which covered the history of the twelve Imams and jurisprudential books such as *al-Muqni'a*.[7] He died in Baghdad in 413/1022 and was buried near the shrine of the seventh Shi'i Imam, al-Kadhim. His student Sharif al-Murtada (d. 436/1044) became the leader of the *Imami* school after him. It is at this point that we see *usul al-fiqh* developing which is a systematic theory in deriving law using linguistic, analytical, philosophical and theological tools.[8]

It is also important to note that at this time, Baghdad was under control of the Buyids (322/934–446/1055) who were sympathetic towards the Shi'i.[9] This period allowed Shi'i scholars and seminaries considerable freedom to expand and flourish. Scholars were not persecuted and were free to express their beliefs and ideas. Eventually Baghdad became the centre for Shi'i learning. Hence, in comparison to the traditionist era which was marked more by restriction and compiling narrations (to safeguard the *Twelver Imami* thought), the era of the jurist was marked by freer expression and analysis due to the freedom that the Buyids allowed as well as the need of the time to contextualise the *hadith*.

As an example, Sharif al-Murtada, the teacher of Shaykh al-Tusi, had opened a seminary and library called *Dar al-Ilm* (which existed during the year 381/991–449/1057) meaning the 'house of knowledge.' The library contained over 80,000 books and Shaykh al-Tusi had access to these for the 13 years during which he lived with his teacher.[10] After the demise of Sharif al-Murtada, Shaykh al-Tusi succeeded him as the head of the Shi'i community. The Abbasid caliph, al-Qaim Billah (422/1031–467/1075), after attending al-Tusi's lectures, was so impressed that he appointed him to the court's chair of teaching *kalam* (theology) in Baghdad, which used to be Shaykh al-Mufid's position.[11]

Baghdad was by then renowned as the centre of intellectual discourse and it was there that many trends of rationalist thinking developed. During this period, the depth of the religious discussion was at its greatest and the notable Shi'i theologians used the rationalist tools and methods quite effectively. Arguably, al-Mufid, al-Murtada and al-Tusi greatly developed *usul al-fiqh*.[12] Al-Mufid wrote an *usul al-fiqh* book called *Mukhtasar al-Tadhkira bi Usul al-Fiqh,* which is included in Abu al-Fath Muhammad b. Ali b. Uthman al-Karajiki's (d. 449/1057) *Kanz al-Fawa'id.* Furthermore, Sharif al-Murtada wrote *al-Dhari'ah ila Usul al-Shari'ah*. These books were extremely influential for their time and gave al-Tusi firm foundations in which to develop the interpretation of *usul al-fiqh* further in his book *al-Uddah*. With so much scholastic activity in Baghdad, we find Shi'ism impacted the surrounding scholarship and social milieu. One example of this is reported by ibn al-Jawzi in which we are told of the *adhan* (call to prayer) in the mosques of Karkh and Kadhimiyyah including verses recited only in the Shi'i *adhan*.[13]

What this shows is that Baghdad and then Najaf (following the sectarian troubles that came at the time of the Seljukids that forced al-Tusi out of Baghdad and to Najaf) were major sources of Shi'i knowledge and many scholars emerged from there exemplifying the trend of producing *ulama* grounded in religious interpretation. This trend is exemplified during the IlKhanid period (13th–15th centuries) where the *hawza* of Najaf moved to al-Hilla. This was during the time of the Shi'i scholars, Ibn Idris (d. 598/1202), Sayyid b. Tawus (d. 664/1266), Muhaqqiq al-Hilli (d.676/1278) and his nephew, Allama al-Hilli (d. 725/1325). The *hawza* remained there for a while before returning to Najaf, where it remained for several centuries, although Shi'a scholarship developed elsewhere (and expanded into other regions such as Qum). One of the best examples of this time was Muqaddas al-Ardabili (d. 1585)[14], who stayed in Najaf and refused offers by the Safavid government to act as an adviser to it in Iran but this did not affect the trend of other *hawzas* producing grand scholars such as as al-Shahid al-Awwal (d. 785/1384) and al-Shahid al-Thani (d. 965/1558) in Jabal Amil, Lebanon and Muhaqqiq al-Sabzawari (d. 1089/1679) in Isfahan, Iran.

A crucial turning point occurred during the time of Shaykh Muhammad Baqir b. Muhammad Akmal (1206/1791–2) known as Wahid al-Bihbahani where the *hawza* moved to Karbala. He was born in Isfahan in 1116/1704–6 or 1118/1706–7 then moved with his father to Karbala, where he had considerable scholarly success.[15] Bihbahani established a victory for the *usuli* school of thought over the *akhbari* school of thought due to his important theories in *usul al-fiqh*. The *usuli* school of thought believes the Qur'an and Sunnah can be methodologically interpreted according to the science of *usul al-fiqh*. Contrary to the formalistic and unquestioning nature of akhbarism, usulism advocates that the Qur'an and Sunnah can be subject to theoretical and jurisprudential analysis in solving evolving human problems. Akhbarism is the school of thought that believes no one has the right to refer directly to the Quran and to interpret it. Only the infallible Shi'i Imams have such a right. One's duty is to refer to their *ahadith*. Only those parts of the Quran that have been explained in *hadith* may be referred to for legal purposes; other parts whose exegesis does not exist in hadith may not be acted upon. [16]

This victory of the *usuli* or rationalist school of thought would have important consequences for the mindset of the *ulama* in the way they understood the domain of religion as capable of being interpreted but most importantly, that this interpretation was religiously permissible. This meant the role of a scholar was not merely rooted in memorising *hadith* or deriving edicts for the religious and spiritual affairs of a human being. Rather, the scholar would be able to use *usul al-fiqh* to derive legal norms for social and political problems because the Qur'an had become a universal tool for application and not a book of imitation, as *akhbaris* believed.

Through Bihbahani's efforts, *usuli* ideas began to be taught in most of the seminaries of the shrine cities and many *akhbari* students converted. He trained a generation of *mujtahids* who dominated religious life in both Iraq and Iran, spreading *usuli* thought and significantly reducing the influence of *akhbari* legal doctrine. Bihbahani was the teacher of several important Shi'i scholars such as Sayyid Muhammad Mahdi Bahrululoom (d. 1211/1797) author of *Masabih al-Ahkam*, Sayyid Ali al-Tabatabaei, author of *al-Riyad al-Masa'il* (d. 1231/1816)[17], al-Muhaqqiq al-Qummi author of *Qawanin al-Usul*[18] and Shaykh Ja'far Kashif al-Ghita[19] (d. 1227/1813), author of *Kashf al-Ghita*, another important *fiqh* textbook.[20]

The *hawza's* move back to Najaf and its progression during the nineteenth century

It is interesting to note that even when the *hawza* moved back to Najaf from al-Hilla and Karbala, the strong academic tradition of studying, writing and carrying out ritual duties continued. One example was Sayyid Bahrululoom[21], who came from a family of scholars having studied under his father Sayyid Murtada al-Tabatabaei and Shaykh Yusuf al-Bahrani (d. 1185/1772), the author of *al-Hada'iq al-Nadira* and finally under Wahid al-Bihbahani. Sayyid Bahrululoom's legacy was the development of the scholarly tradition by encouraging his students to undertake scholarly duties. He appointed Shaykh Husayn Najaf (d. 1250/1835) for congregational prayers, Shaykh Muhyi al-Din for judicial duties, Sayyid Jawad al-Amili (d. 1225/1811) for writing and himself for teaching *bahth al-kharij*[22] (final studies in jurisprudence that lead to one being a qualified jurist). Even after the death of Bahrululoom, more scholarly families emerged in the nineteenth century such as the Kashif al-Ghita, al-Radi and al-Jawahiri families. This showed that since the creation of the *hawza* of Najaf by Shaykh al-Tusi as well as during its progression, the notion of rigorous study in traditional Islamic sciences continued.

Perhaps a good example of how much importance analytical religious sciences had in the *hawza* is the concept of *ijtihad* (the employment of effort to derive a law from its sources). In many academic works, this term is described vaguely and does not depict the rigorous and pious nature to attain this scholarly level. For example, Litvak states that,

> the *ijazat ijtihad* itself was not sufficient for acquiring widespread recognition. Theoretically, certain additional conditions were necessary for a jurist to qualify as an "absolute marja" (*mujtahid mutlaq*) or a fully qualified (*jami al-sharayat*) *mujtahid*. These qualifications were command of Arabic grammar and syntax, of fiqh, of legal opinions (*fatawa*), and of the consensus (*ijma*) on legal and doctrinal issues. In addition, the mujtahid needed to have fair knowledge of Qur'anic exegesis (*tafsir*), hadith and biographies of its transmitters (*'ilm al-rijal*), logic, and theology (*kalam*).[23]

It appears that Litvak's definition of a *mujtahid* and the necessary requirements to become one is unclear because what he has listed as qualifications are what every *hawza* student would study. A *mujtahid*, however, has to be *jami al-sharayat* and his *ijtihad* should be performed in the fields of *ilm al-fiqh* and *usul al-fiqh*, more than the other Islamic sciences. These fuller qualifications actually refer to a *mujtahid's* character traits through self-development such as his piety and trustworthiness, not just his *hawza* credentials, which is what Litvak implies.

The aforementioned concepts of *ijtihad* and *mujtahid*, however, did not remain purely within the domain of scholarship and self-development. Sahib al-Jawahir (d. 1266/1850) and Shaykh Murtada al-Ansari (d. 1280/1864) can be regarded as pivotal turning points in introducing such a trend. This is because Shaykh Muhammad Hasan al-Najafi (known as Sahib al-Jawahir) became the supreme *marja* after the death of Kashif al-Ghita (mentioned above). Although he is particularly known for authoring *Jawahir al-Kalam*, one of the most important Shi'i *fiqh* encyclopaedias, the idea of him being the religious authority within the *hawza* system and wider community was a key change in the role of the *alim* from a *hawza* scholar to a scholar functioning more in the public domain. In fact, this notion of the 'public scholar' is highlighted by the *marja* who succeeded him, Shaykh al-Ansari.

In the final few days of Sahib al-Jawahir's life, he was asked who would succeed him as the next *marja*. So he assembled his sons and students at his house and in the presence of several senior *ulama,* he called forward Shaykh Murtada al-Ansari and announced him as his successor.[24] Shaykh al-Ansari was known for his teaching and piety and in particular, his new legal methodology outlined in his book *al-Rasa'il* (also known as *Fara'id)* made *usul al-fiqh* more accessible to students. This greatly influenced the *hawza* curriculum during his lifetime and after. Specifically, al-Ansari himself demonstrated the application of his methodology in his book *al-Makasib,* which dealt with commercial law.

Al-Ansari's distinction in *usul* and *fiqh* made him the most sought after teacher in Najaf for hundreds of Arabs and non-Arabs.[25] However, it is important to note that al-Ansari's selection as the next religious authority exemplifies a prominence in religious status amongst lay people, in addition to his already towering scholarly achievements at that time. It is precisely the official recognition of both Sahib al-Jawahir and al-Ansari as popular religious authorities (extending their authority to people), not merely *hawza* religious authorities that sowed the seeds for an *alim* to exercise his powers beyond the scope of a *hawza.* It is at this point we come to Mirza Shirazi who did just that.

The reason for mentioning the development of scholarship from the time of the twelfth Imam to the early scholarly period of Najaf was to show how religious guidance began to be assumed in the hands of the Shi'i *ulama*. In particular, the development of jurisprudence as a primary subject to legally guide the Shi'i community at that time is a good example of the increasing freedom a scholar had to derive laws relevant to the social, political and cultural life of people. Naturally, this increased both his scope and standing within the Muslim community. Perhaps one of the best examples of such a scholar is Mirza Shirazi, who exemplified the continuing *hawza* tradition of Shi'i scholarship. I will now analyse his background, move to Samarra and role in the Tobacco Protest of 1890.

Mirza Shirazi's early studies and his rise to prominence

Mirza Shirazi was the son of Sayyid Mahmud al-Shirazi. He was born in Shiraz, Iran on 25th April 1815 and started his studies there. At the age of 15 he began teaching the standard *sutuh*[26] text of *Sharh al-Lum'a*[27] and two years later, he migrated to Isfahan where he studied under Shaykh Muhammad al-Taqi, the author of *Hidayat al-Mustarshidin fi Sharh Ma'alim al-Din* and several other *mujtahids* before deciding to move to Najaf at the age of 29. He attended the classes of Shaykhs Ali and Hassan Kashif al-Ghita as well as Sahib al-Jawahir. Interestingly, Sahib al-Jawahir sent a letter to the ruler of the Fars region when Mirza Shirazi returned there for a short while, informing him of the rank of Mirza Shirazi and foreseeing a great future for him.[28] Following Sahib al-Jawahir's death, he became a premier student under Shaykh Ansari. Shaykh Murtada al-Ansari used to call him *Agha Buzurg* (the bigger master) in recognition of his knowledge and became one of his most brilliant and highly regarded students.[29] Usually al-Ansari taught without allowing interruption but the exception was when Mirza Shirazi had a comment and this showed al-Ansari's recognition for Mirza Shirazi's knowledge.[30]

Shaykh Murtada al-Ansari was the supreme *marja* but after his death in 1846, his best students from amongst the Arabs and Persians met at Mirza Habib-Allah Rashti's house, of which Mirza Shirazi was amongst them. Al-Ashtiyani mentions that the Azari Turks favoured Sayyid Husayn Kuhikamari and even followed him during his life,[31] although he died soon afterwards. It is at this point that Mirza Shirazi became the undisputed *marja*. He was recognised as such when Nasir al-Din Shah (1831–96), the Shah of Persia, visited Najaf and wanted Shirazi to come and see him. When the latter refused, they agreed to meet at the shrine of Ali b. Abi Talib as a compromise.[32]

As Mirza Shirazi came to prominence, he moved to Samarra in September 1874 where he established a *hawza* and taught luminaries of the Shi'i world for more than two decades. There are several theories as to why he decided to move there, which I shall tackle in the next section, but Mirza Shirazi's migration helped develop Samarra from a small shrine city into a prosperous centre of learning. Many students and pilgrims flocked to the city which consequently experienced an economic boom, with Shirazi receiving a large number of monetary contributions. The status of Shirazi's *hawza,* which rested on his own reputation, became one of the prominent centres of Shi'i learning along with Najaf.[33] It was Mirza Shirazi's own intellectual rigour, which was also recognised by his peers, that established his status as a leading scholar of his time. Some of Shirazi's famous graduates were al-Akhund al-Khurasani[34], Sayyid Kadhim al-Yazdi[35], Mirza Husayn al-Naini[36], Sayyid Ismail al-Sadr[37], Sayyid Hasan al-Sadr[38], Shaykh Muhammad Taqi al-Shirazi[39], Shaykh Fadhlullah al-Nuri[40] and Shaykh Muhammad Ali al-Jamali.[41] Several of these scholars played a key part in the Constitutional Revolution of Iran 1905–11.

Mirza Shirazi's move to Samarra

The reason for Mirza Shirazi's move to Samarra is not beyond dispute, and is usually discussed by scholars rather than documented in books. One opinion is that he wished to elevate Samarra by creating *hawzas* and improving its scholarship, in line with Najaf, Karbala and Kadhimayn. A second opinion is that he did not set out to reside in Samarra but having arrived there and seeing his students following him, being allowed more opportunity to teach and the general receptive mood of the city, he decided to see out the rest of his life in

Samarra. It is possible that there is a combination of all of these elements at work but what is clear is that he wanted to establish a legacy of intellectual heritage for the Shi'a of Samarra.

Furthermore, the conditions in Najaf made life difficult for him and the demands on his time were overwhelming. There was a famine in Najaf in 1871, which led to food prices soaring, causing severe hardship on the populace. Mirza Shirazi appointed people to distribute aid among the poor, scholars, traders and virtually all classes of society. Though the expense was huge, the result was that the price of staple foods decreased to tolerable levels in Najaf. However, this led to people seeing Mirza Shirazi as the first point of resort in the event of problems or a crisis. People even came to ask him to pay the 100 Ottoman Lira (a large sum at the time) required for their children to be exempted from army service.[42] The situation became increasingly difficult as Mirza Shirazi realised that even some of the wealthy notables in Najaf were encouraging the needy people to go and see him rather than helping these people themselves. With these increasing pressures and demands on him, Mirza Shirazi decided to leave Najaf on a visit to Karbala in Rajab 1290/1874.

After his visit to Karbala, he called for his family to join him there and left for Samarra with the intention of the visitation of 15th Shaban (birth anniversary of the twelfth Shi'i Imam, Muhammad al-Mahdi). He stopped off in Kadhimayn and spent a few days there, leaving for Samarra at the end of Shaban, arriving there just before the start of Ramadhan. As far as people knew, he travelled there for *ziyarah* of the Imams and would return soon. However, a year passed and he was still in Samarra, so a few of his students went to visit him after Ramadhan 1291/1875 to enquire about his intentions. It appeared Mirza Shirazi intended to stay in Samarra and upon receiving news of this, students from Najaf and elsewhere steadily joined him in Samarra until the ranks of students were swollen with luminaries and it became the premier centre of learning, superseding all others.[43]

The Tobacco Protest 1890

The Tobacco Protest was a Shi'i cleric-led revolt in Iran against an 1890 tobacco concession granted by Nasir al-Din Shah to the Western imperial power of Great Britain. The protest climaxed in a widely-obeyed December 1891 *fatwa* against tobacco use issued by Mirza Shirazi.[44] The boycott was one of the first times the Iranian religious elite succeeded in forcing the government to retreat from a policy to the extent that Vali Nasr writes, 'the Shi'a *ulama* were Iran's first line of defence against colonialism.'[45] Nasr's statement is highly apt because it neatly encapsulates the gradual transition of the Shi'i *ulama* to political scholars. Furthermore, the very fact that the Shi'i *ulama* were against colonialism is crucial because, according to them, Nasir al-Din Shah had the image of a colonialist or a colonialist cooperative.

According to businessmen and some of the *ulama*, the Shah's action of conceding a complete monopoly over the production, sale and export of all Iranian tobacco to a British businessman in March 1890, was an affront to justice and Iran as the control of resources were being handed over to a foreign agent.[46] This led to Mirza Shirazi issuing a *fatwa* in 1891 forbidding the use of tobacco after the establishment of a British-owned tobacco monopoly and succeeded in forcing its cancellation.[47] The courage of Mirza Shirazi is evident because, despite him being a scholar, he chose to enter the political and social arena in order to protect the businessmen of his own country. This, of course, is not tantamount to him being a political leader or necessarily being interested in politics, but it does demonstrate the notion that a scholar cannot always remain aloof from social issues and has to manage pressures from his local community.

However, Mirza Shirazi's actions were not without challenges. Nasir al-Din Shah had built close links with the Western imperial powers of that time, in particular the British. Nasir al-Din Shah succeeded his father, Muhammad Shah Qajar, in 1848. He decided to improve the education, transport and communication industry of Iran but based on Western models, investment and expertise.[48] He was particularly fond of Europe, visiting it three times.[49] The relationship between Nasir al-Din Shah and the West meant Western imperial powers had a financial stake in Iran, which could not be removed so easily. The unfortunate consequence of the protest was that it left Iran with its first foreign debt; £500,000 was owed to the British-owned imperial bank as exorbitant compensation to the company. The movement was the first successful mass protest in modern Iran, combining *ulama*, intellectuals, merchants and townspeople in a coordinated movement against government policy.[50] However, there were economical and political consequences to be dealt with in the aftermath of the protest.

There are those who argue that this was a failing of Mirza Shirazi, or that he was under the influence of other scholars. For example, some state that Mirza Shirazi's *fatwa* was under the influence of Sayyid Jamal al-Din al-Asadabadi, known as 'al-Afghani', who 'claimed Afghan birth and upbringing, probably in order to ensure a favourable reception among Sunni Muslims and to have more influence in the Sunni world than he would have had as an Iranian who had a Shi'i education in Iran and in the Shi'i shrine cities of Iraq.' [51] Shakib Arslan, in his note on the *Hadira al-Alam al-Islami,* thought that the letter which had been sent by al-Afghani was one of the reasons for the tobacco verdict. However, Mirza Shirazi issued his verdict before the arrival of that letter and as a *mujtahid* he would probably not have issued such an important statement without being definite about it.[52] It is here I would argue one has to appreciate the intellectual and spiritual rigour of Mirza Shirazi and his emphasis on justice. Trying to protect local people from undue foreign influence which creates economic injustices is a huge challenge, particularly for a scholar, but the need for justice to prevail in society is one of the central teachings of the Shi'i faith. This was the basis on which Husayn b. Ali refused to give allegiance to Yazid b. Mu'awiyah in Karbala, Iraq leading to his martyrdom. I think it is important to appreciate this kind of spiritual dimension behind Mirza Shirazi's actions, particularly as he studied in Shi'i *hawzas* which emphasised such teachings.

The Tobacco Protest elevated Mirza Shirazi 'to unprecedented authority over both ordinary believers and the entire religious establishment in Iran and Iraq. It transformed him from the preeminent and most influential *mujtahid* among other leaders into the acknowledged head of the *ulama,* whose authority was accepted by most other exemplars.'[53] Equally important, it added a political dimension to his authority. Here, it is important to point out that this elevation in status was not brought about by Mirza Shirazi himself. As I have indicated earlier, Mirza Shirazi came from the Shi'i *hawza* tradition, which was essentially educationalist and spiritualist in nature. Though with the subject of *usul al-fiqh*, a *mujtahid* would be required to give guidance on legal and social matters, this did not necessarily occur on the basis of political authority or political interest.

Meir Litvak aptly sums up Mirza Shirazi's attitude to the Tobacco Protest,

> Mirza Hasan Shirazi's role in the 1891 Tobacco Protests is often cited as an example of the importance of the shrine cities as oppositional centres. Shirazi himself took action against the monopoly fairly late and only after repeated exhortations by other 'ulama' and the merchants ... [the *fatwa*] appeared only in December 1891, after the campaign in Iran was well under way ... in fact before the crisis, Shirazi had been known for his lack of interest in politics.[54]

It is perhaps accurate to say that Mirza Shirazi was motivated by justice in involving himself in the Tobacco Protest, but with an attitude of political disinterest.

Despite Mirza Shirazi's educationalist nature as above, the public and scholarly reaction towards the tobacco concession brought about the politicisation of the Shi'i leadership and marked an improvement in the relations between the *mujtahids* in Iraq and the Qajars before the Constitutional Revolution of Iran between 1905–11, where the real struggle began between the two main rivals of *al-Mashruta* and *al-Mustabidda*. The former movement was called *al-Mashruta* because it took the articles of a constitution to be conditions (*shurut*) that the king must observe in dealing with his subjects, an idea that stems from the theory of social contract made popular in Europe after the French Revolution (1789–99), which gradually spread to Turkey and Iran.[55] However, there was an opposing movement called *al-Mustabidda*. They were called by this name because they believed the constitution was a deviant and irreligious innovation and they opposed democracy and the imposition of a constitution on the monarch *(istibdad)*.[56]

The ideas of the constitutional movement led by al-Akhund al-Khurasani had its roots in Mirza Shirazi's participation in the Tobacco

Protest and were exemplified by the studentship of Mirza Naini, the notable jurist, who wrote a book entitled *Tanbih al-Umma wa Tanzih al-Milla*. The constitutional movement was a

> struggle [that] first surfaced in Iran at the end of the nineteenth century in response to domestic crisis caused by Europe's attempts to dominate Iran's economy and politics. The ineffectual effort to resist European interference underscored the debilitating effects of arbitrary rule and political authority and how it should be deployed to solve the country's problems. The result was the Constitutional Revolution of 1906, which was perhaps the first movement directed at establishing accountable and representative government, one that would meet the demand for strong state institutions, rule of law and individual rights.[57]

The death of Mirza Shirazi and his intellectual legacy

Mirza Shirazi died on 20th February 1895 in Samarra and his death did not merely represent the death of a scholar. It was the death of a public reformer and a people's servant.[58] The transportation of his coffin was extraordinary. It took eight days to move it from Samarra to Najaf. The procession used to stop regularly at each town, where a great number of locals welcomed them in their own way. In the end the coffin reached the holy town of Najaf where Mirza Shirazi was laid in peace in his own graveyard adjacent to the holy shrine.[59] The multifaceted role of Mirza Shirazi left an indelible imprint on the status of the *hawza* in Samarra. The *hawza* had become the prime centre of Shi'i learning with bright graduates and an enduring intellectual heritage. More than that, his participation in the Tobacco Protest 1890, though motivated primarily by justice rather than governance, influenced the mindset of his students and the *ulama* after him to consider social and political affairs as important. The Constitutional Revolution of Iran 1905–11 is a prime example of his continuing influence after his death, along with the concerted efforts by his students to engage with constitutional and political issues. He left a legacy of scholarship, pragmatism and social engagement.

It is a shame that despite the number of students he produced in Samarra, there were still threats from the Ba'athist regime. For example, there were over 100 *mujtahids* residing and teaching in Samarra well into the 1960s (such as Shaykh Mujtaba al-Lankarani, one of the foremost teachers in the *hawza*) until the purge of the scholarly classes and prominent families was initiated by the Ba'athist regime. Some, such as Shaykh Ridha Hamadani[60] (a prominent *mujtahid* in Samarra), are buried there and his grave is still frequented by visitors today. Another example is the Naeb family who held offices in the town and owned land, guest houses, hotels, endowments and other establishments that served both the people of and visitors to Samarra. These were usurped by the Ba'athist regime and have still not been returned to their rightful owners.[61] It is clear that Samarra suffered from the forced exodus of these scholars and prominent families who, for generations, have helped to make Samarra, the landmark it is today. Mirza Shirazi was one of these central figures and his legacy developed the intellectual heritage of Samarra, which has survived through his students.

Notes

1. See Husayn, Jassim., *The Occultation of the Twelfth Imam: A Historical Background* (London, 1982), ch: 2.
2. Al-Tusi, Muhammad b. al-Hasan. *Fihrist Kutub al-Shi'a wa Usuluhum wa Asma al-Musannifin wa Ashab al-Usul* (Qum, 2000), p. 443.
3. Al-Fadhli, Abd al-Hadi., *Tarikh al-Tashri al-Islami* (Qum, 2006), pp. 238–50.
4. Al-Hilli, Hasan b. Yusuf b. Mutahhar., *Khulasat al-Aqwal (Qum,* 2002), p. 101.
5. Al-Najashi: *Rijal al-Najashi*, p. 385.
6. Al-Hilli: *Khulasat al-Aqwal*, p. 248.
7. Modarressi, Hossein., *An Introduction to Shi'i law* (London, 1984), p. 43.
8. Ibid, p. 40.
9. Howard, Ian K. A., "Tahdhib al-Ahkam' and 'Al-Istibsar' by Al-Tusi', *Al-Serat: A Journal of Islamic Studies*, 2:2 (1976). Available online at: http://www.al-islam.org/al-serat/default.asp?url=Tusi-howard.htm
10. It has been reported from ibn al-Athir in his *al-Kamil fi al-Tarikh*, that Sharif al-Murtada's library was the third largest in Baghdad after Shapur's *Dar al-ilm*, the first being *Bayt al-Hikma* founded by the Abbasid Caliph Harun al-Rashid. For further information on the extensiveness of the library, see al-Tusi, Muhammad b. al-Hasan, M., *Talkhis al-Shafi* (Qum, 1974), vol 1, p. 9.

11. See Howard: 'Tahdhib al-Ahkam.'
12. See al-Sadr, Muhammad Baqir., *Principles of Islamic Jurisprudence* (London, 2003), pp. 33–35.
13. It has been reported that when describing the change of the adhan from including the line *haya ala khaiyr al-a'mal*, meaning 'hasten to the best of practices' to instead adding the line *al-salatu khaiyru min al-nawm* meaning 'prayer is better than sleep' into the morning prayer, at the time when the Sunni Seljuks were seizing control of the area and asserting their authority. al-Tusi, Muhammad b. al-Hasan, M., *Talkhis al-Shafi* (Qum, 1974), vol 1, p. 10.
14. Modarressi: *An Introduction to Shi'i law*, p. 51.
15. Gleave, Robert., Inevitable Doubt: *Two Theories of Shi'i Jurisprudence* (Leiden, 2000), p. 10.
16. See Mutahhari, Murtada., 'The Role of Ijtihad in Legislation', *Al-Tawhid Journal*, Vol IV, No.2. http://www.al-islam.org/al-tawhid/default.asp?url=ijtihad-legislation.htm
17. He is the founder of al-Hujja family in Karbala, the cousin and son-in-law of Wahid al-Bihbahani and the author of *Riyad al-Masail* which 'was an important application of the new *usul* methodology in *fiqh*.' Litvak, Meir., *Shi'i Scholars of Nineteenth Century Iraq* (Cambridge, 1998), p. 50.
18. *Qawanin al-Usul* is one of the most technically profound books in *usul al-fiqh*.
19. He is the founder of Kashif al-Ghita family in Najaf and author of Kashf al-Ghita, one of the most important *Imami fiqh* books.
20. For further information on the impact of Bihbahani, see Gleave, Robert., *Inevitable Doubt: Two Theories of Shi'i Jurisprudence* (Leiden, 2000), p. 11.
21. Born in 1742 in Karbala, he is the grandfather of the Bahrululoom family in Najaf and author of several important books in which he contributed theories in *fiqh, usul al-fiqh and ilm al-rijal*. Examples are *al-Masabih* and *Fawaid al-Rijaliyyah*.
22. Al-Amin, Muhsin., *A'yan al-Shi'a* (Beirut, 2000), vol 10, p. 159.
23. *Litvak: Shi'i Scholars of Nineteenth Century Iraq*, pp. 104–5.
24. Mahbuba, Ja'far., *Madi al-Najaf wa-Hadiruha* (Najaf, 1955–58), vol 2, p. 134.
25. *Litvak: Shi'i Scholars of Nineteenth Century Iraq*, pp. 70–75.
26. *Sutuh* is the second stage of studies in a *hawza*.
27. *al-Lum'ah al-Dimashqiya* was written by Muhammad Jamal al-Din al-Makki al-Amili (1334–1385), commonly referred to as *Shahid Awwal* (the first martyr) as he was the first martyred scholar of Islam. Shahid Awwal wrote al-Lum'ah, a textbook of jurisprudence still being taught in seminaries today, in seven days whilst awaiting his martyrdom in prison.

28. Mahallati, Zabih Allah., *Maathir Al-Kubara Fi Tarikh Samarra*, (Qum, 2005), vol 2, p. 56.
29. Al-Amin, Muhsin., *A'yan al-Shi'a,* (Beirut, 1983), vol 5, p304.
30. Ibid, p305. It is also reported that Ansari said he teaches for the sake of three individuals, one of whom was Shirazi. See Mahallati: *Maathir Al-Kubara Fi Tarikh Samarra*, vol 2, p. 55.
31. Ibid and see al-Tehrani, Aqa Buzurg. *Tabaqat A'lam al-Shi'a* (Mashhad, 1984), p. 438.
32. Ibid.
33. Nakash, Yitzhak., *The Shi'is of Iraq* (Oxford, 1995), pp. 262–8 and see al-Wardi, Ali., *Lamahat Ijtimaiyyah min Tarikh al-Iraq al-Hadith,* (Baghdad, 1969), vol 3, pp. 88–90.
34. His notable work *Kifayat al-Usul* is studied even today and has necessitated elucidatory footnotes and commentaries. Many *ulama* of repute have attended to this need, and nearly 120 commentaries exist to explain what Akhund had to say. Akhund Khurasani also gave a *fatwa* in favour of the Constitutional Movement in Iran (1905-11) which was adopted in the state constitution.
35. Author of *Urwat al-Wuthqa* and famous for his anti-constitutionalist stand during the Iranian Constitutional Revolution of 1905–11
36. In his major contribution to *usul al-fiqh*, he differed in many matters with Akhund al-Khurasani, disputing the latter's conclusions. Many students were trained by him in *fiqh*. He is also famous for his political treatise called *Tanzih al-Ummah.*
37. Sayyid Ismail al-Sadr is the grandfather of the well-known Sadr family.
38. Father of Iraqi Prime Minister, Sayyid Muhammad al-Sadr
39. Leader of the 1920 revolution in Iraq, which liberated Iraq from colonial powers.
40. Later executed in Iran for his role in the constitutional movement in 1909.
41. Uncle of Iraqi Foreign and Education Minister Dr Fadhil al-Jamali. *Mara'ashi* in his introduction to *Al-Takmilah* by Hasan al-Sadr mentions many more of the luminaries that attended in Samarra. al-Sadr: *Takmilat Amal al-Amil*, p. 20.
42. Mahallati: *Maathir Al-Kubara Fi Tarikh Samarra*, vol 2, p. 61.
43. Ibid, p. 56
44. al-Wardi, Ali., *Lamahat Ijtimaiyyah min Tarikh al-Iraq al-Hadith* (Baghdad, 1969), vol 3, pp. 94–95.
45. Nasr, Vali., *The Shia Revival: How Conflicts Within Islam Will Shape the Future* (New York, 2006), p. 117.
46. Avery, Peter et al., *The Cambridge History of Iran* (Cambridge, 2003), vol 7, p. 195.

47. Dawani. Ali., *Nahdat Rawhaniyun Iran* (Tehran, 1983), vol 1, p. 92.
48. Avery: *The Cambridge History of Iran*, vol 7, pp.177–198.
49. Sykes, Percy., *A History of Persia*, (London, 1915), p. 395.
50. Avery: *The Cambridge History of Iran*, vol 7, p. 169.
51. Ibid, pp192-5 and see Lapidus, Ira., *A History of Islamic Societies* (Cambridge, 2002), p. 516.
52. Al-Amin: *A'yan al-Shi'a,* vol 4, p. 215.
53. Litvak, Meir., *Shi'i Scholars of Nineteenth Century Iraq* (Cambridge, 1998), p. 86.
54. Ibid, p. 172.
55. al-Wardi: *Lamahat Ijtimaiyyah,* vol 3, p. 103.
56. Al-Juburi, Kamil Salman., *Sayyid Muhammad Kazim al-Yazdi* (Qum, 2006), p. 167.
57. Gheissari, Ali and Nasr, Vali., *Democracy in Iran: History and the Quest for Liberty* (New York, 2006), p. 23.
58. al-Wardi: *Lamahat ijtimaiyya,* vol 3, p. 99.
59. al-Sadr. Hasan., *Takmilat Amal al-Amil* (Qum, 1985), p24.
60. Author of *Misbah al-Faqih*, which is an important textbook in contemporary *hawza* studies in *fiqh* al-istidlali
61. Interview with Mustafa al-Naeb, London, September 2009.

CHAPTER 6

AMILI PERSPECTIVES OF THE *HAWZAS* OF SAMARRA AND NAJAF: SHARAF AL-DIN AND MUHSIN AL-AMIN

Pascal Missak Abidor

In the late 1920s, an Amili cleric living in Najaf, Muhsin Sharara, published what Ende has called 'the most radical and detailed criticism of the teaching methods and cultural climate in Najaf ever written by a Shi'i.'[1] As an alternative to Najaf, Muhsin Sharara proposed that Samarra be made the seat of Arab Shi'i learning. The dichotomy of criticism against Najaf and praise or reverence for Samarra and its clerics appears to be a recurring theme in Shi'i writings by early-twentieth century Shi'a from Jabal Amil. Drawing upon autobiographies, travel accounts and contemporary chapters I propose to outline Amili perspectives on Samarra and Najaf during the early twentieth century as well as to demonstrate that these ideas not only emerged from personal experience but from the historical reliance of Jabal Amil upon Najaf for the production of its *mujtahids*. In the end, the reform of religious education in Najaf did occur due in no small part to the Amili reformists. This Chapter will demonstrate the obvious yet overlooked role of Amili clerics in the reform of education in Najaf.

Indeed, it can be shown through an examination of Amili Shi'i scholars' perspectives of the religious educational establishments (*hawzas*) of Samarra and Najaf that although Samarra was a major centre of religious learning from 1874–95, the impact of its *hawza* was lasting upon the Shi'i community. I have chosen to look at Amili scholars as the basis of this Chapter because the implications of broader religio–scholastic developments are often overlooked in studies on Lebanese Shi'i history in the late Ottoman and French Mandate periods. Furthermore, this study demonstrates the rapidity with which Samarra lost its relevance as a centre for religious learning. As this is a broad subject some limitations of this study need to be explained. Regarding chronology, the period at hand is limited in scope to the late-nineteenth and early-twentieth century. This period is significant because it is the last in which the traditional religious elite of Shi'i Lebanon had significant sway and influence in their community in the absence of Shi'i political parties. As of the mid–late twentieth century, the religious leadership of the Lebanese Shi'i community takes a different shape, with the rise of organised Shi'i movements and the influence of Revolutionary Shi'i thought after 1979. The late-nineteenth to early-twentieth centuries are also a time of reawakening for the Lebanese Shi'i religious and secular elite as they sought to mould their community while recovering from the decline of the previous centuries and coping with the emerging state structures. Lastly, the late-nineteenth century represents the brief time in which the supremacy of Najaf as the centre of Arab Shi'i religious learning was effectively challenged by Samarra. As for Amili scholars, I have chosen the two most important and prominent of the time: Sayyid Abd al-Husayn Sharaf al-Din and Sayyid Muhsin al-Amin, who were both part of the traditional religious elite of Jabal Amil (South Lebanon). These particular scholars have provided prolific writings including autobiographical materials, which form the basis of this study.

Samarra as a centre of religious learning

Though Samarra is significant to Imami-Shi'i Islam as a place of pilgrimage, it was only in the late-nineteenth century that it achieved status as a centre of religious learning. In fact, this was only a brief period of time (circa 1874–95) and came about due to the presence of the major religious scholar Ayatullah Mirza Hasan Shirazi (d. 1895). Shirazi was originally based in Najaf but had moved to Samarra in 1874. The move can briefly be explained as an attempt to achieve sole leadership of the Shi'i community by avoiding competition with other prominent clerics in Najaf and establishing himself as the centre of a *hawza* in a city that had none.[2] As will be evidenced below, Shirazi's move greatly changed the fortunes of Samarra. Today, Mirza Hasan Shirazi is known in scholarship for his role in the Tobacco Protest of 1890–91. In response to the controversy caused when Nasir al-Din Shah granted a tobacco concession over the crop in the Persian Empire to British subject, Major G. F. Talbot, Shirazi issued a widely popular and followed *fatwa* prohibiting the use of tobacco thereby ending the prospect of the British profiting from their concession.[3] Within the history of Shi'i theology, this event is viewed as a major turning point in the history of clerical authority, granting the concept of religious leadership (*riyasa al-imamiyyah*) a new 'political dimension.'[4]

At the same time that Shirazi was making a name for himself through his unprecedented involvement in politics, two clerics from Jabal Amil began their higher religious education in Iraq. Sayyids Abd al-Husayn Sharaf al-Din and Muhsin al-Amin would go on to become important clerics in their own right but in the early 1890s they were only beginning the long process of attaining the qualification to perform *ijtihad* and becoming high-level jurists.

Sharaf al-Din

Sayyid Abd al-Husayn Sharaf al-Din (1873–1957) was an Iraq-born Amili from a long line of religious scholars. Numerous ancestors of his have been written about in works like *A'yan al-Shi'a* by Muhsin al-Amin and *Amal al-Amil* by al-Hurr al-Amili. He was a distant relative of Musa al-Sadr and Muhammad Baqir al-Sadr.[5] Abd al-Husayn Sharaf al-Din's forefathers emigrated to Persia from Jabal Amil to take part in the spread of 'state-sponsored' Shi'i Islam by the Safavid empire.[6]

Sharaf al-Din spent a year in Samarra during the early stages of his higher religious education. Between 1890 and 1891 Sharaf al-Din moved from Kazimiyya to Samarra. While in Samarra, Sharaf al-Din was fully subsumed within the educational milieu created by Shirazi. He had two teachers in the city, Shaykh Baqir Haydar and Sheikh Hasan al-Karbala'i.[7] Each of these men was also a student of Shirazi.[8] Within his own family, Sharaf al-Din joined in Samarra an uncle, Abu Muhammad al-Zaki and a distant cousin, Sayyid Isma'il al-Sadr.[9] Abu Muhammad had moved from Najaf to Samarra with his teacher, Shirazi, in 1874.[10] In the same year, Sayyid Isma'il moved from Isfahan to Samarra to study under Shirazi as well.[11]

Sharaf al-Din's stay in Samarra lasted only a year due to the instability that came to the city during the Tobacco Protest. He does not describe his departure as voluntary, instead saying the situation 'obligated/forced' (*awjaba*) him to leave. In his account of the Tobacco Protest, Sharaf al-Din mentions few particulars of its history and context, referring to the affair only as a *fitna* (discord, civil strife, sedition). Instead, he focuses on the power wielded by Shirazi in the matter and the fear and greed in the reactions of the Ottomans, Qajars and British.

Based on Sharaf al-Din's writings, it is implicitly clear that he viewed the educational relevance of Samarra as inextricably linked to Shirazi. Any mention of Samarra is always linked with Shirazi and his *hawza*.[12]

Figure 1 Abd al-Husayn Sharaf al-Din (1873-1957)

His uncle and distant cousin left Samarra within a year of Shirazi's death. Some of their more important students, those worth mentioning in a biography, were first met while in Samarra.[13] Outside of the Shirazi period, Sharaf al-Din makes no other mention of Samarra. He is fairly detailed in his accounts of his relatives' actions and educations so the absence of Samarra in biographical work from before or after the Shirazi period would indicate that even if they had gone there, it did not relate to education and was otherwise insignificant.

Muhsin al-Amin

Sayyid Muhsin al-Amin (1867–1952) was an Amili cleric from the town of Shaqra. He moved to Najaf while in his twenties to continue his religious education following four years of his studies' lapsing after the death of his teacher.[14] Al-Amin had much briefer but equally telling experiences in Samarra. In his autobiographical writings there are accounts of three visits to Samarra, two visits during Shirazi's lifetime and one occurring in 1933–4. Muhsin al-Amin visited Samarra twice in his first two years in Iraq, in 1891 before Shirazi became involved in the Tobacco Protest and in 1893.[15] Al-Amin limits his discussion of Shirazi and the Tobacco Protest to Shirazi's entry in *A'yan al-Shi'a*. Unlike Sharaf al-Din, who implicitly connects Shirazi with the Samarran educational establishment, al-Amin is unequivocal on the matter. In his 1891 encounter he describes throngs of people, *ulama*, students, travellers and pilgrims coming to visit Shirazi.[16] In 1893, al-Amin was able to sit with Shirazi and ask him questions on jurisprudence.[17]

Muhsin al-Amin's equation of Samarra with Shirazi is clear in his detailed description of the city's development following Shirazi's arrival there:

> Before he lived there, Samarra was a small village. After he lived there it prospered remarkably and houses and suqs (markets) were built [there]. Foreigners lived there as well as people seeking a livelihood, the number of [foreign] delegates increased and the number of students and teachers was not to be overlooked . . .[18]

Shirazi had schools and *aswaq* (markets) built as well as the first bridge to cross the Tigris since the Abbasids – all using funds that were collected from visitors or sent to him from India and other places.[19] Shirazi had also anonymously provided monthly stipends to the town's poor families and bankrupt merchants. He extended his influence beyond the city by giving monthly stipends to promising students outside of Samarra.[20]

Despite all of his efforts, Shirazi's institutions suffered from the common problem of collapsing after their founder's death. The schools closed shortly after his death and within a few years, the markets that were built would become dilapidated. Cynically, al-Amin mentions that the bridge remained in use though in disrepair as the town had come to rely upon the money it brought in.[21] The decline in Samarra's fortunes was directly related to Shirazi's death. Without him, the centre and chief fundraiser of the educational establishment was gone as was the added attraction that had greatly increased the number of pilgrims to Samarra.[22]

Many years later, in early 1934, al-Amin visited Samarra again and in his travel diaries he provides a report on the state of religious education in the city. At this point Samarra or Shi'i Samarra, was a shell of its former self under Shirazi. While religious instruction was still offered, the number of students who travelled to the city to pursue higher education had dwindled greatly. According to al-Amin, there were barely 40 émigré (*muhajirin*) students, so poor they could not afford government issued bread, compared to Shirazi's day when the city was 'teeming' with students.[23] During Muhsin al-Amin's first visits to Samarra, he noted that Shirazi had a bridge built to subvert the extortion of the locals who would force travellers to pay high prices by demanding payment in the middle of the Tigris. According to al-Amin, the locals profited from the bridge after Shirazi's death while allowing it to fall into disrepair, biding their time until it fell apart and they could return to their original scam.[24] By the 1930s, however, the price to cross the Tigris was a set amount of 20 fils collected by and for the government in Baghdad.[25]

Critiquing religious education in Najaf and Samarra

Both Sharaf al-Din and al-Amin spent the vast majority of their higher education in Najaf. It should be noted that though Sharaf al-Din started

Figure 2 Sayyid Muhsin al-Amin (1867–1952)

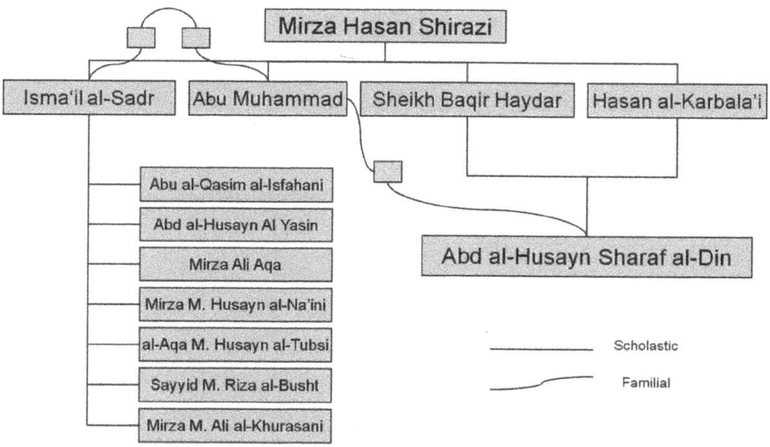

Figure 3 The Sharaf al-Din/al-Sadr family in Samarra

his studies in Samarra before going to Najaf, Muhsin al-Amin went directly to Najaf. Al-Amin's decision could be attributed to the larger number of Amilis in Najaf and the tendency for social groupings in the centres of learning to follow 'ethnic and regional divisions'.[26] Al-Amin indicates that he was capable of choosing to take a teacher's course based solely on whether it had enough Amili students.[27] Muhsin al-Amin was part of an Amili student group that refused to accept anyone who was not from Jabal Amil.[28] Sharaf al-Din's decision would have been skewed by the fact that he was born in Iraq and had family members already living in Samarra. Despite having a number of the same teachers in Najaf, the two men had different opinions of the city.[29] Besides praise for his teachers, Sharaf al-Din appears to have had little to comment on the nature of religious education in Najaf. Educational reform was of little importance to Sharaf al-Din and he saw no problem with the system in Najaf just as he saw little reason to work toward ameliorating the educational situation in Lebanon.[30] Al-Amin, however, was highly critical of education in Najaf, providing a seven point list of problems with the system. In summary, these issues related to poor regulation of students' qualifications to take courses, unqualified teachers, improper division of topics, obsessions with the hypothetical aspects of jurisprudence, neglect of the science of hadith and *isnad* (chain of transmission) and the de-emphasis of the requisite mastery of Arabic.[31] These problems were partially due to the competition between the *ulama* in the major centres of learning 'for students, prestige, funds, and influence' in the community.[32] The relationship between the students' freedom and the teachers' competition was bi-directional, however, as the students' freedom to choose teachers encouraged the competition amongst those teachers to attract more students.[33] Any reform with the view of rectifying these problems was made especially difficult due to the fact that these levels of courses were driven entirely by *mujtahid*s with no supporting bureaucracy.[34]

In 1928, Muhsin Sharara, an Amili religious student in Najaf, published a chapter in the Lebanese Shi'i journal *al-Irfan* critiquing the suitability of Najaf as a centre of religious learning. In this chapter, Sharara proposed looking at Mirza Hasan Shirazi as an inspiration for moving the centre of religious learning to Samarra – an idea that was not well received by the people of Najaf.[35] Other ideas of Muhsin Sharara concerning the adaptation of the system to the needs of modern times would later be iterated by others, including Muhsin al-Amin.[36] Sharara's critique of Najaf was all-encompassing including descriptions of the poor public health situation there compared to the healthier environment and climate in Samarra.[37] The fact that his grandfather died of tuberculosis that he had contracted while in Najaf no doubt played a part in this assessment.[38]

Whether it was meant to be seriously considered or not, it can be seen in the accounts of our two preceding jurists that Sharara's proposal vis-à-vis Samarra was anachronistic. By 1928, Samarra had long lost the relevance to Shi'i higher education it had gained as well as any links with Shirazi. Shirazi's son, Ali, had remained in Samarra with a small group of followers until his own death in 1920.[39] At some point during the First World War, Hasan Shirazi's student and successor, Muhammad Taqi Shirazi, had left Samarra to relocate to the safety of Karbala.[40] As we have seen, only a few years after Sharara's chapter, Muhsin al-Amin's account of Samarra shows a severely deteriorated educational establishment. Lastly, the more accepted solution to the problems with education in Najaf had been to work towards reform – an effort that Muhsin al-Amin and other Amilis supported.[41]

Despite the brevity of these Amili scholars' encounters with Shirazi and Samarra, the influence of the latter on the former should not be discounted. During their time studying in Iraq, Shirazi was the only scholar-jurist to be the undisputed and sole *marja al-taqlid* (source of emulation, supreme exemplar) for the Shi'i community.[42] Al-Amin and Sharaf al-Din left Iraq in 1901 and 1904, respectively, seeing religious leadership divided amongst a number of *mujtahids* in the last few years of their stay.[43] Following Shirazi's death,

Figure 4 Muhsin Sharara

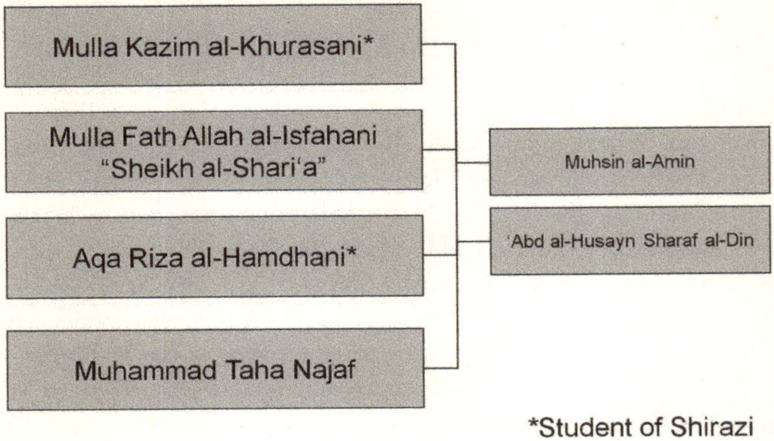

Figure 5 Common teachers between al-Amin and Sharaf al-Din

leadership of the Shi'i community was divided until 1908–09 when a series of *mujtahid*s achieved sole leadership of the community before leadership was divided again until the arrival of Ayatollah Burujirdi in 1946.[44] It is through the first three of these sole *maraji* that Shirazi's legacy would continue for a time, as they had all been his students.[45] The tendency towards the consideration of the broader theological and jurisprudential situation within Shi'i thought when examining the Shi'i community in nineteenth and twentieth century Iraq and Iran should also be applied to the Shi'i community of Lebanon.

The impact of Shirazi's legacy on Amili clerics

Thus considered, Shirazi's legacy was long lasting for the Amili clerics. Most obvious was the submission of the Amili clerics to the emulation (*taqlid*) of his students. Sharaf al-Din and al-Amin both deferred to the authority of Shirazi's student and successor, Mirza Muhammad Taqi Shirazi. Taqi Shirazi issued two important *fatawa* that prohibited Muslims from electing non-Muslim leaders and calling for the excommunication (*takfir*) of Muslims who took a position in government. These *fatawa* played no small part in the support of the Amili religious elite for attachment to Syria instead of Lebanon, a country with Christian leadership and dominance and the refusal of both Muhsin al-Amin and Abd al-Husayn Sharaf al-Din to serve as president of the newly formed Shi'i court in the French Mandate of Lebanon.[46] Before any of this, however, al-Amin and Sharaf al-Din studied under students of Shirazi.[47]

If we consider al-Amin and Sharaf al-Din as part of and beholden to the progression of clerical authority in Shi'i Islam, Shirazi's influence can be seen in their reformist tendencies. Each of these men represents different trends that can be interpreted as emanating from Shirazi's legacy. Sharaf al-Din was highly engaged in the politics of the Shi'i community in Lebanon during the Mandate era.[48] Unsurprisingly, his account of Samarra and Shirazi focuses upon the political impact of Shirazi's actions, providing a detailed description of Ottoman, Qajar, and British responses. The precedent of political activism set by Shirazi would have been a major factor in influencing as well as allowing Sharaf al-Din's behaviour. Al-Amin, on the other hand, focused upon the transformations Shirazi achieved in Samarra and its educational establishment. Though politically quietist, Al-Amin's legacy was in two fields: the reform of religious practice[49] and the establishment of lasting schools and other social institutions in Syria and Lebanon.[50] One certainly sees the influence of Shirazi in the latter and there are strong parallels between Shirazi's transformation and the development of Samarra for the Shi'i community there and al-Amin's transformation and development of the Shi'i community of Damascus.

Notes

1. Ende, Werner., 'From Revolt to Resignation: The Life of Shaykh Muhsin Sharara' in *Humanism, Culture, and Language in the Near East*, ed. Asma Afsaruddin and A.H. Mathias Zahniser (Winona Lake, 1997), pp. 61–70.
2. Litvak, Meir., *Shi'i Scholars of Nineteenth-Century Iraq: The 'Ulama' of Najaf and Karbala'* (Cambridge, 1998), p. 83.

3. Lambton, Ann., 'The Tobacco Regie: Prelude to Revolution I', *Studia Islamica* 22 (1965), pp. 119–157 and 145 – see preceding pages for details of the events surrounding the granting of the concession and the lead up to Shirazi's *fatwa*. See also Keddie, Nikki., *Religion and Rebellion in Iran: The Iranian Tobacco Protest of 1891-1892* (New York, 1966), p. 96. Keddie states that there is debate as to the actual provenance of Shirazi's *fatwa* with opinions ranging from it originating with Shirazi to Shirazi only later approving the *fatwa* after it had been issued in his name. This debate is irrelevant to the topic at hand and for simplicity I have adopted the standard history of the Tobacco Protest.
4. Ammanat, Abbas., 'In Between the Madrasa and the Marketplace: The Designation of Clerical Leadership in Modern Shi'ism' in *Authority and Political Culture in Shi'ism*, ed. Said Amir Arjomand (New York, 1988), p. 117.
5. Sharaf al-Din, Abd al-Husayn., *Bughyat al-Raghibin fi Silsal Al Sharaf al-Din* (Beirut, 1991). Volume 1 of this family history provides detailed bibliographic information about many members of the Sharaf al-Din / al-Sadr line.
6. Abisaab, Rula., *Converting Persia: Religion and Power in the Safavid Empire* (New York, 2004), p. 151.
7. Sharaf al-Din: *Bughyat al-Raghibin*, vol 2, p. 67.
8. Al-Amin, Muhsin., *A'yan al-Shi'a* (Beirut, 2000), vol 8, p. 448.
9. Sharaf al-Din: *Bughyat al-Raghibin*, vol 2, p. 66.
10. Ibid, vol 1, p. 300.
11. Ibid, vol, pp. 193–194.
12. Sharaf al-Din: *Bughyat al-Raghibin* - an examination of the work shows this.
13. Sharaf al-Din: *Bughyat al-Raghibin*, vol 1, p. 306 and 195.
14. Al-Amin: *A'yan al-Shi'a*, vol 15, p. 320 – the teacher was Musa Sharara.
15. Ibid, vol 3, p. 445. Within his autobiography, Muhsin al-Amin conflates these two visits in to one but describes two distinct visits in Shirazi's entry in *A'yan al-Shi'a*. See vol 15, p. 324.
16. Ibid, vol 15, p. 324.
17. Ibid, vol 8, p. 445.
18. Ibid.
19. Ibid
20. Ibid, vol 8, p. 447 – al-Amin says that Shirazi's heir in matters of *usul al-fiqh*, Mulla Kazim al-Khurasani, as a student who received a stipend until Shirazi's death.
21. Ibid, vol 8, p. 445.
22. Litvak: *Shi'i Scholars*, pp. 90–91
23. al-Amin, Muhsin., *Rihlat Muhsin al-Amin* (Beirut, 2001), p. 123.

24. Al-Amin: *A'yan al-Shi'a*, vol 8, p. 445.
25. Al-Amin: *Rihlat*, p. 123.
26. Litvak: *Shi'i Scholars*, p. 33.
27. Al-Amin: *A'yan al-Shi'a*, vol 15, p. 328.
28. Ibid, vol 15, p. 330.
29. Sharaf al-Din: *Bughyat al-Raghibin*, vol 2, pp. 71–77; Al-Amin: *A'yan al-Shi'a*, vol 15, p. 354. The teachers being: Mulla Kazim al-Khurasani, Muhammad Taha Najaf, Aqa Riza al-Hamdhani, Mulla Fathallah al-Isfahani 'Sheikh al-Shari'a'.
30. Mervin, Sabrina., *Un Réformisme Chiite, Ulémas et lettrés du Jabal 'Âmil (actuel Liban-Sud) de la fin de l'Empire ottoman à l'indépendance du Liban* (Paris, 2000), p. 182.
31. Al-Amin: *A'yan al-Shi'a*, vol 15, pp. 325–326.
32. Litvak: *Shi'i Scholars*, p. 22.
33. Litvak, Meir., 'Madrasa and Learning in Nineteenth-Century Najaf and Karbala' in *The Twelver Shia in Modern times: Religious Culture & Political History*, eds. Rainer Brunner and Werner Ende (Leiden, 2001), pp. 58–78, 72.
34. Mervin, Sabrina., 'The Clerics of Jabal Amil and the Reform of Religious Teaching in Najaf Since the Beginning of the twentieth Century' in *The Twelver Shia in Modern times: Religious Culture & Political History*, eds. Rainer Brunner and Werner Ende (Leiden, 2001), pp. 79–86, 79.
35. Ende, Werner., 'From Revolt to Resignation: The Life of Shaykh Muhsin Sharara' in *Humanism, Culture, and Language in the Near East*, ed. Asma Afsaruddin and A.H. Mathias Zahniser (Winona Lake, 1997), pp. 61–70, 64–66.
36. Mervin: 'The Clerics of Jabal Amil', pp. 81–82
37. Ende: 'The Life of Muhsin Sharara', p. 65.
38. Mervin: *Un Réformisme Chiite*, p. 99. His doctor order him to return to Jabal Amil where the climate was better. This was the second option offered to him by the doctor, the first being a guaranteed cure which was, unfortunately, more than Musa Sharara could afford.
39. Al-Amin: *A'yan al-Shi'a*, vol 12, p. 439; Litvak: *Shi'i Scholars*, p. 90.
40. Al-Amin: *A'yan al-Shi'a*, vol 13, p. 449.
41. Mervin: *Un Réformisme Chiite,* pp. 212–228.
42. Mussavi, Ahmad Kazemi., 'The Institutionalization of *Marja'-i Taqlid* in the Nineteenth Century Shi'ite Community', *Muslim World* 83 (1994), pp. 279–99, 291.
43. Al-Amin: *A'yan al-Shi'a*, vol 15, p. 337; Sharaf al-Din: *Bughyat al-Raghibin,* vol 2, p. 104.
44. Litvak: *Shi'i Scholars*, pp. 90–91; Mussavi: 'Institutionalization of *Marja'-i Taqlid*', p. 292; Momen Moojan., *An Introduction to Shi'i Islam* (Connecticut, 1985), pp. 321–322.

45. Al-Amin: *A'yan al-Shi'a*, vol 8, pp. 448–449 - Mulla Kazim al-Khurasani, Sayyid Kazim al-Yazdi, Mirza Muhammad Taqi al-Shirazi.
46. Chalabi, Tamarra., *The Shi'is of Jabal 'Amil and the New Lebanon: Community and Nation State 1918 – 1943* (New York, 2006), pp. 141–42.
47. Sharaf al-Din: *Bughyat al-Raghibin*, vol 2, pp. 71–77; Al-Amin: *A'yan al-Shi'a*, vol 15, p. 354.
48. Ibid, p. 141.
49. For information on this see: al-Najafi, Muhammad al-Qasim Husayni., *Thawrat al-Tanzih* (Beirut, 1996); Ende, Werner., 'The flagellations of Muharram and the Shi'ite *'Ulama'*, *Islam* 55 (1978), pp. 19–36; Mervin: *Un Réformisme*; Weiss, Max., 'The Cultural Politics of Shi'i Modernism: Morality and Gender in Early twentieth-Century Lebanon,' *International Journal of Middle East Studies* 39 (2007), pp. 249–270.
50. See relevant chapters in Al-Amin: *A'yan al-Shi'a*, vol 15, pp. 297–466; Mervin, Sabrina. *Autobiographie D'un Clerc Chiite du Gabal 'Amil* (Damascus, 1998). Mervin, *Un Réformisme Chiite* – a number of the schools and institutions Muhsin al-Amin established are still open and operating to this day.

PART III

SAMARRA IN WIDER IRAQI DISCOURSE: SECTARIANISM, POLITICS AND CITIZENSHIP

CHAPTER 7

SECTARIANISM IN RECENT IRAQI HISTORY: WHAT IT IS AND WHAT IT ISN'T

Peter Sluglett

This Chapter will attempt to discuss the phenomenon of Iraqi sectarianism in historical terms showing that while sectarian consciousness has in some sense always existed, this should not be extrapolated into permanent sectarian antagonism. Sunni–Shi'i tensions were virtually non-existent and relatively unimportant until Saddam Hussein's regime exacerbated them in the course of the Iran–Iraq war. In addition, while it is true that the Sunnis were favoured by the British under the Iraqi mandate and monarchy, there was no real sense of persecution. I will explain how the Sunnis came to be preferred by the British and how the Shi'a of early-modern Iraq were on the whole not eager to be co-opted into the modern state. It is also important to stress that contemporary tensions have not existed 'from time immemorial' and are largely a product of unwise external intervention. However, it is equally important to realise that the tensions would not have risen to the surface had there not been some underlying substance to them. Thus, the notion *maku farq baynana, kulluna Iraqiyin* (there is no difference between us, we are all Iraqis) has some element of wishful thinking.

Religious identity

Iraqis often say, *maku farq baynana, kulluna Iraqiyyin* which means Sunnis, Shi'a, Kurds, Christians, Turcomans and Yazidis are united by being Iraqis. One of the broader implications of this is that however great the misery in which Iraqis were living under the regime of Saddam Hussein or of the imposed sanctions of the UN (or US), Iraqis are painted as people basking in some kind of non-sectarian harmony for most of the period before the American invasion in 2003. As the story goes, the American occupation effectively revived sectarianism, which had by then become largely dormant. The main consequence of this turned out to be, on the one hand, the promotion of the interests of the Shi'a (and the Kurds of course) over those of anyone else and on the other, discrimination against the Sunnis, whom the Americans, in their ignorance, found it convenient to label *en masse* as Ba'athists or crypto-Ba'athists. One of the long term consequences of this mistaken and insensitively applied policy has been the creation, by the Americans, of an Iraqi government composed largely (or at least most significantly) of religious Shi'a with strong ties to Iran. As in almost all cases of this kind, there is some truth in this version of events but also a great deal of error and I want to try to unpack these elements as best I can.

In the first place, sectarian or religious affiliation and identity are very different notions in the Middle East and the Muslim world compared to Europe or the United States. For the most part, in present-day Europe and North America, religious affiliation is largely an act of personal choice. It is not generally expected that an individual should be affiliated *with any religion at all* (except in some especially tight-knit communities). Although this varies considerably between different European and American contexts, there is generally a fairly strict separation of religion and state. This is because the state does not permit religion or religious institutions to play a significant role in public life (perhaps in the case of France) or it is the duty of the state to see to it that its citizens are free to practise the religion of their choice as private individuals (perhaps in the case of America). It may even be both these reasons.

However, in the Islamic world, religious affiliation for both Muslims and non-Muslims is significantly a matter of community of origin, faith or sect into which an individual was born, rather than a matter of deliberate personal choice. Thus a Middle-Eastern Muslim or Christian is a Muslim or Christian because his or her parents were Muslims or Christians, rather than because he or she has voluntarily espoused Islam or Christianity. One major consequence of this is that an individual's identity as a Muslim or a Christian or a Jew has no necessary connection with belief. So you may well be an atheist but your identity card will say that you are a Muslim or a Christian because that was what you were born. In many cases your community of origin will be obvious from your names, first and last.

The second major point is that since Iraqis are born into different religious sects and ethnicities, an individual's identity is not constant. At different times and in different circumstances, some aspects of an individual's identity assume greater importance than others. So in the face of war or invasion from outside, sectarian identity will become less important than national identity i.e the notion of 'being Iraqi' in the face of external threats. Similarly, if a sect or ethnic group is suffering persecution then sectarian or ethnic identity will come to the fore. This idea has been stated very clearly by the Lebanese writer Amin Maalouf:

> In every age there have been people who considered that an individual had one overriding affiliation so much important in every circumstance to all others that it might legitimately be called his 'identity'. For some it was the nation, for others, religion or class. But one only has to look at the various conflicts being fought out all over the world today to realise that no one allegiance has absolute supremacy. When people feel their faith is threatened, it is their religious affiliation that seems to reflect their whole identity. But if their mother tongue or their ethnic group is in danger, then they will fight ferociously against their own co-religionists. Both the Turks and Kurds are Muslims, though they speak different languages; but does that make the war between them any less bloody? Hutus and Tutsis alike are Catholics, and they speak the same language, but has that stopped them

> slaughtering one another? Czechs and Slovaks are all Catholics too, but does that help them to live together?[1]

I would also like to quote a passage by Ussama Makdisi (writing about the history of nineteenth century Lebanon):

> From the outset … it is imperative to dispel any illusion that sectarianism is simply or exclusively a native malignancy or a foreign conspiracy. Sectarianism can be narrated only by continually acknowledging and referring to both indigenous and imperial histories, which interacted – both colluded and collaborated – to produce a new historical imagination.[2]

There are two other factors at work in the context of more-or-less contemporary Iraq – both revolving around the way the 'master narrative' is constructed. The first is that like other colonial powers in the past (particularly the British in India[3]) the US has used the existence of sectarian hostility to justify the continuation of its presence. US representatives say 'there will be civil war if we withdraw too quickly' just as the British considered their own presence essential in order to prevent communal conflict between Hindus and Muslims. This opinion cannot be dismissed as being entirely without foundation. However, the conflict in Iraq is so complex and so baffling particularly to the (inevitably) unspecialised journalists who report it that they take the very human line of least resistance in trying to simplify it and to make it comprehensible to themselves as well as their audience.[4] So one will often find stories starting with assertions such as 'Shi'a think …', 'Sunnis fear …' 'Kurds are trying to obtain …' with no proper attribution for these generalisations which become 'analyses'.[5] Motivation is all too often ascribed to some axiomatic behaviour pattern or on the grounds that they 'all hate each other' (and that 'they', unlike 'us', are completely irrational).

Finally, it is also the case that a great deal of the fighting in Iraq over the past few years has been *intra*-Shi'i. In the south, there has been a lot of conflict between the militias of those Shi'i groups who seek some kind of federal structure for the oil-rich southern provinces and other Shi'i groups (based mainly in Baghdad and central Iraq) who are bitterly opposed to anything of the kind.[6] It is no secret that there are profound enmities between the followers of Muqtada al-Sadr (almost all of whom stayed in or could not leave Iraq during the Ba'athist period), the supporters of Ayatullah Abd al-Aziz al-Hakim (the head of the Supreme Council for Islamic Revolution in Iraq – SCIRI) and sections of the Maliki government. It is also quite clear that these often deadly disagreements are political, not doctrinal or religious.

V. P. Gagnon's *The Myth of Ethnic War: Serbia and Croatia in the 1990s*,[7] is very helpful in trying to get to grips with the phenomenon of sectarianism. It is specifically useful in helping us understand the mechanisms that cause people who have lived next door to each other for years (who have also intermarried or collaborated politically), suddenly to turn on one another. The kinds of violence which took place in the Balkans in the 1990s and continues in Iraq today almost always breaks out in circumstances under which state power has collapsed and there is a hiatus or transition; a relatively ordered past gives way to a suddenly uncertain future. Indeed, journalists and others tended to explain the conflict in Yugoslavia in terms of the unleashing of ancient ethnic hatreds which were never very far below the surface. Here are two quotations that point towards a rather different reality,

> ... the violence of the Yugoslav wars of the 1990s was part of a broad strategy in which images of threatening enemies and violence were used by conservative elites in Serbia and Croatia; not in order to mobilize people but rather as a way to *demobilize* those who were pushing for changes in the structures of economic and political power that would negatively affect the interests of those elites. ... This ... enabled conservatives to maintain control of existing structures of power, as well as to reposition themselves by converting state-owned property into privately held wealth, the basis of power in the new system of a liberal economy.[8]

And,

> If we can learn anything from Balkan history, it is that ethnic identities and the meanings attributed to them are fluid. This is a region where coexistence was the norm, where homogeneity

> has historically not been a prerequisite for peace, and where violence was most often a tool used by outsiders in order to deal with social and/or political realities that they did not like and could not otherwise control. ... In response elites fomented and provoked conflict in ethnic terms in order to change the meanings of ethnic identities and the nature of ... the relationships between people who identify in common ethnic terms ...[9]

This kind of analysis is extremely helpful in our attempts to understand what is happening in Iraq. It is of course undeniable that from Iraq's inception as a state and for much of the first twenty or thirty years of its existence, the Sunni Arabs, who constituted what can generously be estimated as a quarter of the total population, exercised a virtual monopoly over its political and administrative functions. On the other hand, in spite of this evident imbalance, whose most obvious corollary was the very limited representation of the Shi'a in government, public service and in the upper echelons of the military, this was not, or at least was not simply, a *religious* divide. This is because the Sunni Arab leadership before and after 1958 did not have a religious agenda; most of the individuals who formed part of it were secular or agnostic. It is worth reminding ourselves once again that these labels are essentially descriptive of whatever sect an individual may happen to have been born into rather than an expression of religious belief. Although a small group of Sunnis did indeed monopolise public office, it was also the case that until the army became sufficiently large and/or competent to defeat tribal rebellions in the mid-1930s, the Iraqi regime under the mandate and monarchy (1920–58) depended on a close partnership between the Sunni politicians in Baghdad and the great tribal landowners of the south and centre, all of whom were Shi'as.[10] What I will do now is to try to outline the process by which the Sunnis came to dominate the political, administrative and military structures of the modern Iraqi state.

The political climate of Iraq

In the late Ottoman period, the area that now forms Iraq consisted of the three Ottoman provinces of Basra, Baghdad and Mosul. These were ruled (at least after 1831) by governors sent out from Istanbul.[11] Even after the introduction into Iraq of the modernising reforms of the Tanzimat under Midhat Pasha in the late 1860s, most governors' terms of office were fairly short. The result was that both the governors themselves and the Ottoman state as an institution relied substantially on informal partnerships with the local urban elite, almost all of whom, except the great landowners of the rural south, were Sunnis. As the Ottoman bureaucracy expanded and hereditary landownership became more widespread after the introduction of the provisions of the Ottoman Land Code of 1858, members of the Sunni Arab nobility became part of a bureaucratic and military 'aristocracy of service' acting as intermediaries between the Ottoman state and its subjects. As a Sunni institution, the Ottoman Empire had a somewhat ambivalent attitude towards Shi'a (especially the Shi'a of Iraq – given their numbers, their demographic concentration and the presence of the *atabat* i.e holy thresholds) and tended only to employ Sunnis, Christians and Jews in government service. The Ottoman governors Najib Pasha and Namiq Pasha succeeded in ending the semi-autonomous status of Karbala and Najaf by their attacks on the two cities in 1843 and 1852 respectively. However, after this the *atabat* were generally left to their own devices by the central government for the remainder of the Ottoman period. In particular, 'Abd al-Hamid II's pan-Islamic agenda and his repeated calls for Muslim unity created fairly cordial relations with the Iranian court and the Iraqi Shi'i clerical hierarchy.[12]

When the educational reforms of the Ottoman *tanzimat* (reorganisation) arrived in Iraq in the last decades of the nineteenth century, few Shi'a attended the newly established modern state schools. Rather, such Shi'a, if they could afford it, sent their children to private schools run or at least supervised by the clergy. Furthermore, given Shi'i attitudes towards the Ottoman (or indeed any) state (i.e the basic notion that the temporal state functioned as a kind of necessary evil to be endured until the coming of the twelfth Imam), Shi'a did not regard state service as a particularly noble calling. Thus very few of them joined the burgeoning ranks of the Ottoman bureaucracy between 1870 and 1914 and fewer still became officers in the Ottoman Army. Hence, when the Iraqi state was created in 1920, Sunni Arabs continued to supply the main cadres for the administration and the officer corps. Such individuals were recruited from the old notable families (which included both urban absentee landlords and tribal leaders in central and western Iraq) and from the ranks of more *nouveaux riches* ex-Ottoman officers and officials. Since so few Shi'a were either available for such positions or perhaps more importantly, deemed competent to be able to serve in them, the result was the gross under-representation of Shi'a in the civil service in proportion to their numbers in the population as a whole. For similar reasons, the same situation occurred in all the ministries of the pre-1958 period.[13]

It was also the case that, in their desire to control Iraq, the British (to simplify a much more complex reality) generally found the Sunnis the more congenial partners and for their part both the Sunni aristocracy and the Sunni *nouveaux* seemed happy enough to transfer their loyalties almost seamlessly from the Ottomans to the British. Faysal, the new king of Iraq, came from a leading Sunni family in the Hijaz and his principal Iraqi supporters were all Sunnis. Some of these supporters were partly members of the service aristocracy and some partly from the ranks of the Ottoman officers who had gathered around him during the Arab revolt and in his time in Syria during 1918–20. In stark contrast, the *marja-i taqlid* (source of imitation), Ayatullah Muhammad Taqi Shirazi, issued a *fatwa* on 1 March 1920 asserting that service under the British was unlawful. In addition, many of the leading clergy of the *atabat* had been closely involved in the events of the Iranian Constitutional Movement, which had temporarily managed to impose a Constituent Assembly and a Constitution on the Qajar monarchy in 1906.[14]

It is important to add that in the early-twentieth century, many members of the small Sunni Arab bureaucratic and military elite were influenced, to a greater or lesser extent, by embryonic ideas of Arab nationalism. I say embryonic because the strength and deep-rootedness of the Arab nationalist movement as a phenomenon has been greatly exaggerated after the fact. Suffice it to say that Arab nationalism does not, generally, much antedate its reinvention by Sati' al-Husri in the 1920s; there is little hard evidence of the strength or universality of the ideology before the collapse of the Ottoman Empire. This is quite comprehensible when we take into account the conquest or take-over of Algeria, Tunisia, Egypt and Tripolitania by Britain, France and Italy in 1830, 1881, 1882 and 1911. These were catastrophic events which would have caused many Arabs (the vast majority of whom were Sunni Muslims like the Ottoman Turks) to have regarded the Ottoman Empire as 'the only remaining political force capable of forestalling European colonial ambitions'.[15]

In addition, by their espousal or perhaps their promotion of the Hashemite cause in 1915, the British seem to have backed the wrong horse – at least to the extent that they believed themselves to have been tapping into a broader movement of potential resistance which was largely a figment of the imagination of a few professionally anti-Ottoman British intelligence enthusiasts. These individuals managed to convince their superiors that the Hashemites were a sort of 'Islamic aristocracy' whose name resounded throughout the Muslim world but that is another story.[16] However heavy-handed the official narrative of nationalist historiography has been, even its most diehard proponents cannot disguise the fact that there were no widespread manifestations of anti-Ottoman sentiment (let alone the potential for an anti-Ottoman revolt) either in wartime Syria or in wartime Iraq where such displays would obviously have received either covert or overt British backing.

Shi'i participation

Shi'i interest or participation in such activities was of a rather different order. It is better described as 'anti-imperialist' than 'Arab'. It is also important that the 'Shi'i leadership' at this stage, apart from Ja'far' Abu al-Timman, consisted mostly of members of the clerical hierarchy. On the other hand, the fact that many Shi'i clergy had been profoundly opposed to the secularising ideology of the Young Turks did not stop them rallying to the Ottoman cause as soon as the British landed in southern Iraq at the beginning of the First World War; the *ulama* (scholars) of Karbala and Najaf immediately declared a *jihad* (act of striving) against the invaders in November 1914.[17] At the same time, the inhabitants of the *atabat* (like most Syrians) seem to have been almost completely indifferent to Sharifian propaganda urging all Arabs to join with the British in throwing off the Ottoman yoke.

In February 1919, Ayatullahs Muhammad Taqi al-Shirazi and Shaykh al-Shari'a al-Isfahani wrote two letters to President Woodrow Wilson, seeking his aid against Britain and the British occupation. The second letter, dated 21 February, contains the following passage:

> The desire of all Iraqis, as [members of] a Muslim nation is that they should be given the liberty to choose a new independent Arab and Islamic state, with a Muslim king assisted by a national assembly. As far as the question of a protectorate (*wisaya*, i.e. this letter antedates the term mandate, *intidab*) is concerned, it should be up to the national assembly to accept it or reject it, after the convening of a peace conference.[18]

Similar sentiments continued to be expressed in various petitions submitted to the British-occupation authorities in the run up to what has become known in somewhat grandiose terms as 'The Great Iraqi Revolution of 1920'. Furthermore, the words 'independent Arab and Islamic state' or 'independent Islamic state' crop up again and again. British reports routinely portrayed the Shi'i *mujtahids* as extremists, fanatics and reactionaries irrevocably opposed to progress, presumably in an attempt to deflect attention from their core (and ultimately unacceptable) demand for independence. Of course, given their previous linkages to the Ottoman state, it was almost inconceivable that the Sunni 'aristocracy of service' should seriously associate themselves with what they considered to be a Shi'i independence movement. If this succeeded, it would almost certainly undermine the foundations of their own power. This explains the Sunni elite's almost eager alignment, almost immediately after the revolution of 1920, with the British mandatory authorities, its ready embrace of the ideology of Arab nationalism and rather later, the notion of a united fertile crescent under Hashemite rule.

Of course, both those who promoted Arab nationalism and the content of the doctrine itself underwent important qualitative changes with the passage of time. In the case of the Sharifian officers who threw in their lot with Faysal and the Iraqi state after 1920, their original patriotic and nationalist attitudes (in the sense of aspirations for independence from Ottoman rule) are not in doubt. Furthermore they could and did argue, at least at the beginning of the 1920s, that however faintly Iraq might resemble an independent state, it was at least 'more Arab' in its administration and more of a formally coherent entity than the three provinces had been under Ottoman rule. By the end of the 1920s, however, it was clear that such politicians as Nuri al-Saeed and Ja'far al-Askari had become content merely to accommodate themselves to the exigencies of British policy. The result was that whatever Arab nationalist credentials they might once have possessed gradually ceased to count in their favour among most Iraqis. The mainstream of Arab or Iraqi national awareness passed to different groups, who developed their own roots among the population by merging the desire for Arab or Iraqi independence with other more immediately relevant political and social aspirations.

In addition, the struggle for national independence in Iraq under the mandate and monarchy (that came to engulf all but a very few privileged members of Iraqi society) gradually became embedded in an essentially secular way of thinking – whether 'socialist' or 'nationalist'. Of course, this kind of secularism had been developing during the *tanzimat* and the late Ottoman period, aided by the promulgation of the *mecelle* (civil code) and the Ottoman constitution. An important by-product of this in independent Iraq (as in republican Turkey) was that within the new parameters of the nation state, many people gradually came to feel more conscious of their identity as Iraqis than as Sunnis or Shi'a. This sense of national identity gathered increasing momentum after the Second World War and especially in the years before and immediately after the Revolution of 1958. During this time, sectarian barriers began to disappear, were less politically and socially significant, and there was a fair amount of inter-sectarian marriage. Examples of this melting pot tendency are the huge national demonstrations against the Portsmouth Agreement of 1948, the crowds who turned out to support Abd al-Karim Qasim in 1959 and the fact that it was the Shi'a of Kadhimayn who were the most numerous of those who rushed into the streets of Baghdad to defend Qasim's (almost entirely Sunni) government against the Ba'athist coup of February 1963. What I have just described here would probably gain nods of approval among those (particularly) older Iraqis, long resident outside the country, who would very much agree with the sentiment *maku farq baynana, kulluna Iraqiyyin* (there is no difference between us, we are all Iraqis). What would soon distort or destroy this atmosphere would be the growing and, to my mind, entirely pernicious influence of pan-Arabism and Ba'athism in Iraq, especially after the overthrow of the government of Abd al-Karim Qasim in 1963.

Arab nationalism and US intervention

The clandestine or illegal Iraqi political arena had long been polarised into two principal camps. The first were the Arab nationalists (including, by the middle 1950s, a handful of Ba'athists) whose vision for the future, greatly encouraged by the Egyptian revolution of July 1952, was of Iraq becoming part of a more-or-less extensive unified Arab state. The second were the Communists whose vision for the future of Iraq could be summed up as a secular, socialist, independent state. Of the two, the Communists enjoyed far greater credibility, had superior organisation and manpower, and were well known for having led the opposition to the monarchy since the late 1940s. Let us look into this a little more closely.

The notion that pan-Arabism had broad appeal in interwar Iraq has become part of the standard account of Iraqi history but it is questionable whether the doctrine was quite as widely accepted as has been claimed.[19] The ethnic and sectarian composition of Iraq makes it difficult to imagine that an essentially Sunni Arab vision of the Arab-Islamic world would have been the doctrine of choice of a population whose composition was more than half Shi'a and at least one fifth Kurdish. This is magnified when we consider that this composition was also extremely poor,[20] for whom the kinds of ideas which I have just summarised were largely irrelevant in addressing their poverty, illiteracy and social and economic deprivation. Apart from enjoying a certain vogue among some members of the urban Sunni middle class and among army officers, I very much doubt whether such ideas were widely shared before or even after the Second World War. Apart from a single demonstration on the occasion of the visit of a well-known

British Zionist (Sir Alfred Mond) to Baghdad in 1928, the Palestine cause (always a useful barometer of pan-Arab feeling) had not been espoused to any noticeable extent by any Iraqi government or political organisation before the Palestine rebellion of 1936.

Given the inevitability of national liberation or decolonisation in all parts of the colonised world, the US's attitude was to ensure that the process would prove as palatable to US interests, especially as Iraq's potential as a major oil producer was very evident by the late 1940s. Hence the US's fear of the rise of the left trumped its otherwise more humanitarian instincts to support the emergence of just and democratic societies. This resulted in the US championing a string of more or less dreadful military dictatorships throughout the developing world – a process that only began to be reversed with the restoration of democracy in southern Europe (Spain, Portugal, Greece) and in southern and central America in the 1980s and 1990s. The Middle East was too important both strategically and economically to allow this to happen and for the most part, potentially leftist or left-leaning regimes were replaced by national-socialist dictatorships or in the case of Iran under the Shah, by an autocracy that became increasingly less benevolent as the years passed. The CIA and British intelligence were behind the coup that overthrew Musaddiq and restored the Shah in 1953 and in the Ba'athist coup which overthrew Abd al-Karim Qasim in Iraq in February 1963. Furthermore, the CIA had been in touch with members of the Ba'ath party, most probably including Saddam Hussein (since his days in exile in Egypt in the late 1950s), on the grounds that the party could be regarded as the 'force of the future' and it was virulently anti-Communist. Evidently, it was thought that some form of partnership could be forged between the United States and the incoherent but fundamentally non-revolutionary forces of Arab nationalism and this shrewd calculation proved in many ways uncannily correct, both for Egypt and for Iraq.

Perhaps the most unfortunate consequence of this pathological fear or hatred of local Communists and leftists, which the Cold War encouraged if it did not actually engender, was that secular opposition was driven underground almost everywhere in the Middle East. In such circumstances, politics either became extraordinarily dangerous or degenerated into sycophancy. Opposition to or criticism of the regime or of the leader's policies became tantamount to treason and could be punished as such. In consequence, whatever opposition there was drifted into the hands of religious organisations of various kinds, including those that arose within mosques. This is because in Islamic countries, governments cannot close down the mosques.

To return to what I stated earlier in this Chapter, in its manifestation in Iraq, Ba'athist pan-Arabism was a Sunni phenomenon. This was not what happened next door in Syria where the most enthusiastic and earliest supporters of Ba'athism were Alawites, Isma'ilis and Greek Orthodox Christians. The subtext of Iraqi Ba'athism came to be that only Sunni Arabs were 'real' Arabs and thus full members of the rest of the Arab world. This gradually revived the notion that the Shi'as were 'really' foreigners i.e *ajam,* Persians or of Persian origin. This offensive claptrap began in earnest with the Ba'athist coup in 1968 but not much of it really mattered until the Iranian revolution in 1978–9 and the war between Iran and Iraq in 1980. At this point, the Ba'ath began to make the Iraqi Shi'i a dangerous fifth column of potentially pro-Iranian sympathisers or traitors and to perpetuate the myth that they were 'really' Iranian.

The danger that the Iranian Revolution represented for Saddam Hussein and his regime turned almost all Iraqi Shi'as in to potential enemies of the state and was one of the major reasons for the Iran–Iraq war, which lasted for most of the 1980s. Of course, as has often been noted, the war was actually fought between Iraqi Shi'i conscripts on one side and Iranian Shi'i conscripts on the other. Anti-Shi'i hostility on the part of the regime continued into the 1990s and 2000s. At the same time, as law and order gradually broke down and citizens were exposed to increasing arbitrariness (and could no longer rely on the conventional institutions of the state), they turned even more towards primordial pre-state organisations such as family, tribe, kin and sect. This was in order to protect them both from the state and from each other. In addition, since the Communists had effectively been killed off or driven abroad some decades earlier, it was only the clandestine Shi'i parties (especially *al-Da'wa*) who put up any serious opposition to Saddam Hussein and the Ba'ath between 1991 and 2003.

When the Americans invaded Iraq in 2003, they had been egged on by a group of secular Shi'a in exile in Washington, led by the charming 'Rolex wearing opportunist' Ahmad Chalabi. He was just the kind of person that US policy makers envisaged putting in charge of the new democratic Iraq which would miraculously emerge after decades of the most appalling repression. Chalabi himself had left Iraq in 1958 at the age of 10, Ayad Allawi had not been to Iraq since 1978 and rather more honourable individuals like Kanaan Makiya and Ali Allawi had left in the mid-1970s – long before the utter breakdown of the social and moral order which took place in the 1990s and early 2000s. Chalabi, who may well have believed his own rhetoric, told his audiences at the Pentagon just what they wanted to hear, that troops would be regarded as liberators, showered with flowers and so on and so forth. What none of them seems to have understood was the profound changes which a combination of the aftermath of the Kurdish and Shi'a uprisings of 1991, the UN sanctions and Saddam Hussein's steadily increasing paranoia, had wrought upon Iraqi society.

As I have stated, the Iraqi state collapsed or was not present in much of southern Iraq throughout the 1990s and early 2000s. This was partly due to the sanctions and partly to 'the regime's withdrawal from the social sphere'. Young people had few employment prospects, given the absence or deterioration of educational facilities and the fact that they were no longer accepted into the army. They lacked the capital or social contacts necessary to migrate in search of greater opportunities so 'menial jobs and criminal activity appeared to be their only horizon'. Such individuals, in their 20s and early 30s, were attracted to the Sadrist movement just as they had been to the populist message of Sadr's father, Muhammad Sadiq al-Sadr (whom the regime assassinated in 1999). 'By eradicating the Islamist parties in the early 1980s, isolating the *marjaiyyah* and retreating itself from society, the regime generated huge appeal for the particular form of religious-based mobilisation engineered by Sadr in the 1990s [and continued by his son in the period after the invasion].' All in all, Iraqi Shi'i society 'displayed a relatively high degree of social organisation, in comparison with both the Sunni and the progressive component of Iraqi society ... this specificity largely contributed to its ascendency in post-2003 Iraq'.[21]

Reviving sectarianism

In the first years of the occupation and after the fiasco of the Coalition Provisional Authority, the Americans, without fully understanding the implications of what they were doing, proceeded to reinvent or revive sectarianism. They did this by organising a system of *de facto* sectarian quotas and second, by establishing a government in Baghdad composed largely of people with a generally religious rather than secular bent who had sat out the 1980s and 1990s either in London or as guests of the Iranian regime in Tehran. In short, this was a government from which the Sunnis, not all of whom had been well treated by Saddam Hussein and his circle, came to feel completely excluded. The complexity of the entire issue is well illustrated in a recent article by Peter Harling who notes that one of the principal flash points of the *intifada* (uprising) in southern Iraq against the regime in 1991 was the Sunni enclave of Zubayr. He also lists the names of individual Ba'athists in the south who made use of their local knowledge and connections to put down the rising. These were Muhsin Khudhir al-Khafaji, Muhammad Hamza al-Zubaydi, Karim Hasan al-Tamimi, Aziz Salih al-Khafaji, Mizban Khudhir Hadi, Qa'id al-Awadi and Hasan Ali al-Amiri, *all of whom were Shi'is.*[22] As we know, very few of those in charge of planning the Iraq fiasco in Washington between late 2001 and early 2003 were seriously encumbered by any real knowledge of the recent history and politics of the Middle East and were happy to accept views which fitted neatly into their own preconceptions about the region and into their vision for the future of Iraq.

After the overthrow of the regime, some degree of de-Ba'athification was obviously necessary but it should have been selective rather than wholesale since it was certainly not the case that all Sunnis were implicated in the terrible crimes of the old regime. It was also true that party membership was more or less obligatory for those above a certain level in any state organisation. Furthermore, it was unfortunate that the direction of the process was given over to individuals whose neutrality was very much open to question and who had a vested interest in rooting out Ba'athists, both real and imaginary. The US's sledge-hammer tactics in this and other respects had the effect of convincing mid-level

Sunnis that they had little to look forward to in a post-Saddam Iraq. In addition, the fact that a whole army of some 400,000 troops had been demobilised without either its weapons being collected or any arrangements being made for its sustenance, brought both the Sunni insurgency and later the Mahdi Army into being.

Therefore, the daily horrors of Sunnis killing Shi'a and vice versa is far less a matter of time-immemorial grievances or ancient hatreds, as many commentators would have us believe. It is far more a matter of specific politico–historical conjunctures which have come into being as a result of terrible repression, ignorance and stupidity, which some less than high-minded individuals came to take deadly advantage of for their own ends. For these reasons, it will be a very long time before anything remotely resembling civil society can be built in Iraq.

Notes

1. Maalouf, Amin (trs. Barbara Bray)., *In the Name of Identity*, (New York, 2000), p. 13. {Original title *Identités Meutrières*, Paris, 1996}
2. Makdisi, Ussama., *The Culture of Sectarianism: Community, History, and Violence in Nineteenth-Century Ottoman Lebanon*, (Los Angeles, 2000), ch:1, 'Religion as the site of the colonial encounter.' http://publishing.cdlib.org/ucpressebooks/view?docId=ft2r29n8jr&chunk.id=ch1&toc.depth=1&toc.id=ch1&brand=ucpress
3. Cf. 'After the uprising of 1857, in which Hindu and Muslim soldiers fought together to restore the Mughal emperor, the British went to great lengths to create an intricate taxonomy of caste, class and religion, a patchwork of conflicting interests which apparently could only be held together by the higher logic of imperialism. The British insisted almost hysterically on the hostility between Hindus and Muslims, and by the time decolonisation came, this had been internalised by the most influential members of both communities.' Deb, Siddhartha., 'Enemy Citizens' *London Review of Books*, (1 January 2009), p. 40.
4. In addition, 'embedded' reporters often judge that neither their editors nor their readers will understand if they *do* try to tell the story in more nuanced terms. Personal communication with C J Kirkpatrick (February 2009).
5. See Visser, Reidar., 'The Sectarian Master Narrative in Iraqi Historiography: New Challenges since 2003,' unpublished paper presented to the colloquium on *Writing the History of Iraq: Historiographical and Political Challenges* (Geneva, 6–8 November 2008).

6. 'Another, deeply ingrained fault line opposes the Middle Euphrates to the far South. Shi'ite representation has long been the preserve of elites originating from central Iraq, and resented by [those on] the periphery'. Of course, all the *atabat* are located in central, not southern, Iraq. See Peter Harling, 'Building on Sand? Buttressing the Saddam-era body of Knowledge', unpublished paper presented to the colloquium on *Writing the History of Iraq: Historiographical and Political Challenges* (Geneva, 6–8 November 2008).
7. Gagnon, Valere Philip., *The Myth of Ethnic War: Serbia and Croatia in the 1990s* (Cornell University Press, Ithaca and London, 2004), xv.
8. Here the parallel with Iraq, the sense of the state patrimony being at play between competing groups ('les enjeux' in French) is particularly striking.
9. Gagnon: *The Myth of Ethnic War*, xvi–xviii.
10. See Sluglett, Peter., *Britain in Iraq: Contriving King and Country* (New York, 2007), ch:6, 'Tenurial, Revenue and Tribal Policy', pp. 161–81.
11. Contrary to much current received wisdom, 'Iraq', certainly the area south of Mosul to the Gulf, was a more or less unified political entity under the authority of whoever controlled Baghdad for most of the period between the Abbasids and the First World War, so the notion that it is 'artificial' is not quite accurate. The only major exceptions to this were the period between c. 1530 and c.1690, when there were *four* distinct provinces (Baghdad, Basra, Mosul and Shahrizor): 'In 1850 Mosul was added to the Iraqi core, while for 12 years Basra was separated from it. Then from 1862, the *vilayet* of Baghdad was again the state structure of a single Iraqi entity corresponding almost exactly to the modern state. This arrangement more or less to the 1880s, when Mosul and Basra were separated, *and for 30 years – and for the first time in its history – Iraq assumed the tripartite structure that has become entrenched in Western historiography as the basic administrative pattern of 400 years of Ottoman rule*' (my italics). See Visser, Reidar., 'Historical Myths of a Divided Iraq', *Survival*, 50/2, (April–May 2008), p. 99. In the same article, Visser shows convincingly (pp. 96–97) that the Ottomans did not divide the provinces purely along sectarian (or ethnic) lines.
12. See particularly Nakash, Yitzhak., *The Shi'is of Iraq*, (New Jersey, 1994), pp. 13–48, pp. 55–56; Nakash shows in some detail that the conversion of most of the tribes of southern Iraq took place relatively recently. The complexity of Ottoman-Shi'i relations is discernible in Deringil, Selim., 'The Struggle Against Shi'ism in Hamidian Iraq; a Study in Ottoman Counter-Propaganda', *Die Welt des Islams*, 30 (1990), pp. 45–62.
13. See Sluglett, Peter., *Britain in Iraq …*, Appendix I, 'A Note on Shi'i Politics', pp. 219–32.

14. There is a detailed account of these events in Abrahamian, Ervand., *Iran Between Two Revolutions* (New Jersey, 1982), pp. 50–101.
15. See Masters, Bruce., *Christians and Jews in the Ottoman Arab World: the Roots of Sectarianism* (Cambridge, 2001), p. 176.
16. In April 1918, Sir Percy Cox characterised Sharif Husayn as 'a figure who carries no weight in Iraq, where only the most distant interest is taken in him.' See 'Memorandum of 22 April 1918', India Office, *Letters, Political and Secret* 10, 4722/18/5064. In addition, at least as far as 'Abdullah ibn Husayn was concerned, his interest in the alliance with Britain lay more in its potential to increase the family's standing in the Arabian peninsula than in ventures in the 'Arab lands further north'. See Wilson, Mary C., *King Abdullah, Britain and the Making of Jordan* (Cambridge, 1987), p. 31. There is also no real sense in which the Hashemite family could be considered as 'representing the Arabs.'
17. See Ende, Werner., 'Iraq in World War I: the Turks, the Germans and the Shi'ite *mujtahids*' call for jihad', in Rudolph Peters (ed.), *Proceedings of the Ninth Congress of the Union Européenne des Arabisants et Islamisants, Amsterdam 1978* (Leiden, 1981), pp. 57–71.
18. Quoted in Pierre-Jean Luizard, 'Le mandat britannique en Irak: une rencontre entre plusieurs projets politiques', in Méouchy, Nadine and Sluglett, Peter (eds.)., *The British and French mandates in comparative perspectives/Les mandats français et anglais dans une perspective comparative* (Leiden, 2003), pp. 363-64 (my translation of Luizard's French). More generally, see the same authors' *La formation de l'Irak contemporain : le rôle politique des ulémas chiites à la fin de la domination ottomane et au moment de la construction de l'Etat irakien,* Editions du CNRS (Paris, 1991).
19. See for example, Simon Reeva S., *Iraq Between Two World Wars; the Creation and Implementation of a Nationalist Ideology*, (New York, 1986) or Eppel, Michael., 'The Elite, the Effendiyya, and the Growth of Nationalism and Pan-Arabism in Hashemite Iraq', *International Journal of Middle East Studies,* 30, ii, (1998), pp. 227–50.
20. In a survey carried out in 1953, a British medical expert described the Iraqi fallah as a 'living pathological specimen' and estimated average life expectancy at between thirty-five and thirty-nine years. Professor M. Critchley, quoted in Gabbay, Rony., *Communism and Agrarian Reform in Iraq* (London, 1978), p. 29.
21. The quotations in this paragraph are from Peter Harling's paper, 'Building on sand …' quoted above (note 6).
22. 'Saddam Husayn et la débâcle triomphante. Les ressources insoupçonnés de Umm al-Ma'ârik', in *L'Irak en perspective, Revue du Monde Musulman et de la Méditerranée,* 117-118 (2007), pp. 157–78, here pp. 168–9.

CHAPTER 8

SECTARIAN COEXISTENCE IN IRAQ: THE EXPERIENCES OF THE SHI'A IN AREAS NORTH OF BAGHDAD

Reidar Visser

Studies of the Shi'a of Iraq have tended to focus on what is often described as the Shi'i 'heartland' – the Euphrates area with the holy cities of Najaf and Karbala. The far south and Basra, the tribes along the Tigris and the Shi'a of Baghdad (with Kadhimayn) have also been quite amply covered. However, there are also important areas with Shi'i connections north of Baghdad: the holy city of Samarra, as well as Shi'i communities (some Arabs but also Turkmen and Fayli Kurds) living in places such as Dujayl, Balad and Mandali and other scattered localities in the provinces of Diyala and Kirkuk. It is the aim of this Chapter to explore the historical experiences of these communities, ranging from peaceful coexistence in long periods to episodes of extreme friction such as the Ba'athist massacre of hundreds of innocent Shi'a in Dujayl in 1982. More recently, Shi'i issues in northern Iraq have come into focus as a consequence of the Kirkuk question (where some of the Shi'i Islamist parties have embraced the Turkmen cause) as well as the situation in Diyala (where the boycott of the January 2005 local elections led to a strong Shi'i role in provincial government despite their status as a minority). The main argument in the Chapter is that there exists in Iraq a *longue durée* legacy of coexistence between Sunnis and Shi'a that is challenged only rarely and generally unsuccessfully. As a consequence, political projects that seek to reject this coexistence tradition have tended to fail – whether they are peaceful political projects like the attempt to create federal entities that would erect fences between Iraqis on the basis of sects (particularly the Region of the Centre and the South scheme promoted between 2005 and 2007 by the Islamic Supreme Council of Iraq) or acts of savage destruction, like the attack on the holy Shi'i shrine in Samarra on 22 February 2006.

The Ottoman legacy

Whereas the Ottomans in theory considered the Shi'a to be infidels and potential fifth columnists for the Persian state, their practices as administrators in Iraq generally and north of Baghdad in particular, attest to a culture of pragmatism and an overriding concern for peaceful sectarian coexistence within the Ottoman Empire.

With respect to Iraq as a whole, the trend towards tolerance and indeed inclusion of the Shi'a within the Ottoman state was more evident than is often realised, even quite early on. One example is the poet, Abd al-Jalil al-Tabataba'i, who lived in Basra and Qatar and other parts of the Ottoman Gulf in the early-nineteenth century. In the 1830s, after the Ottoman reconquest of Muhammara (a town on the Shatt al-Arab on the opposite side of Basra in present-day Iran), Tabataba'i lauded the operation as 'a conquest which makes the lands of the King shine; a conquest whereby all of Iraq *(arja al-iraq)* is in control of all its parts'.[1] The quote is noteworthy not only for its pro-Ottoman tenor but also for the focus on Iraq as the object of the poet's eulogy. The latter aspect was by no means unique. A friend of Tabataba'i would emulate him later in the 1840s as he extolled the landscapes of the Euphrates in a poem in his honour called *dhikrayat al-huqul* (memories of the fields): 'What urged me on', the writer says, 'was the goodness of Iraq and its people'.[2] Tabataba'i is listed in the great lexicon of Shi'i writers of Aga Buzurg al-Tihrani.[3]

As for Samarra itself in the second half of the nineteenth century, it was, in contrast to areas like Najaf and Karbala, very much within the firm control of the Ottomans. The Ottomans regularly appointed officials to the town just as they would to any other town in the Baghdad *vilayet* (province). Nevertheless, during the initial years after the move to the city in 1875 by the leading Shi'i cleric of Najaf, Hasan al-Shirazi, the Ottomans actually contributed to the development of Shi'i infrastructure in the city. Apparently, the state was involved at first in refurbishing the two Shi'i shrines in the city, referring to the process as the 'renovation of the mosques of Hasan al-Askari and the Imam Mahdi' (*Bagdad Vilayeti Samarra Kazasinda Bulunan Imam Hasan El-Askeri ve Imam Mehdi Camilerinin Tamiri*).[4] This seems to have been all part of an initiative towards rapprochement between the Shi'a and Sunni that had been initiated by Abdulhamid II after his accession in 1876 and which also involved reconstruction of Shi'i sanctuaries in Najaf.[5]

Later in the 1880s, signs of friction between the local Sunni community and the growing Shi'i element did become apparent and the mufti of Samarra was active in denouncing the increased Shi'i activity. However, still in 1886, the Ottoman state was involved in constructing a bridge across the river with the aim of improving access for Iranian pilgrims.[6] When in the early 1890s a counter-campaign was initiated, it featured perfectly pacific tactics: the Ottomans tried to strengthen Sunnism at Samarra but they did so primarily through sending more Sunni teachers, opening new schools and according Sunni Sufi leaders (such as Muhammad Saeed al-Naqshbandi) prominent roles.[7] Some lower-ranking Sunni officials were not as acquiescent and, in 1894, instigated local mobs to attack the Shi'a; two Shi'i students were killed. The Ottomans were later punished by their own government for these transgressions and the Shi'a of Samarra remained in dialogue with the Ottoman government about improvements to the shrines as late as in 1906.[8] British sources, too, emphasise the essentially episodic character of the 1894 incident.[9]

It has been maintained that much of the Shi'i population of Samarra was a student population that left after the death of Hasan al-Shirazi in 1895. However, a Shi'i element clearly persisted beyond that. Gertrude Bell, in 1909, described it thus:

> Samarra town is like a toy – a broken toy. It stands in the open plain above the river, all walled round with a high wall above which rise the tiled minarets and golden dome of the Mahdi's tomb. But when you get inside you find the enclosure is half empty and inside the wall are large open spaces covered with dirt and ruins. A large part of the population consists of very fanatical Persians – they have been quite nice to me, but then I haven't bothered them much. All the windows looking onto the streets are bricked up and most of the dwellers in the houses are I think dead, anyway there is no one and nothing to be seen as you ride down the silent little ways. But just at the mosque door there are a few tea houses with grave Persians and ragged Arabs sitting in them and smoking narghilehs. They all gave me the salaam as I passed and I was careful not to look too curiously through the gate of the mosque where the big chain hangs under the blue and yellow tiled archway. For you may not enter unless you are of the Faith.[10]

Bell's characterisation of the Shi'a as 'fanatical' is very typical of her – she used the term all the time and her rather strained and stereotypic way of commenting on the Shi'i community reflected the fact that she never really managed to establish personal ties with the higher ranks of the Shi'i clergy. Her designation of the Shi'a in Samarra as a mainly 'Persian' community may have greater credibility, even if she would often conflate 'Persian' and various forms of 'fanaticism' in her writings.[11] However, even if the Shi'i population of Samarra may have had a strong Persian contingent at the time, Shi'i satellites with a clearer Arab character could also be found north of Baghdad where they remained vibrant throughout the late Ottoman period. There were for example important Shi'i settlements at Dujayl, Balad and Khalis. In all of these places, the Ottomans exercised normal governmental control (Balad was the site of a particularly prosperous land plot owned by the Ottoman sultan personally and governed as *sanniyeh*) but few if any incidents of a sectarian nature have been reported.[12] People from Dujayl and Khalisi would travel to the holy cities and become important contributors to Shi'i culture and its scholarly hierarchy. These included the descendants of Aziz al-Khalisi, a famous settler in Khalis in the nineteenth century, such as Mahdi al-Khalisi, a prominent cleric of the early twentieth century.[13] When Claudius James Rich travelled through these 'outlying' Shi'i areas in the early-nineteenth century, he reported several Shi'i tombs that were still maintained and served as sites of pilgrimage.[14]

Finally, the Shi'i presence extended into the Turkmen and Kurdish areas, even though individuals from these areas were less intimately connected with the Shi'i high culture of the holy cities of the Iraqi plains and there is simply less information available about them. Many Lurs and Faylis living in the eastern borderlands held Persian nationality. The existence of a Fayli community (*Feyli taifesi*) in Kirkuk was noted by the Ottomans in 1910; others were just counted as members of a tribe (*Feyli asireti*).[15] The Shabak were noted by travellers in the 1880s[16] and described by the historian of the British mandate Stephen Longrigg as speaking 'a Kurdish dialect and . . . thought to profess a heretical type of Shi'ism.'[17] The Turkmen Shi'i community of Tall Afar has been described in some sources as pro-Ottoman,[18] although there is also evidence that Ottomans worked hard to bring some of the Shi'a of Shaykhan back to the Hanafi fold, again using education as their primary tool.[19] Tuz Khurmatu had a strong Shi'i Turkmen community and a regular Ottoman administration at the *nahiye* level, most often subordinated to Kirkuk.

What this record shows is two things. Firstly, Ottomans were in control of Samarra and most other Shi'i areas in the north of Iraq. Had they wished to do so, they could easily have implemented harsh policies to reduce the influence of Shi'ism in these areas and the Ottomans were indeed worried about the spread of Shi'ism. However, despite their comparatively powerful position in these parts, their means for resisting Shi'ism were entirely peaceful. Typically, they did not question the Shi'i right to have a place of worship in Samarra but they would, on occasion, resist Iranian agency in bringing about renovation. This happened in 1886 when Ottoman authorities declared that any repair works should be carried out by the Ottoman state and not by Persian merchants.[20] Relations cannot have been too strained, however, because two years later, Persians would once more apply for permission for improvement works on the shrines.[21] One contributing factor in this may have been the considerable financial contribution made by visiting pilgrims to the local economy and to the state, including burial taxes levied in the holy cities.[22] It was not unusual for the Ottomans to furnish armed guards for the ships that conveyed Shi'i pilgrims from abroad to Karbala when they traversed dangerous tribal areas in the south of Iraq – in other words a case of the Sunni state protecting the Shi'a against Shi'a.[23] Still in 1907, the Ottomans expressed interest in the revenues that accrued from Shi'i pilgrimage traffic to Iraq, including Samarra. In sum, the few episodes of open friction apart,[24] the rise of Samarra in a period when the Ottomans did indeed have concerns about the spread of Shi'ism attests to a climate of relative inter-sectarian tolerance quite different from that of Europe during the confrontation between Catholicism and Protestantism in the sixteenth and seventeenth centuries.

Iraqi identity in the writings of Kazim al-Dujayli

In the period of the Iraqi monarchy, these patterns of coexistence in the north were largely perpetuated. In the 1930s, Ayatollah al-Naini, one of the leading Shi'i scholars at the time, considered moving to Samarra after a split with his main competitor, Ayatollah Isfahani; again this seems to be a testament to an atmosphere where mobility outside the Shi'i core areas was considered perfectly feasible and not something that would threaten the safety of the ayatullahs.[25] Similarly, peaceful religious mobilisation among the Shi'i of Kirkuk, including performance of the *ta'ziyeh* (theatrical re-enactment) ritual drama, was reported in the 1920s.[26] It is noteworthy that when the Persians expanded their presence in certain parts of Iraq during the monarchy (especially with schools in Basra, and Baghdad/ Kazimayn), Samarra and other northern areas were not affected.[27] As late as 1966, construction of new Shi'i mosques were reported in Tuz Khurmatu.[28]

The corollary to this trend was the creation of intimate links between the Shi'a and Iraqi nationalism. In fact, this process dates back to before the formal creation of the modern Iraqi monarchy in 1921, as exemplified by the writer Kazim al-Dujayli (circa 1884–1970) who had family ties to the Shi'i areas between Baghdad and Samarra. Before the First World War, he was a prominent contributor to *Lughat al-Arab*, an Arabic magazine that was published in Baghdad under the editorship of Anastas al-Karmali and an important contributor to early iterations of Iraqi nationalism.

One of the articles by Dujayli from around 1911 deals with Shaykh Uthman b. Sanad al-Basri (circa 1766–1826), an early-nineteenth-century author from Najd who lived in Basra.[29] In the opening paragraph, Dujayli explains why he is interested in writing about Shaykh Uthman from the distant coastal city of Basra, 'the twelfth and thirteenth centuries [*hijri*] are among the most beautiful centuries that Iraq has experienced'. In this period, the author remarks, there was an intellectual blossoming in Iraq, as exemplified by families such as the Haydari, Suwaydi, Alusi, Azri, Shawi, Umari, Qazwini, Bahr al-Ulum, Taliqani, Tabataba'i, Bahrani, Asfur, Jaza'iri, Hilli, Shahristani, Yasin, Tabaqchali and Kawwaz. Among individuals singled out for praise are Muhammad Faydi al-Zahhawi, Haydar al-Hilli, Humadi Nuh, Jabir al-Kazimi, Husayn al-Ashari, Jafaar al-Hilli, Salih al-Tamimi, Mulla Umar Ramadan al-Hiti, Khalid al-Naqshbandi and Ulu al-Din al-Mosuli. In other words, Dujayli sees an intellectual heritage connected to the area he calls 'Iraq' that incorporates Sunni and Shi'i writers from Basra to Mosul with his heroes featuring prominent representatives of both sects.

Dujayli is fully aware of these sectarian categories. He explains that al-Basri was a Sunni, more specifically belonging to the Maliki school of jurisprudence and with a strong attachment to that school. He had, in Dujayli's own words, a sectarian leaning: *maliki al-madhaba mutaasaban jiddan*. However, Dujayli is far more interested in Basri and his historical writings such as *Matali al-Saud fi Tarikh Dawud*, which deals with the rule of the mameluke pashas of Baghdad in the late eighteenth century when their rule encompassed much of the territory of modern Iraq. This book, Dujyali tells his readers, is important because it sheds lights on 'the lives of Iraqis, both the Bedouins and the settled ones (*hadar*)' from the 1770s to the 1820s. Dujayli also praises Basri for his other works, including collections of biographies that included notables from the 'Iraqi lands' (*al-bilad al-iraqiyya*).

While writing amicably about his compatriot of the opposite sect, Dujayli was not suppressing his own Shi'i sectarian identity either. For example, in the same period, he contributed articles about the libraries of Najaf and also wrote about Ashura celebrations in Najaf and Karbala. Dujayli did not shy away from talking about problems of the past such as the misdeeds by the Abbasids against the Shi'a. However, he concludes that the 'Shi'a of Karbala are freer today than at any point'.[30] Later, he would become a prominent Iraqi nationalist – among the first to praise Faysal I upon his arrival in Basra[31] with diverse contributions to the growing field of Iraqi nationalist literature.[32] How unexceptional his stance was among the Shi'a is indicated by other Shi'i publications from the pre-1914 era where the Iraq theme was similarly highlighted; examples include the *Iraqiyyat* collection published in Saida in Lebanon in 1912.[33]

The non-Arab Shi'a and post-2003 politics

In the early-twentieth century, at least some of the non-Arab Shi'i communities in the north of Iraq were associated with heterogeneity and even heresy. For example, in 1927, a British observer wrote about the 'unorthodox semi-pagan [Shi'i] sects of Kirkuk'.[34] This changed gradually during the twentieth century as communication with the holy cities in Iraq increased, and the process intensified after 2003 as Shi'i Islamist parties tried to expand from their traditional bastions into the northern areas.

Arguably, the Ba'athist regime was itself responsible for forging ties between the established Shi'i Islamic parties and the non-Arab Shi'a of Iraq. Through a series of indiscriminate deportations of people holding Iranian nationality or being of Iranian descent, the Fayli community was targeted between 1969 and 1971, possibly in an attempt by the regime to alter the demographic balance in the Kurdish-dominated north during the ongoing conflict with the Kurds.[35] Later, during the Iran–Iraq war, Dujayl was targeted and collectively punished after a 1982 assassination attempt against Saddam Hussein whilst he was visiting the town; it should be stressed however that although the Ba'athists directed accusations against a

Daawa cell in Dujayl, they punished Sunnis of the mixed Shi'i/Sunni Khazraj tribe in Dujayl too – in itself an indication that sectarian coexistence had survived at the local level. At any rate, both the opposition Supreme Council for the Islamic Revolution in Iraq (SCIRI) as well as the Iranian leadership showed particular interest in Iraq's northern Shi'a. Khomeini himself reportedly singled out Mandali as a 'suppressed region' in Iraq alongside Basra[36] and in 1984, SCIRI arranged separate processions (*mawakib*) for the Iraqi Fayli refugees in Tehran.[37] In 1986, a Shi'i Shaykh of Kurdish origins and a member of SCIRI's central committee said that in the case of a change of regime in Iran, no autonomy (*al-hukm al-dhati*) would be needed; the rule of Islam (*hukm al-islam*) would be sufficient.[38] Later, Shi'i Turkmen would become important allies of SCIRI, such as for instance Abbas al-Bayati. Still, it has to be stressed that other Turkmen Shi'a did reasonably well during the Ba'athist years. Symbolically, at least, there was room for Turkmen Shi'ism and the regime made a point of celebrating the legacy of the medieval Turkmen poet Mehmet Suleyman Fuzuli Baghdadi as a quintessential Iraqi hero with both Sunni and Shi'i connections.[39] Nevertheless, government actions in the 1970s such as cutting the northern Euphrates areas off from the old, sprawling Baghdad governorate (which had previously extended as far north as Takrit) and making them part of the new Salahaddin governorate, must have been seen by local Shi'a as an act of isolating them from their co-religionists in and around Baghdad. In addition, this subjected them to a local government in which Sunni dominance was more pronounced.

The fall of the Ba'athist regime in 2003 and the subsequent opening up of the political process in Iraq brought Arab and non-Arab Shi'a closer together. The established Shi'i political parties soon incorporated symbolic references to the non-Arab northern Shi'i satellites in their political rhetoric, as seen in Muqtada al-Sadr's appeal to the Turkmen of Kirkuk in anti-federal demonstrations in early 2004. This can also been seen in references to Tall Afar in Abd al-Aziz al-Hakim's speech during the launch of his Shi'i federalism scheme (a single federal entity of nine Shi'i-majority governorates between Basra and Baghdad) in Najaf in August 2005. While these overtures have had a certain effect, not everyone in the targeted Shi'i communities have readily accepted the idea of their amalgamation into a wider Iraqi Shi'i family at the expense of links to their ethnic community and indeed their notions of a primary Iraqi national identity.

The Shabak community in the Nineveh governorate offers examples of this dualism. On the one hand, on several occasions members of the community have moved towards mainstream Shi'i Islamism. An example is in terms of the way Ashura is celebrated and through processions signalling Shi'i solidarities (as seen not least in the wake of the Samarra attack in 2006). In these contexts, Shabak politicians often employ traditional Shi'i symbolism such as the colours of green and black and images of the Shi'i imams. Similarly, many Shabak leaders have performed highly publicised pilgrimages to Najaf and Karbala. In 2005, Hunayn al-Qaddo, an important Shabak community leader, joined the Shi'i Islamist United Iraqi Alliance and his vote was reportedly decisive in the initial contest over the UIA premiership in 2006, when Adil Abd al-Mahdi lost to the incumbent candidate, Ibrahim al-Ja'fari.

There is also a second, equally important tendency among the Shabak. To many Shabak politicians, a central goal since 2003 has been to define themselves as an Iraqi ethnic community first and foremost with rights to special representation on an ethno–linguistic basis. In tandem with this, Shabak particularism combined with Iraqi nationalism have often been highlighted at the expense of their Shi'i identity. For example, Hunayn al-Qaddo has expressed fierce resistance to some of the more sectarian schemes of SCIRI such as creating a new federal map of Iraq largely based on ethno–sectarian divisions.[40] Fearing attempts by the Kurds to assimilate them, many Shabak see an Iraqi nationalist framework as a safer bet for the future and while he is still a member of the UIA, Qaddo has on some occasions voted with the nationalist bloc of parties that includes both secularists and breakaway elements from the Sunni and Shi'i Islamist alliances – as happened with the vote in the Iraqi parliament on various incarnations of the local elections law in the summer and autumn of 2008.[41] On leading Shabak websites, like *alshabak.net*, the symbolic content tends to be ethnic and local rather than religious in character.

Similar tendencies can be seen among many Turkmen and Faylis who still prefer Iraqi nationalist and/or ethnic micro-categories of identities to pan-Shi'i ones. Additionally, there are some who have responded positively to the constant advances by the Kurds to bring these important grey-zone communities into their pan-Kurdish schemes; this tendency has been more prominent in the case of the Faylis who had suffered particularly under the Ba'ath. For example, while both Turkmen and Faylis were with the UIA in 2005, Islamic parties representing these communities chose to ally themselves with Nuri al-Maliki's coalition ticket (*dawlat al-qanun*) in the 31 January 2009 local elections, including Abbas al-Bayati who in many contexts had been a key ally of Islamic Supreme Council of Iraq (ISCI) in the past. Maliki's separate ticket has featured a catch-all profile designed to reach wider than traditional Shi'i audiences. It also incorporates strongly Iraqi nationalist and centralist tendencies that mark a breach with other parts of the UIA, such as the pro-federal and strongly decentralist Supreme Council (now the ISCI.) In the Kirkuk issue, Bayati has sided with the Iraqi nationalist parties who demand a transitional power-sharing regime with reserved quotas for Arabs, Turkmen and Christians in order to reverse Kurdifying policies in the governorate since 2003.[42] Even Badr members from northern Iraq have signalled unhappiness with the pro-Kurdish policies of SCIRI/ISCI, preferring instead an Iraqi nationalist position over the Kirkuk issue.[43]

In general, the relationship between these Shi'i peripheries of Iraq and the holy cities offers certain parallels to the situation seen in post-communist Azerbaijan, where contact with the seats of Shi'i learning in Iraq and Iran had been less extensive for a long period and when the pull factor from parties with strong secular traditions was considerable. Still, where Azerbaijan is almost monolithically Shi'i, the established Turkmen parties in Iraq are often Sunni-dominated and closely linked to Turkey. This may open up a special potential for Islamists seeking to attract Shi'a on a sectarian basis. In the 2009 local elections, all the main Shi'i Islamist parties fielded candidates in northern governorates with substantial Shi'i minorities (i.e. in Salahaddin, Diyala and Nineveh but not in Anbar).

The case for hope

The history of Iraq's 'northern' Shi'a shows communities that they have mostly been intimately integrated into their local societies and often were in the vanguard when Iraq began moving towards a more integrated national society in the early twentieth century. The Shi'a of the north have generally lived at peace with their Sunni neighbours and have on the whole been enthusiastic supporters of a common Iraqi identity framework.

Against the backdrop of this legacy, cases of extreme brutality and aggression against the Shi'i communities in the north (as witnessed in the Dujayl massacre following the failed assassination attempt against Saddam Hussein during a visit in 1982 and in the destruction of the holy Shi'i shrine of Samarra in 2006), are grotesque exceptions to the general patterns of coexistence that have prevailed. Those who carried out these transgressions deviated so clearly from historical traditions of tolerance in Iraq that they could never win popular approval for their crimes. This is why it is so wrong to portray the Samarra tragedy as 'the end of Iraq' as some writers do.[44] At the same time, Shi'i Islamist parties should take note of the fact that some of their more sectarian projects, like establishing Shi'i territorial contiguity in a new Shi'i federal entity, have not proven particularly popular among many northern Shi'i, many of whom tend to hold on to Iraqi nationalism as their preferred mode of political action. The limits of sectarian loyalties linking the people to the Shi'i-dominated government are such that in 2008, incredible as it may sound, many Shi'i residents of Dujayl reportedly expressed a desire for a return to the days of the Ba'athists. In their view, despite the horrors of 1982, the days of the Ba'athists offered more stability and prosperity overall.[45] While sectarian coexistence in northern Iraq was never without its problems, this commitment to a common territorial framework among Shi'a and Sunni in the north alike is an important factor that both Iraqi politicians and the international community should take into consideration as they deliberate the best ways of shaping a new democratic future for Iraq.

Notes

1. al-Tabataba'i, Abd al-Jalil., *Diwan* (Cairo, 1966), p. 70.
2. *Ibid.* p. 264.
3. al-Tihrani, Muhammad Muhsin Aga Buzurg., *Al-Dhari'a ila Tasanif al-Shi'a*, vol. 17 (Beirut, 1983), entry no. 654.
4. Ottoman archives, I. SD. 42/2253. 21/12-1295/16 (December, 1878).
5. Litvak, Meir., *Shi'i Scholars of Nineteenth-Century Iraq* (Cambridge, 1998), p. 166.
6. Ottoman archives, MV 12/86. 4/1-1304/20 (October, 1886).
7. On Naqshbandi, see Eich, Thomas., 'Patterns of the 1920 Rising in Iraq: The Rifa'iyya tariqa and Shiism', *Arabica* vol. 56 (2009), pp. 112–19. Eich also shows how other Sufis were more oriented towards ecumenism, and how Sunnis as early as in the 1850s would travel on pilgrimage to Shi'ite sites, including Samarra. See also Eich, Thomas., *Abu l-Huda as-Sayyadi: Eine Studie zur Instrumentalisierung Sufischer Netzwerke und Genealogischer Kontroversen im Spätosmanischen Reich* (Berlin, 2003), p. 120.
8. Ottoman archives, I. EV 39/1324-S11.
9. UK National Archives, FO 195/1841. Mockler to the British Embassy in Istanbul (10 August 1894).
10. Getrude Bell to her mother (18 April 1909).
11. Gertrude Bell to her father, (1 November 1920).
12. There were sanniyeh properties at Dujayl too.
13. See entry no. 1553 in vol. 11 of al-Tihrani, Muhammad Muhsin Aga Buzurg, *Al-dhari'a ila tasanif al-Shi'a*. Other northern Shi'ites noted in the annals of the holy cities of Najaf and Karbala include Ali b. Muhammad Aliwi al-Dujayli (circa 1810).
14. See Rich, Claudius James., *Narrative of a Residence in Koordistan* (London, 1836).
15. Ottoman archives, DH. MUI 16-3/15. 6/1-1328/18 (January 1910).
16. Sachau, Eduard., *Reise in Syrien und Mesopotamien* (Leipzig, 1883), p. 354.
17. Longrigg, Stephen Hemsley., *Iraq 1900 to 1950* (Oxford, 1953), p. 9
18. Fuccaro, Nelida., *The Other Kurds: Yazidis in Colonial Iraq* (London, 1999), p. 53.
19. Ottoman archives, Y. MTV 68/90. 19/4-1310/9 (November 1892).
20. Ottoman archives, MV 21/68. 22/10-1304/14 (July 1887).
21. Ottoman archives, YA. RES. 46/5. 26/4-1306/30 (December 1888).
22. Lorimer, John Gordon., *Geographical and Statistical Gazetteer of the Persian Gulf, Oman and Central Arabia* (Reading, 1908), p. 869.
23. UK National Archives, FO 195/2020. Loch to Currie (23 April 1898).
24. The Ottomans referred to the 1894 incident in Samarra as a *haditha* (an occasion) which emphasised its highly extraordinary character.

25. UK National Archives, AIR 23/267. Special Service Officer Baghdad to Air Headquarters (6 August 1930).
26. National Archives of India, BHCF 7/15/3/VIII. Abstract of Intelligence (16 June 19).
27. See al-Barrak, Fadhil., *Al-Madaris al-Yahudiyya wa-al-Iraniyya fi al-Iraq* (Baghdad, 1984).
28. See Kerkuklu, Mofak Salman., *The Turkmen City of Tuz Khurmatu* (Turkey, 2008).
29. Saint-Elie, Anastase-Marie de., *Lughat al-Arab*, vl, (Najaf, 1911), pp. 180–6.
30. Ibid vl, p. 294.
31. UK National Archives, CO 730/3. *Intelligence report* (July 1921).
32. Bashkin, Orit., *The Other Iraq: Pluralism and Culture in Hashemite Iraq* (Palo Alto, 2009), p. 48.
33. See Iraqiyyat, *Wa Huwa Mukhtar min Shi'r Ashrat Shuara min Mashahir al-Iraq* (Saida, 1912).
34. Middle East Centre, St. Antony's College, University of Oxford: Private papers collection, Edmonds 3/1. Special report, circa 1927, draft.
35. Babakhan, Ali., *L'Irak 1970–1990: Déportations des chiites* (n.p., 1994) pp. 46–9.
36. *Liwa al-Sadr*, 9 October 1983 (Tehran, 1983), no. 123.
37. Ibid, 3 October 1984 (Tehran, 1984), no. 168
38. Ibid, 17 December 1986 (Tehran, 1986), no. 280.
39. See for example al-Amiri, Thamir Abd al-Hasan., *Mawsuat al-Ashair al-Iraqiyya* (Baghdad, 1992), pp. 230–1.
40. In some contexts, SCIRI has also sought to bring together the governors of all the eleven governorates where Shi'ites dominate local governorate, i.e. including Baghdad and Diyala. Baghad is constitutionally barred from joining other governorates in a federal region, whereas SCIRI's disproportionate influence in Diyala is a result of the widespread Sunni boycott of the January 2005 local elections.
41. "Iraqi Minorities Get Special Representation in the Provincial Elections Law", www.historiae.org/minorities.asp, (3 November 2008).
42. *Al-Bayyina al-Jadida* (8 July 2009).
43. 'Sii Türkmenler: Türkiye bizi hic görmedi', *Zaman*, (31 January 2005).
44. Galbraith, Peter., *The End of Iraq* (New York, 2006).
45. 'Dujail Residents Miss Saddam', 13th October 2008 (Reuters, 2008).

CHAPTER 9

CITIZENSHIP AND IDENTITY: A CASE STUDY OF SHI'I MUSLIMS IN SAMARRA AND WIDER IRAQ

Amal Imad

The fall of the Berlin wall is a historic event that still reminds us of the triumph of capitalism and liberal democracy over socialism. Since then, liberal democracy could be regarded as an ideal form of government. It can be argued that liberal democracy lays down a particular set of universal rights which is to be granted and protected by the state. Through its emphasis on equality and the rule of law, citizens theoretically are treated as individual rational beings pursuing their interests, have the right to political participation. The idea of universal and equal citizenship in the liberal democracy can be predicated upon the premise that citizens are 'abstract', 'disembodied' and 'culturally disembedded' entities.[1] Therefore, despite liberal democracy's emphasis on the natural rights and agency of human beings, it often does not take immediate consideration of factors of ethnicity, race and gender which affect the realisation of these rights.

Citizenship, taken as a solely liberal construct, requires citizens to practise their rights and responsibilities independent of their own ethnic, political and social identities. The emergence of diverse group rights for political representation in the last three decades, such as religious–ethnic minorities as well as women's groups, indicates that common identities and interests have often been subject to attempts to suppress them under the banner of equal citizenship and justice. This is a point made by scholars such as Young and Kymlicka who have argued that group identities and politics of differences should be taken seriously by the democratic institutions in the decision-making process in order to make citizenship more inclusive.[2] The emergence of group identities based on religion, race, gender and language is considered by many scholars, such as Friedman, Littleton, Morley and Robins, to be in conflict with the citizenship. This is mainly due to the universalistic nature of citizenship as compared to the particularistic aspects of group identities.[3]

On the other hand, scholars such as Isin and Wood view citizenship as more inclusive of group identities. According to them, citizenship is a set of practices through which citizens formulate and claim new rights or struggle to expand or maintain existing rights.[4] This is an interesting notion as it posits citizenship as a means to understand, discuss and critically explore the claims of groups and their identities. Identity is a complex notion, related to how people understand and conceive of themselves individually and in relation to other individuals and groups. It is a combination of internal perceptions and external actions, attitudes and behaviour. Similarly, citizenship identity is a self perception of an individual as citizen with the same rights and responsibilities as other citizens. However, the issue of citizenship identity provokes crucial questions such as, do some people think they are treated as second-class citizens? Do they feel they are discriminated against and not considered to be equal to other citizens? Most importantly, the issues related to citizenship identity deal with finding effective solutions for equality and justice in the society.

This Chapter aims to explore the historical experiences of Iraqi Shi'i Muslims before, during and after the Saddam era. It probes into the question of how the status of the Iraqi Shi'i population as equal citizens has been affected throughout history to present day Iraq. It endeavours to explore the effects of various policies on the recognition, belonging and identities of Shi'i Muslim citizens in Iraq. Finally, the Chapter uses Samarra as a case study to explore why it is important for Iraqi Shi'i citizens to project their religious identity in the realm of political and public spheres after the fall of Saddam's regime.

Iraqi Shi'ism

Shi'ism is not only a religion; it also has social, cultural and political dimensions that exist within the society in which the faith is manifested. In Iraq, Shi'ism has a presence in almost every stratum of society – from clerical and tribal classes to bourgeoisie, politicians and modern intellectuals. Iraqi Shi'i intellectuals and activists have been a salient part of both Iraqi history and contemporary politics including both communist and nationalist parties. The cultural elements of Iraqi Shi'a such as their social customs, rituals, motifs and literature are not confined at the communal level but have been a part of public and political spheres resulting in conflicts and rivalry. Apart from the religious history of Shi'ism through the presence of the family of Prophet Muhammad and the *hawza* of Najaf started by Shaykh al-Tusi in the early eleventh century[5], Shi'ism saw a further resurgence during the eighteenth and nineteenth centuries. This was due to the settlement of tribes in Najaf and Karbala. The conversion of tribesmen to Shi'ism was the starting point for the process of the configuration of the Shi'i state and this played a significant role in bringing the various ethnic groups together, which led to the expansion and development of a new Iraqi Shi'i society. The hierarchal structure of the newly formed Shi'i state in the southern part of Iraq was such that the economic and financial resources were controlled by the Shi'i elite members. Amongst these elite members were the *mujtahids,* who were in charge of the monetary funds derived from religious taxes and donations.[6] Through religious guidance and rituals, the *mujtahids* maintained unity amongst the tribesmen and established a religious–political entity. The Shi'i law served as a source of knowledge for daily social and economic activities. Hence, the religious identity of the tribesmen settled in the southern part of Iraq was intertwined with their political identity. In the twentieth century, the *mujtahids* formulated a model for the establishment of the Islamic government, which was terminated due to the British occupation and installation of the Sunni monarchical state in Iraq.[7]

Interestingly, a prominent jurist residing in Samarra, Mirza Shirazi, attempted to increase political representation amongst *mujtahids* and co-operated with the Sunni Sharifians in the Tobacco Protest of 1890. However, the collaboration was short lived as the conflict between the Shi'i *mujtahids* and Sunni government intensified due to the establishment of the Iraqi Sunni monarchy. Under the Sunni monarchy, Baghdad became the apparent centre, abating the significance of cities like Najaf and Karbala, isolating *mujtahids* on the policy of separating religion from the state and declining the opportunities for the Shi'a in politics. As the participation of the *mujtahids* diminished in politics, the Sunni government gained more control over the Shi'i institutions such as *waqf* property (religious endowment) and *madrassahs*.[8] Such policies had an unfavourable effect on the participation of Iraqi Shi'i citizens in politics and public sphere.

Iraqi nationality and citizenship were affected enormously by the British after the collapse of the Ottoman and Safavid empires and creation of Iraqi and Iranian territories. Since then, the issues of citizenship rights and identity have been exploited by both the Iraqi and Iranian government, especially during the Iran–Iraq war (1980–88). For example, the Ba'ath regime during the Iran–Iraq war deported many Iraqi Shi'a to Iran due to their past links with the Persian Empire. Many Iraqi Shi'a have been denied the right of citizenship as they encountered the possibility of banishment or oppression in their own homeland because of their active participation in the public and political sphere.[9] Iraqi Shi'ism is distinctive from its neighbouring Iranian Shi'ism due, in large part, to the prevailing influence of Arab culture and identity. Historically, Shi'ism has often been mainly related to the Persian culture and placed in opposition to the Sunni Ottoman culture due to political contests between the two empires. The formation of the present day territory of Iraq has its roots in the severe contention between the leading empires of the nineteenth and twentieth centuries. Iraq had been a battle ground for a long time in history (particularly since the sixteenth century) between the Shi'i

Safavid and the Sunni Ottoman Empire. In the sixteenth century, the Safavids conquered Iraq in order to control the Shi'i holy cities such as Najaf and Karbala. However, their reign was short-lived and Iraq was soon occupied by the Sunni Ottoman Empire. During the long rule of the Sunni Ottoman Empire, the majority Shi'i population of Iraq was deprived of economic and political resources. Young men selected for the military colleges in Istanbul and government positions were mainly Sunnis. The Sunni population was given privileges to experience economic and political power.[10] Such prejudice against the Shi'a caused increasing tensions between the two religious communities.

The current boundaries of Iraq were created by British officials in cooperation with the Sunni Arab army of Husayn in 1921, Sayyid Husayn b. Ali (the Sharif of Makkah), after the collapse of the Ottoman Empire. The Iraqi population, including the Sunni and Shi'a, revolted against the British occupation, due to which the British decided to set up a monarchy. Iraq soon became an Arab monarchical state with a majority Shi'i population and sacred shrines in Najaf, Karbala and Samarra. According to Nakash, the British rulers considered Iraqi Shi'i religious leaders of Najaf and Karbala as a threat and extremely influential over the large Shi'i population.[11] In order to subdue the political power of the Shi'i leaders, the British created an independent monarchy in Iraq while they maintained the mandate and installed Faisal b. Husayn b. Ali al-Hashemi as King of Iraq in 1921. Since the official members under the power of King Faisal were few, many Ottoman officers were appointed to collaborate and share power. Therefore, the formation of the Iraqi monarchy paved the way for non-Iraqi Sunni officers to take control of the new state excluding the local majority Shi'i population. Moreover, the power hierarchy and the social structure that developed during the Ottoman era was maintained and preferred during the rule of the British Empire.

The preference of the Sunni leadership over the majority Shi'i population weakened Iraqi Shi'i identity and citizenship. During the rule of King Faisal many Shi'i leaders who raised their concerns against the monarchy were forced to leave Iraq and remain politically inactive. A series of monarchs ruled after the death of King Faisal and many military coups followed during 1930–50. In 1968, the Ba'ath party, which was against the communist Iraqis and backed by America, took control of the government. The party was mainly led by Sunnis, and pan-Arabism was the main ideology of the party with great emphasis on Iraqi nationalism.[12] Therefore, since the twentieth century, the political involvement of the Shi'a was often limited, which made many feel like second-class citizens with inferior rights compared to other citizens in their own state.

The Ba'ath party

In 1979, Saddam Hussein became the leader of the Ba'ath party and under his leadership, the Shi'a and Kurds were not included in the government and faced brutal oppression and mistreatment. During Saddam's regime, government policy was often aimed at restricting the religious activities of the Shi'i population and weakening Shi'i culture within Iraqi society. The government suspected the Shi'i population, especially in the southern region, of having links with their Iranian counterparts. In order to control the activities of the Iraqi Shi'i, the cities of Karbala and Najaf were renovated, which caused damage to the bazaar area around the shrines, bringing great economic difficulties to many of the Shi'a. Many Shi'i madrassahs were also damaged as the libraries were destroyed and the *ulama,* as well as the students, were arrested. At the time of Iran–Iraq war, many community and religious leaders of the Iraqi Shi'a were kept under strict surveillance and sometimes even persecuted or killed.

Although the Ba'ath party portrayed itself as secularist and nationalist, it was a medium for Sunni supremacy and dominance. According to Nasr, Fuller and Franke, the Shi'a were mercilessly assaulted, the areas populated by majority Shi'a were neglected, lacked public services, major clerical families were executed and their alimentary wetland was drained.[13] These adverse conditions made many Iraqi Shi'i move from the areas near the Tigris and Euphrates to the slums of Baghdad. The Ba'ath party also banned many Shi'i festivals and many religious leaders were murdered. Although there were some Shi'i political organisations existing, they were banned under the Ba'ath regime. The Ba'ath regime was initially against the involvement of the tribes in developing the political structure. However, during the 1980s, Saddam Hussein collaborated with many Sunni tribes in order to mobilise the war effort against Iran. The tribes soon gained favour from the ruling elites in return for their support and loyalty. After the second Gulf war, the Ba'ath party increasingly depended on the Sunni tribes for security. The growing power of tribes in the government further intensified tensions between the Sunni and Shi'i communities. The increasing tribal power soon turned the Iraqi government into a family enterprise. The lack of support from the government meant that the Shi'a and the Kurdish communities had to deal with unemployment and harsh punishments alone. Under such circumstances, many Iraqi Shi'i fled to Iran where they founded political organisations such as *al-Da'wa* and the SCIR with the help of the Iranian government. These organisations were against the policies of the Ba'ath regime and aimed at putting an end to the Saddam's hostile regime.

The Islamic revolution of Iran in 1979, had devastating effects on the conditions of the Shi'a in Iraq, as Saddam Hussein's regime understood the revolution as a threat to the Sunni ruling regime. Indeed, Saddam became the new President of Iraq in 1979, and his policies became more discriminatory and harsh towards Shi'i scholars, political organisations and activists. Perhaps the most pertinent example of this is the imprisonment and torture of Ayatullah Muhammad Baqir al-Sadr in 1980. Sadr was a jurist, philosopher and ideological founder of *al-Da'wa* party in Iraq. Saddam feared Sadr's increasing influence and eventually had him executed. His sister, Amina Sadr b. al-Huda, was also imprisoned, tortured and executed. It has been alleged that Sadr was killed by having an iron nail hammered into his head and then being set on fire.[14] In addition, many young and old men and women were killed on a massive scale in Iraqi Shi'i cities by Saddam's regime to prevent any kind of revolt or revolution.[15]

Although the Shi'a constituted a majority in Iraq, they had less access to economic resources and have often been excluded from political power. It is important to understand that people in Iraq mainly identify themselves with respect to their inherited communal allegiance, with their religious leaders playing a vital role as their representatives and means of communication with the government. Therefore, the connection of individual Iraqi citizens with their Shi'i religious leaders helps maintain group identities. The main economic support and income for the Iraqi Shi'i communities is from pilgrims who come from various parts of the world to visit holy cities in Iraq such as Najaf, Karbala and Samarra.[16] It should be acknowledged that the Iraqi Shi'i were nationalist and fought against the Iranian Shi'i during the eight years of the first Gulf war. Moreover, many Iraqi clerics including Grand Ayatollah Ali al-Sistani are not in complete favour of the form of Islamic republic idealised by Ayatullah Khomeini where the supreme power lies in the hands of clergymen. It is also vital to remember that the Iraqi Shi'i are Arabs and became a majority as the Arab nomadic tribes settled down in Iraq in the nineteenth century. Both the Sunni and Shi'a population of Iraq consider themselves as Iraqi nationalist though their political aspirations are different, dating back to the time when the monarchy was established by the British. While the Iraqi Shi'i promote distinctive Iraqi Arab nationalist identity, the Sunni minority prefer pan-Arabism which extends to Arab states beyond the territories of Iraq.

Throughout history, many Shi'i writers expressed their views against the ideology of modern secular Arabism and had to face a life of exile. They argued that the Sunni minority rulers, who had come from outside and had no links with the local majority Shi'i Iraqi tribes, had given a new version of Western national identity to Arabism. However, for the majority Shi'i population, the word Arabism was related to the attributes inherited from one tribal generation to another. In order to dismiss the nationalist view of the Shi'i population, the Sunni rulers associated Shi'ism with heresy incited by the Persian detestation for the Arabs. The Ba'ath regime employed the word *shu'ubi* (tribal people) to present the Shi'i population as rejecters of Arab nationalism, and as their opponents. The term *shu'ubiyyah* was used during the Iran–Iraq war in the 1980s to raise questions related to Shi'i identity and belonging to the Iraqi society and Arab nation. The Ba'ath regime represented themselves as the proponents of Arab nationalism against the Persians and depicted the Shi'i population as opponents by associating them with the Islamic Republic of Iran. Hence, Saddam Hussein was the leader of the Arab nation fighting against the Persians to protect the Arab culture from being taken over by the Persians. In such an ideological war, the Iraqi Shi'i who did not fight against the Ba'ath party were categorised as 'good' Shi'i, making the rest of them 'bad' Shi'i.

In the 1990s, when the Sunni rulers of the Ba'ath party were trying to gain control of the southern part of Iraq populated by a Shi'i majority, a number of news articles discredited the identity of the Iraqi Shi'i by linking them to either Iranian or Indian origins. The education system of the Shi'i colleges was also attacked since they were considered as promoting foreign Iranian religion amongst Iraqi students.[17] Therefore, the Iran–Iraq war in the 1980s and the use of the term *shu'ubiyyah* as a strategy for maintaining power by the Sunni minority politicians created a strong sense of Iraqi identity and citizenship amongst the Shi'i Iraqis. The intense resistance of the Shi'i population to the political strategy of labelling them as outsiders or enemies has brought them into a constant power struggle with the minority Sunni rulers. Indeed, in the Gulf war of 1991, the civil disturbance in the Shi'i southern region was repressed through horrific violence, and the discovery of piles of graves of Shi'i fighters and civilians demonstrates the level of tension, animosity and aggression between the Sunni government forces and Shi'i fighters.[18]

This persistent power struggle amongst the diverse citizens of Iraq had been suppressed under Saddam's regime but is now waiting to be unleashed. Given the history of how modern Iraq was created and came to be ruled by Sunni minority rulers, the invasion and occupation of Iraq by the US and its coalition forces gave the suppressed Iraqi Shi'i the chance to compete in full swing for political power to reassert their citizenship and identity.

Invasion of Iraq in 2003

Iraq was invaded by the US and its allied forces in March 2003, with the stated aims of: 1) removing the Ba'athist regime; 2) eliminating any presence of al-Qaeda in Iraq; and 3) destroying any weapons of mass destruction. Removing Saddam Hussein's regime was not a difficult task for the US and its allied forces; the most vital and arduous challenge was (and is) to rebuild Iraq and win the support of the Iraqi people, which was essential to instil democracy in the country. Although there was no concrete long-term plan to rebuild a unified democratic Iraq by the US government, a Coalition Provisional Authority was formed, led by the former State Department diplomat, Paul Bremer. Moreover, the Iraqi people were told that the US and its allied forces would stay in Iraq for a longer time period to destroy the weapons of mass destruction. The lack of planning to provide safety, security, educational infrastructure, public facilities, prevent killing, looting and humanitarian crises in the post-Saddam Iraq, made many Iraqi people critical of the presence of the US and its allied forces. However, the intervention did allow the Shi'a a political voice, which enabled them to raise their concerns as citizens, something which had been denied to them for a long time.

The negative aspects of the invasion, however, are the decline in Iraq's petroleum export, increased civil conflicts, insurgencies against invading forces and many cities experiencing extensive robbery and destruction. Under such circumstances, Iraqi citizens have turned to their tribal leaders, Shi'i clerics and militia leaders for support and protection. As the insurgents grew in strength, the sovereignty of Iraq was transferred from the Coalition Provisional Authority to an interim Iraqi government. However, this US policy did not result in the end of US presence and its allied forces, nor as the killing of civilians due to bomb attacks. The US army was still seen controlling the streets of Iraq and patrolling day-to-day activities of Iraqi citizens. Moreover, continuous presence of the foreign forces made the insurgencies against them eventually gain momentum.[19] After the fall of Saddam's regime, the resistance to the presence of foreign troops has evolved into conflict involving sectarian groups, militias, local and foreign security guards, foreign extremists and Sunni Arab insurgents.

Following the aftermath of the 2003 invasion, an interim government was formed to formulate a liberal constitution in order to transform Iraq into a democracy.[20] This interim government was selected by the Coalition Provisional Authority and was restricted by the laws ordained by it. The interim government was deprived of any jurisdiction over the presence of the foreign troops on the soil of Iraq, which limited their power to act independently and reduced their opportunity to bring economic development, security improvement and their means to pacify the clashes between the sectarian groups. Six years after the invasion, violence, corruption, destruction, religious strife and ethnic conflicts might have been decreasing in one region but increasing in other regions. Iraq was ranked as the 178th most corrupt country out of 180 countries. The presence of al-Qaeda militants has been growing in the northern region of Iraq such as Diyala. The Turkish military units are fighting the Kurds in Iraq, civilians have been a target of ongoing conflicts between the Sunni and Shi'i extremists, and the majority Iraqi population face shortage of clean water, electricity and good quality medical care.[21]

There are a number of factors that have propelled Iraq into a chaotic state. One of the most devastating factors has been the sectarian violence which was unleashed after the US invasion and particularly after the bombing of al-Askariyyain shrine in Samarra in 2006. The collapse of Saddam's regime resulted in problems of law and order and the protection of the ordinary Iraqi citizen. To their great surprise, the US and the allied forces experienced a strong resistance from the Sunni Arab community to the invasion. The Sunni Arab insurgency emerged as a reaction to the coalition invasion and the fall of Saddam's regime soon after the US invasion in 2003. These Sunni insurgents included both nationalist and Islamist extremists. The nationalists struggled to restore and return the power to the Ba'athist government. According to Hashim, this reaction could be due to the perception of the invasion as a threat to the identity and material interests of the Sunni Arab community which was linked to the collapsed regime of Saddam Hussein.[22] The Islamist insurgents, on the other hand, saw the invasion as a threat to Sunni Puritanism. They attacked not only the US forces and its allies but also Iraqi local security guards and civilians from various sects and ethnicities. In mid-2004, the Shi'a, Kurds and more secular Sunni Iraqis became the targets of Sunni Islamist extremists, which endangered the country, dividing it on an ethnic and religious basis, and triggered a civil war.

The fall of Saddam's regime gave rise to a complex political situation in which various sects, tribes and ethnicities engaged in a power struggle amongst themselves. Although many tribal, sectarian and ethnic groups were against the US coaltion forces, it is vital to remember that not all of them adopted the route of violence and insurgent fighting.[23] For example, many Sunni Arab tribal *shuyukh* initially co-operated with the US and its allied forces, but later on resisted them as they did see not their tribal interests protected. The strong support and relationship between the Kurds and US forces also did not last long as their political interests diverged and conflicted with each other.

The establishment of the frameworks for a liberal democracy initially required fair elections through which the Iraqi citizens would be able to vote and elect a government for them to re-establish the war-torn Iraqi society. However, the establishment of local elections and self-rule in provincial cities was put on hold, due to the chaotic situation after the demolition of Saddam's regime. It was instead decided by the US military leaders that they would select and appoint various administrators and mayors to different regions. Most of the appointees were Iraqi military leaders and police officers who would manage the regional matters according to the political interests of the US and its allied forces. They were appointed as mayors of many cities like Najaf, Balad, Tikrit, Samarra and Baqubah.[24] Therefore, the delay of self-rule and local elections highlights that the invasion, which some saw as the advent of more freedom and democracy, could not bring these ideals into fruition without negotiations between various sectarian groups in Iraq battling for political power. However, the clashes between the sectarian groups have to be understood in light of Iraqi history, where some of the groups were denied their right and freedom of opinions, discussions, demonstrations, speeches and publications.

After two years of occupying Iraq, a full-term government was finally established after a series of national elections in 2005. However, the government has still not been able to restore peace and order in the country. The damage done by denying the right of self rule to the Iraqi citizens, and the control of local councils by the foreign authorities, resulted in continuous political turmoil and power struggles amongst various independent leaders, which weakened the civil society and is still a major challenge for the US and its allied forces.[25] The occupation has, however, brought to the fore, many aspects of Shi'i identity which had previously been suppressed and eroded.

Samarra

After the US-led invasion of Iraq, Samarra has come under the control of armed resistance forces making the city a 'no-go zone' for the US occupiers. According to Foulk, Samarra had always been an area of disturbance.[26] By July 2004, it was finally decided that local Iraqi officials would take over the security of Samarra and the US military would be present to provide additional support when and if required. However, this arrangement did not last for long as the US military took over control of Samarra in September 2004. As has been explained by Allawi, the withdrawal of the US and its allied forces from Samarra in 2003 gave opportunities to insurgents to extend their power and control over the city.[27] The local Iraqi guards who were put in charge of the security were poorly trained and unskilled to encounter the insurgents. As a result, security was weakened in Samarra as it came under the strong hold of insurgents, and much of the population of the city, including the Shi'a, suffered accordingly.

After the US armed forces bombarded the city with aircraft and tanks to regain control, Samarra remained a lawless and chaotic city for two months. During these two months, many buildings were destroyed, power and water supplies were cut off, the numbers of kidnappings increased, and many Iraqi and US soldiers were killed in car-bomb attacks. The US forces imposed curfews and houses were searched either by kicking or shooting the doors, causing a great sense of worry and perturbation amongst the people of Samarra. According to the reports of the General Hospital in Samarra, 70 people died, amongst whom 23 were children and 18 were women, during the re-occupation of Samarra by the US-led forces.[28] This turbulence caused Shi'i merchants a great deal of economic difficulty, as the numbers of religious pilgrims to the holy shrines in Samarra dropped. Moreover, the most devastating aspect of the operation to re-take Samarra was the destruction caused to the Golden Dome Mosque, which had a profound effect on not only the Shi'i population of Samarra but also the large numbers of Twelver Shi'a across the globe.

The shrine of Ali al-Hadi and Hasan al-Askari was damaged in a bomb attack in February 2006, and the attacks resulted in a conflict between Shi'i and Sunni Muslims throughout Iraq. Although the identity of the attackers of al-Askariyyain shrine remained unclear, this event aggravated sectarian divisions amongst Iraqis with a strong sense of secular and national identity under Saddam's regime. Moreover, the sectarian divisions and resistance groups against the US coalition forces in Samarra facilitated the presence of extremist groups, many of which had possible links to al-Qaeda. Therefore, the sectarian violence, the furious encounters between the US coalition forces, resistance and extremist groups have culminated in the destruction of the economic, social and political conditions of the city of Samarra and many other cities of Iraq.

Aftermath of the bombings: citizenship and identity in Samarra

The bloodshed caused by the bomb attack of 2006 which destroyed the Golden Dome was followed by another bomb attack in 2007, which demolished the two ten-storey minarets of al-Askariyyain mosque. For many Shi'a around the world, this sacred place is located in an area mainly populated by Sunnis and has been under the strong hold of Islamic resistance groups as well as foreign coalition forces. The safety and protection of the holy places becomes challenging under such circumstances.[29] Furthermore, such attacks on religious places have an adverse impact on people with different religious and ethnic identities living together in a particular location. The bomb attacks on al-Askariyyain mosque elevated anger and hatred amongst Sunnis and Shi'a, adversely affecting sentiments of national identity and instead, making ethnic identities more prominent. As the spirit of being citizens of one democratic state has been diminishing due to various religious communities reprisals, it has become increasingly difficult to make any negotiations and reconciliation amongst them, which is central to the formation of a democratic state.

Soon after the bomb attacks in Samarra, the coalition forces and the Iraqi government sealed the city, making access in and out of the city extremely difficult. At the same time, many people left Samarra in search of a better livelihood.[30] Samarra is an example of the fierce competition for power between the various religious groups in Iraq, which has led the country into a hazardous and chaotic situation. The execution of Saddam Hussein and de-Ba'athification might be essential in the eyes of Western foreign forces for the transition from dictatorship to democracy; however pacification of the ongoing power battle between the Sunni minority and Shi'i majority population is an essential matter for the peace and security of democratic Iraq. The current complications of the Iraqi parliamentary elections for candidates linked to the former Ba'ath party, bombing of important public institutions like ministries and universities regardless of brutal civil deaths, and the recent bomb attacks on Shi'i pilgrims in Samarra, reflect the animosity instilled in the minds of Iraqi citizens through anti-Shi'i policies which have their roots in the history discussed earlier in this Chapter.

The bomb attacks on al-Askariyyain shrine exemplify the intentions of those that wish to threaten the stable identity and citizenship amongst Iraqis. For Iraqi Shi'i citizens in Samarra, al-Askariyyain shrine represents the hub of their religious, social and political ethos. Imam Hasan al-Askari endured house arrest, supervision and repression of his scholarship and guidance by the Abbasid caliph, al-Mutawakkil. His history still resonates with Iraqi Shi'i today because they too consider themselves to have been consistently denied social and political freedom and power by the ruling elite. Al-Askariyyain shrine was a flagship symbol of Shi'i identity, denial of political participation and injustices done to Shi'i Imams. Shi'i Muslims claimed their citizenship through this shrine because it enabled them to claim new rights, or struggle to expand existing rights, based on foundational religious heritage. The shrines symbolise their current struggles, just as their Imams had struggled during their lives, and this gave them impetus to defend their voice as Shi'i Muslims.

The denial of citizenship and identity

Although both the Sunni and Shi'a regard themselves as Iraqi citizens, the policies towards the Iraqi Shi'i population both before and during

Saddam's regime have created a potent rift in Iraqi political and social structures. Furthermore, with the occupation of Iraq by the US and the coalition forces, the situation has worsened as many extremist groups have penetrated Iraqi society from outside the borders of Iraq. The shrine bombings in Samarra are a prime example of this situation and exemplify the long history of persistent denial of citizenship to the Iraqi Shi'a, attacks on their identity and sense of belonging in their own country. Moreover, this is oversimplified in Western media as establishing democracy in Iraq continues to be described in terms of Shi'a and Sunni rivalry.

However, the removal of Saddam Hussein has offered a democratic space for the Iraqi Shi'a, who have long been considered as foreigners and enemies in their own country. Democracy is a way to share power with their fellow citizens, express their loyalty to Iraq as Arabs and obtain access to vital resources as equal citizens without compromising their religious identity. Since their religious identity has been the main reason for their repression and abandonment from Iraqi politics (and Samarra is a pertinent example of this), the current situation in Iraq has allowed many Shi'i citizens to represent themselves as loyal Iraqi Arab Shi'i citizens. Their triumph and peaceful relationships with Sunni and other sectarian groups in Iraq can contribute to the creation of a unique Arab Iraqi identity that will hopefully strengthen over time.

Notes

1. Axtmann, Roland., *Liberal Democracy into the Twenty-First Century: Globalization, Integration and the Nation-State (Political Analyses)* (New York, 1997), pp. 82–83.
2. See Young, Iris Marion., *Justice and the Politics of Difference* (New Jersey, 1990), pp. 116–22 and Kymlicka, Will., *Multicultural Citizenship: A Liberal Theory of Minority Rights (Oxford Political Theory)*, (New York, 1996), pp. 131–52.
3. See Morley, David and Robins, Kevin., *Spaces Of Identity: Global Media, Electronic Landscapes And Cultural Boundaries* (New York, 1995), pp. 83–6.
4. Isin, Engin Fahri and Wood, Patricia K., *Citizenship and Identity* (London, 1999), p. 4 and p. 13.

5. Al-Sadr, Muhammad Baqir., *Principles of Islamic Jurisprudence* (London, 2003), pp. 25–35.
6. Nakash, Yitzhak., *The Shi'is of Iraq* (New Jersey, 2003), pp. 243–4.
7. Ibid, pp. 90–2.
8. Nakash, Yitzhak., *Reaching for Power: The Shi'a in the Modern Arab World* (New Jersey, 2007), p. 5 and p. 271.
9. Jabar, Faleh., *The Shi'ite movement in Iraq* (London, 2003), pp. 69–70.
10. Al-Shawi, Ibrahim., *A glimpse of Iraq* (London, 2006), p. 31.
11. Nakash, Yitzhak., *The Struggle for Power in Iraq* (Summer, 2003), http://www.dissentmagazine.org/article/?article=485,
12. Nakash: *Reaching for Power,* pp. 77–82.
13. See Nasr, Wali., *The Shi'a Revival: How conflicts within Islam will shape the future*, (New Jersey, 2006), p. 187; Fuller, Graham and Francke, Rend Rahim., *The Arab Shi'a: The Forgotten Muslims*, (New York, 1999), pp. 97–99.
14. Shadid, Anthony., *Night Draws Near: Iraq's People in the Shadow of America's War* (New York, 2005), p. 164.
15. Noorbaksh, Mehdi. 'Shiism and Ethnic Politics in Iraq.' *Middle East Policy*, Vol. XV, No.2 (Summer 2008), pp. 53–5. http://www.mepc.org/journal_vol15/96Noorbaksh.pdf
16. Inati, Shams., *Iraq: Its History, People and Politics* (New York, 2003), p. 154.
17. Nakash: *The Struggle for Power in Iraq*, http://www.dissentmagazine.org/article/?article=485
18. Cordesman, Anthony H and Davies, Emma., *Iraq's Insurgency and the Road to Civil Conflict* (Connecticut, 2008), p. 4.
19. Al-Marashi, Ibrahim and Durlacher, Katherine., *Iraqi Perceptions of UK and American Policy in Post-Saddam Iraq* (Nathan Hale Foreign Policy Society, nd), p. 12. http://www.foreignpolicysociety.org/iraq.pdf
20. Burton, Michael, and John Higley. *Elite Foundations of Liberal Democracy* (Lanham, 2006), p. 1.
21. Bilmes, Linda, and Joseph Stiglitz. *The Three Trillion Dollar War: The True Cost of the Iraq Conflict* (New York, 2008), pp. 164–167.
22. Hashim, Ahmed S., *Insurgency and Counter-Insurgency in Iraq* (New York, 2006), p. 18.
23. Heazle, Michael and Islam, Iyantul., *Beyond the Iraq War: The Promises, Pitfalls and Perils of External Interventionism* (Cheltenham, 2006), p. 71.
24. Booth, William and Chandrasekaran, Rajiv., 'Occupation forces halt elections throughout Iraq', *The Washington Post* (June 28th 2003). http://www.iraqwararchive.org/data/jun28/US/wp03.pdf
25. Myerson, Roger., *How to Build Democracy in Iraq* (May 2003), http://home.uchicago.edu/~rmyerson/iraq.pdf, p3.

26. Foulk, Vincent L., *The Battle for Fallujah: Occupation, Resistance and Stalemate in the War in Iraq* (London, 2006), pp. 189–192.
27. Allawi, Ali., *The Occupation of Iraq: Winning the War, Losing the Peace* (London, 2007), p. 291.
28. Harris, Ed. 'Bombs kill 80 in Baghdad a year after shrine attach.' *Evening Standard* (February twelfth 2007) http://www.encyclopedia.com/doc/1P2-3725288.html
29. Cockburn, Patrick., 'Bombing of Samarra shrine sparks fears of reprisals' *The Independent* (June 200 7), http://www.independent.co.uk/news/world/middle-east/bombing-of-samarra-shrine-sparks-fears-of-reprisals-453065.html
30. Garcia-Navarro, Lourdes., 'After Mosque Bombing, Samarra Sunnis remain alienated', *NPR News* (March 2008), http://www.npr.org/templates/story/story.php?storyId=87851320

APPENDIX

SECTION 1

EXCERPTS OF WRITTEN LESSONS OF MIRZA SHIRAZI BY HIS STUDENT, MAWLA ALI RUZODARI, IN 1873[1]

The following four pages in Ruzodari's own handwriting show his notes in Arabic on the subject-matter of *usul al-fiqh* (the science of the principles of jurisprudence) as taught by Mirza Shirazi in 1873.

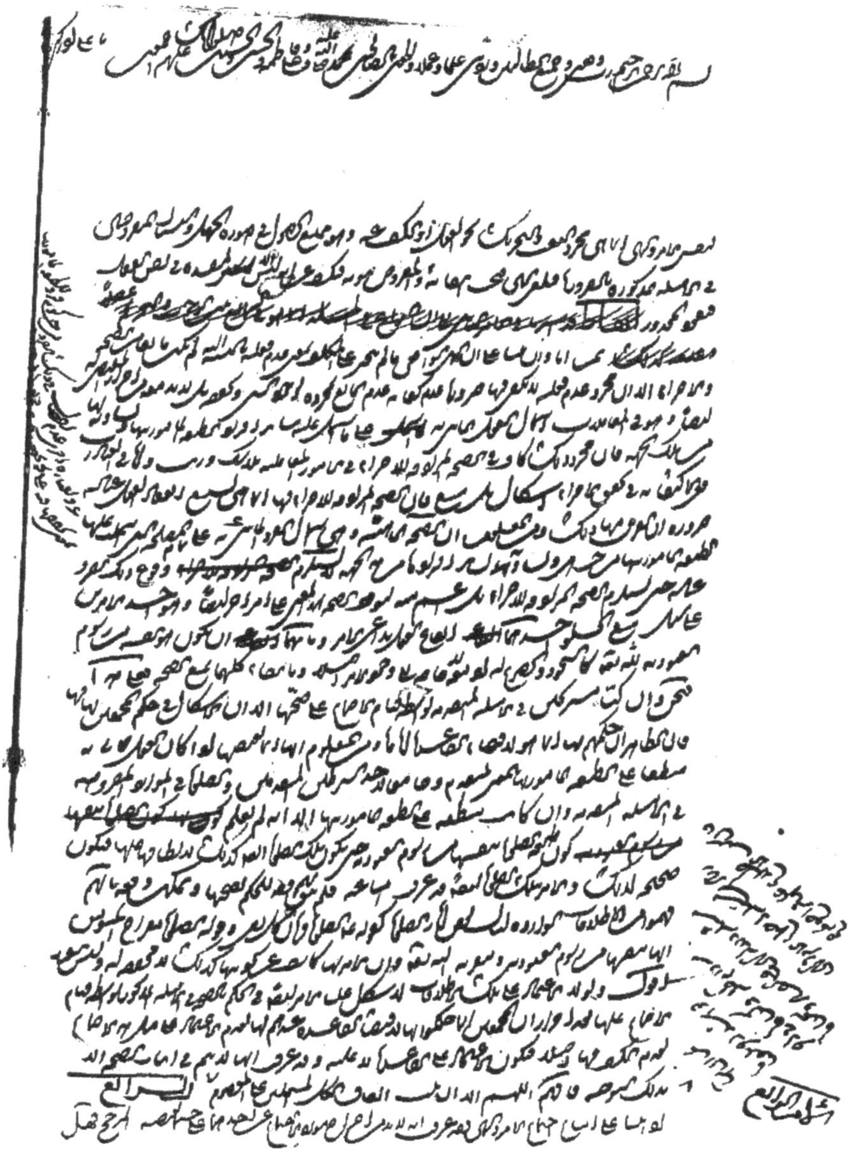

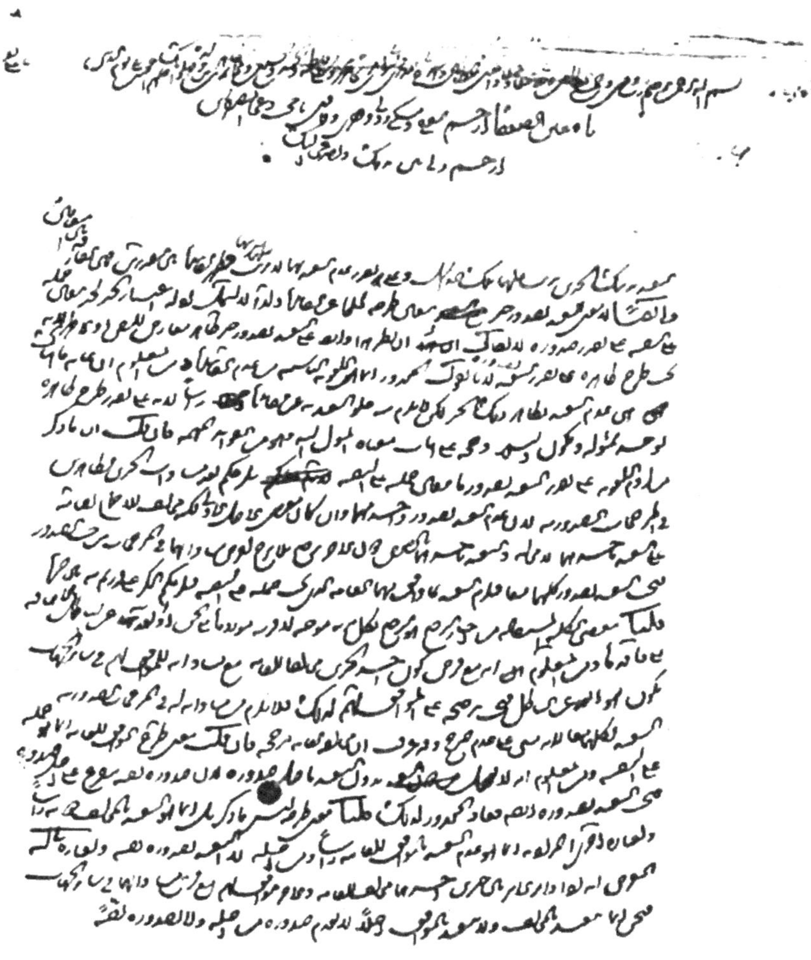

Notes

1. Taken from Ruzodari, Mawla Ali, Written lessons of Ayatullah Muhammad Shirazi (reproduced from the period 1290/1873) (Qum, 2000).

SECTION 2

ZIYARAH OF THE 10TH, 11TH AND 12TH SHI'I IMAMS

This section contains the *ziyarah* (visitation) recitations of the 10th, 11th and 12th Shi'i Imams. *Ziyarah* is a term used for the visitation of the graves of the viceregents of God. These include God's messengers, prophets and their executors. Amongst the Shi'i community, *ziyarah* is also a term that refers to giving salutations to Prophet Muhammad and his family, whether at the grave or from afar. Much of the *ziyarah* literature was recited and transmitted by the Twelve Shi'i Imams and recorded in classical books of Shi'i traditions such as *Bihar al-Anwar*, compiled by Allamah Majlisi in the seventeenth century.

Ziyarah of the 10th Shi'i Imam, Ali al-Hadi[1]

Arabic

السّلامُ عَلَيْكَ يَا أَبَا الْحَسَنِ عَلِيّ بن مُحَمّدٍ الزّكِيّ الرّاشِدَ
النّورَ الثّاقِبَ وَرَحْمَةُ اللّهِ وَبَرَكَاتُهُ،
السّلامُ عَلَيْكَ يَا صَفِيّ اللّهِ،
السّلامُ عَلَيْكَ يَا سِرّ اللّهِ،
السّلامُ عَلَيْكَ يَا حَبْلَ اللّهِ،
السّلامُ عَلَيْكَ يَا آل اللّهِ،

السّلامُ عَلَيْكَ يَا خِيَرَةَ اللّهِ،

السّلامُ عَلَيْكَ يَا صَفْوَةَ اللّهِ،

السّلامُ عَلَيْكَ يَا أَمِينَ اللّهِ،

السّلامُ عَلَيْكَ يَا حَقّ اللّهِ،

السّلامُ عَلَيْكَ يَا حَبِيبَ اللّهِ،

السّلامُ عَلَيْكَ يَا نُورَ الانْوَارِ،

السّلامُ عَلَيْكَ يَا زَيْنَ الابْرَارِ،

السّلامُ عَلَيْكَ يَا سَلِيلَ الاخْيَارِ،

السّلامُ عَلَيْكَ يَاعُنْصُرَ الاطْهَارِ،

السّلامُ عَلَيْكَ يَا حُجّةَ الرّحْمنِ،

السّلامُ عَلَيْكَ يَا رُكْنَ الايمَانِ،

السّلامُ عَلَيْكَ يَا مَوْلَى الْمُؤْمِنِينَ،

السّلامُ عَلَيْكَ يَا وَلِيّ الصّالِحِينَ،

السّلامُ عَلَيْكَ يَا عَلَمَ الْهُدَى،

السّلامُ عَلَيْكَ يَا حَلِيفَ التّقَى،

السّلامُ عَلَيْكَ يَا عَمُودَ الدّينِ،

السّلامُ عَلَيْكَ يَا بْنَ خَاتَمِ النّبِيّينَ،

السّلامُ عَلَيْكَ يَا بْنَ سَيّدِ الْوَصِيّينَ،

السّلامُ عَلَيْكَ يَا بْنَ فَاطِمَةَ الزّهْرَاءِ سَيّدَةِ نِسَاءِ الْعَالَمِينَ،

السّلامُ عَلَيْكَ أَيّهَا الامِينُ الْوَفِيّ،

السّلامُ عَلَيْكَ أَيّهَا الْعَلَمُ الرّضِيّ،

السّلامُ عَلَيْكَ أَيّهَا الزّاهِدُ التّقِيّ،

السّلامُ عَلَيْكَ أَيّهَا الْحُجّةُ عَلَى الْخَلْقِ أَجْمَعِينَ،

السّلامُ عَلَيْكَ أَيّهَا التّالِي لِلْقُرْآنِ،

السّلامُ عَلَيْكَ أَيّهَا الْمُبَيّنُ لِلْحَلالِ مِنَ الْحَرَامِ،

السّلامُ عَلَيْكَ أَيّهَا الْوَلِيّ النّاصِحُ،

السّلامُ عَلَيْكَ أَيّهَا الطّرِيقُ الْوَاضِحُ،

السّلامُ عَلَيْكَ أَيّهَا النّجْمُ اللائِحُ،

أَشْهَدُ يَا مَوْلايَ يَا أَبَا الْحَسَنِ أَنّكَ حُجّةُ اللهِ عَلَى خَلْقِهِ،

وَخَلِيفَتُهُ فِي بَرِيّتِهِ،

وَأَمِينُهُ فِي بِلادِهِ،
وَشَاهِدُهُ عَلَى عِبَادِهِ،
وَأَشْهَدُ أَنَّكَ كَلِمَةُ التَّقْوَى،
وَبَابُ الْهُدَى،
وَالْعُرْوَةُ الْوُثْقَى،
وَالْحُجَّةُ عَلَى مَنْ فَوْقَ الارْضِ وَمَنْ تَحْتَ الثَّرَى،
وَأَشْهَدُ أَنَّكَ الْمُطَهَّرُ مِنَ الذُّنُوبِ،
الْمُبَرَّأُ مِنَ الْعُيُوبِ،
وَالْمُخْتَصّ بِكَرَامَةِ اللّهِ،
وَالْمَحْبُوّ بِحُجَّةِ اللّهِ،
وَالْمَوْهُوبُ لَهُ كَلِمَةُ اللّهِ،
وَالرّكْنُ الّذِي يَلْجَأُ إِلَيْهِ الْعِبَادُ،
وَتُحْيَى بِهِ الْبِلادُ،
وَأَشْهَدُ يَا مَوْلايَ أَنّي بِكَ وَبِآبَائِكَ وَأَبْنَائِكَ مُوقِنٌ مُقِرّ،
وَلَكُمْ تَابِعٌ فِي ذَاتِ نَفْسِي، وَشَرَايِعِ دِينِي،
وَخَاتِمَةِ عَمَلِي وَمُنْقَلَبِي وَمَثْوَايَ،
وَأَنّي وَلِيّ لِمَنْ وَالاكُمْ، وَعَدُوّ لِمَنْ عَادَاكُمْ،
مُؤْمِنٌ بِسِرّكُمْ وَعَلانِيَتِكُمْ، وَأَوّلِكُمْ وَآخِرِكُمْ،
بِأَبِي أَنْتَ وَأُمّي، وَالسّلامُ عَلَيْكَ وَرَحْمَةُ اللّهِ وَبَرَكَاتُهُ.
اللّهُمّ صَلّ عَلَى مُحَمّدٍ وَآلِ مُحَمّدٍ،
وَصَلّ عَلَى حُجّتِكَ الْوَفِيّ،
وَوَلِيّكَ الزّكِيّ،
وَأَمِينِكَ الْمُرْتَضَى،
وَصَفِيّكَ الْهَادِي،
وَصِرَاطِكَ الْمُسْتَقِيمِ،
وَالْجَادّةِ الْعُظْمَى،
وَالطّرِيقَةِ الْوُسْطَى،
نُورِ قُلُوبِ الْمُؤْمِنِينَ،

وَوَلِيّ الْمُتَّقِينَ،

وَصَاحِب الْمُخْلِصِينَ.

اللّهُمَّ صَلِّ عَلَى سَيِّدِنَا مُحَمَّدٍ وَأَهْلِ بَيْتِهِ،

وَصَلِّ عَلَى عَلِيِّ بْنِ مُحَمَّدٍ

الرّاشِدِ الْمَعْصُومِ مِنَ الزَّلَلِ،

وَالطّاهِرِ مِنَ الْخَلَلِ،

وَالْمُنْقَطِعِ إِلَيْكَ بِالامَلِ،

الْمَبْلُوِّ بِالْفِتَنِ،

وَالْمُخْتَبَرِ بِالْمِحَنِ،

وَالْمُمْتَحَنِ بِحُسْنِ الْبَلْوَى،

وَصَبْرِ الشَّكْوَى،

مُرْشِدِ عِبَادِكَ،

وَبَرَكَةِ بِلادِكَ،

وَمَحَلِّ رَحْمَتِكَ،

وَمُسْتَوْدَعِ حِكْمَتِكَ،

وَالْقَائِدِ إِلَى جَنَّتِكَ،

الْعَالِمِ فِي بَرِيَّتِكَ،

وَالْهَادِي فِي خَلِيقَتِكَ

الَّذِي ارْتَضَيْتَهُ وَانْتَجَبْتَهُ

وَاخْتَرْتَهُ لِمَقَامِ رَسُولِكَ فِي أُمَّتِهِ،

وَأَلْزَمْتَهُ حِفْظَ شَرِيعَتِهِ،

فَاسْتَقَلَّ بِأَعْبَاءِ الْوَصِيَّةِ

نَاهِضًا بِهَا وَمُضْطَلِعًا بِحَمْلِهَا،

لَمْ يَعْثُرْ فِي مُشْكِلٍ،

وَلا هَفَا فِي مُعْضِلٍ،

بَلْ كَشَفَ الْغُمَّةَ،

وَسَدَّ الْفُرْجَةَ،

وَأَدَّى الْمُفْتَرَضَ.

اللّهُمّ فَكَمَا أَقْرَرْتَ نَاظِرَ نَبِيّكَ بِهِ فَرَقِّهِ دَرَجَتَهُ،
وَأَجْزِلْ لَدَيْكَ مَثُوبَتَهُ،
وَصَلِّ عَلَيْهِ وَبَلِّغْهُ مِنَّا تَحِيَّةً وَسَلامًا،
وَآتِنَا مِنْ لَدُنْكَ فِي مُوَالاتِهِ فَضْلاً وَإِحْسَانًا
وَمَغْفِرَةً وَرِضْوَانًا
إِنَّكَ ذُو الْفَضْلِ الْعَظِيمِ.

English Translation

Peace be on you,
O Abu al-Hasan,
Ali b. Muhammad,
The pious guide,
The bright light.
And mercy and blessings of Allah (be upon you)!
Peace be on you,
O the sincerely attached friend of Allah.
Peace be on you,
O the confidant of Allah!
Peace be on you,
O the rope of Allah!
Peace be on you,
O he who belongs to the family chosen by Allah exclusively for Himself!
Peace be on you,
O the good of Allah!
Peace be on you,
O the intimate friend of Allah!
Peace be on you,
O the trustee of Allah!
Peace be on you,
O the proof of Allah!
Peace be on you,
O the dearest beloved of Allah,
Peace be on you,

O the light who gives light to other lights!
Peace be on you,
O the pride of the virtuous!
Peace be on you,
O the son of the upright!
Peace be on you,
O the essence of the purified!
Peace be on you,
O the argument of the beneficient!
Peace be on you,
O the essential of the faith!
Peace be on you,
O the master of the faithful
Peace be on you,
O the guardian of the pious,
Peace be on you,
O the symbol of guidance!
Peace be on you,
O the ally of the God fearing!
Peace be on you,
O the mainstay of the religion!
Peace be on you,
O the son of the last prophet!
Peace be on you,
O the son of the first successors!
Peace be on you,
O the son of Fatimah al-Zahra, the prime leader of the
women of the worlds!
Peace be on you,
O the faithful trustee!
Peace be on you,
O the favourite symbol!
Peace be on you,
O the innocent God fearing!
Peace be on you,

O the decisive argument over all people of
every age!
Peace be on you,
O he who studied and interpreted the Holy Quran!
Peace be on you,
O he who taught to distinguish between lawful and
unlawful!
Peace be on you,
O the guardian who always gave sincere advice!
Peace be on you,
O the evident example.
Peace be on you,
O the bright star!
I bear witness,
O my master, oh Abu al-Hasan,
That verily you are the decisive argument of Allah over
mankind,
His representative among the people,
His trusted administrator in His lands,
His witness over His servants,
I bear witness that verily you are the words of piety, door
of guidance and the safe handle,
You are the evident proof for those who are on the earth
and
For those who are deep down in the layers of the soil.
I bear witness that verily you are infallible,
The identity of Allah's grace, free from defects,
The preferred choice of Allah to demonstrate His proofs,
The spokesman of Allah.
The essential principle who protects the people and on
account of whom the social life sustains itself and grows;
I say under oath,
O my master, that I have faith in you,
your forefathers and your children.
I follow all of you in my personal affairs,
in my religious perfomance, in my day-to-day conduct;

My return and my destination are also the same as yours,
I make friends with those who befriend you
I strive against those who oppose you;
I believe in all of you, whether invisible or visible,
In those of you who came first,
In those of you who came last.
My father and mother are at your disposal
Peace be on you and mercy and blessing of Allah (be upon you).
O Allah send blessing on Muhammad and on the children of Muhammad
and send blessing on Thy faithful demonstrator,
Thy sagacious representative,
Thy chosen trustee,
Thy sincerely attached guide,
Thy right path,
The most important approach,
The just and equitable course,
The light of the faithfuls' hearts,
The friend of the God-fearing,
The comrade of the sincere,
O Allah send blessings on our masters, Muhammad and his Ahl al-Bayt,
And send blessing on Ali b. Muhammad, the infallible guide,
Free from errors and faults,
He kept himself aloof from temptations and served Thee,
Tumult and discord seized him,
Troubles and sorrows surrounded Him,
Thoroughly tried and tested,
(but) he endured without complaint
the spiritual guide of Thy servants,
the blessing for the human civilization,
The destination of Thy mercy Thou entrusted him with Thy Wisdom.
He led unto Thy paradise and gave knowledge and wisdom to

Thy created beings and showed them the right path
Whom Thou chose, preferred and elected to take the place of Thy prophet among his ummah
And gave him the responsibility of keeping intact the prescript of His religion.
So, he confidently accomplished the onerous task of his succession,
Allowed it to grow and spread, strengthened its hold,
Difficulties did not confuse him, complications did not obscure his judgement.
He examined and exposed intricate issues
Sealed the loopholes,
Carried out that which has been made obligatory,
O Allah, just as Thou made him a source of delight for Thy prophet,
Raise him to the highest heights and give him the most fitting reward that suits him,
Bless him, convey our greetings and salutations to him.
And give us, on account of our love for him, Thy bounties, favours, amnesty and approval.
Verily Thou art the owner of abundant benefits and bounties.

Ziyarah of the 11th Shi'i Imam, Hasan al-Askari[2]

لسَّلاَمُ عَلَيْكَ يَا مَوْلاَيَ يَا أَبَا مُحَمَّدٍ الْحَسَنَ بْنَ عَلِيٍّ الْهَادِيَ الْمُهْتَدِيَ وَ رَحْمَةُ اللَّهِ وَ بَرَكَاتُهُ
السَّلاَمُ عَلَيْكَ يَا وَلِيَّ اللَّهِ وَ ابْنَ أَوْلِيَائِهِ السَّلاَمُ عَلَيْكَ يَا حُجَّةَ اللَّهِ وَ ابْنَ حُجَجِهِ
السَّلاَمُ عَلَيْكَ يَا صَفِيَّ اللَّهِ وَ ابْنَ أَصْفِيَائِهِ السَّلاَمُ عَلَيْكَ يَا خَلِيفَةَ اللَّهِ وَ ابْنَ خُلَفَائِهِ وَ أَبَا خَلِيفَتِهِ
السَّلاَمُ عَلَيْكَ يَا ابْنَ خَاتَمِ النَّبِيِّينَ السَّلاَمُ عَلَيْكَ يَا ابْنَ سَيِّدِ الْوَصِيِّينَ
السَّلاَمُ عَلَيْكَ يَا ابْنَ أَمِيرِ الْمُؤْمِنِينَ السَّلاَمُ عَلَيْكَ يَا ابْنَ سَيِّدَةِ نِسَاءِ الْعَالَمِينَ
السَّلاَمُ عَلَيْكَ يَا ابْنَ الْأَئِمَّةِ الْهَادِينَ السَّلاَمُ عَلَيْكَ يَا ابْنَ الْأَوْصِيَاءِ الرَّاشِدِينَ
السَّلاَمُ عَلَيْكَ يَا عِصْمَةَ الْمُتَّقِينَ السَّلاَمُ عَلَيْكَ يَا إِمَامَ الْفَائِزِينَ السلاَمُ عَلَيْكَ يَا رُكْنَ الْمُؤْمِنِينَ

السَّلاَمُ عَلَيْكَ يَا فَرَجَ الْمَلْهُوفِينَ السَّلاَمُ عَلَيْكَ يَا وَارِثَ الْأَنْبِيَاءِ الْمُنْتَجَبِينَ
السَّلاَمُ عَلَيْكَ يَا خَازِنَ عِلْمِ وَصِيِّ رَسُولِ اللَّهِ السَّلاَمُ عَلَيْكَ أَيُّهَا الدَّاعِي بِحُكْمِ اللَّهِ
السَّلاَمُ عَلَيْكَ أَيُّهَا النَّاطِقُ بِكِتَابِ اللَّهِ السَّلاَمُ عَلَيْكَ يَا حُجَّةَ الْحُجَجِ
السَّلاَمُ عَلَيْكَ يَا هَادِيَ الْأُمَمِ السَّلاَمُ عَلَيْكَ يَا وَلِيَّ النِّعَمِ السَّلاَمُ عَلَيْكَ يَا عَيْبَةَ الْعِلْمِ
السَّلاَمُ عَلَيْكَ يَا سَفِينَةَ الْحِلْمِ السَّلاَمُ عَلَيْكَ يَا أَبَا الْإِمَامِ الْمُنْتَظَرِ الظَّاهِرَةِ لِلْعَاقِلِ حُجَّتُهُ
وَ الثَّابِتَةِ فِي الْيَقِينِ مَعْرِفَتُهُ الْمُحْتَجَبِ عَنْ أَعْيُنِ الظَّالِمِينَ وَ الْمُغَيَّبِ عَنْ دَوْلَةِ الْفَاسِقِينَ
وَ الْمُعِيدِ رَبُّنَا بِهِ الْإِسْلاَمَ جَدِيداً بَعْدَ الانْطِمَاسِ وَ الْقُرْآنَ غَضّاً بَعْدَ الانْدِرَاسِ
أَشْهَدُ يَا مَوْلاَيَ أَنَّكَ أَقَمْتَ الصَّلاَةَ وَ آتَيْتَ الزَّكَاةَ وَ أَمَرْتَ بِالْمَعْرُوفِ وَ نَهَيْتَ عَنِ الْمُنْكَرِ
وَ دَعَوْتَ إِلَى سَبِيلِ رَبِّكَ بِالْحِكْمَةِ وَ الْمَوْعِظَةِ الْحَسَنَةِ وَ عَبَدْتَ اللَّهَ مُخْلِصاً حَتَّى أَتَاكَ الْيَقِينُ
أَسْأَلُ اللَّهَ بِالشَّأْنِ الَّذِي لَكُمْ عِنْدَهُ أَنْ يَتَقَبَّلَ زِيَارَتِي لَكُمْ وَ يَشْكُرَ سَعْيِي إِلَيْكُمْ
وَ يَسْتَجِيبَ دُعَائِي بِكُمْ وَ يَجْعَلَنِي مِنْ أَنْصَارِ الْحَقِّ وَ أَتْبَاعِهِ وَ أَشْيَاعِهِ وَ مَوَالِيهِ وَ مُحِبِّيهِ
وَ السَّلاَمُ عَلَيْكَ وَ رَحْمَةُ اللَّهِ وَ بَرَكَاتُهُ

At this point visitors may kiss the holy tomb, put their right and then left cheek on it, and say the following:

اللَّهُمَّ صَلِّ عَلَى سَيِّدِنَا مُحَمَّدٍ وَ أَهْلِ بَيْتِهِ وَ صَلِّ عَلَى الْحَسَنِ بْنِ عَلِيٍّ الْهَادِي إِلَى دِينِكَ
وَ الدَّاعِي إِلَى سَبِيلِكَ عَلَمِ الْهُدَى وَ مَنَارِ التُّقَى وَ مَعْدِنِ الْحِجَى وَ مَأْوَى النُّهَى وَ غَيْثِ الْوَرَى
وَ سَحَابِ الْحِكْمَةِ وَ بَحْرِ الْمَوْعِظَةِ وَ وَارِثِ الْأَئِمَّةِ وَ الشَّهِيدِ عَلَى الْأُمَّةِ الْمَعْصُومِ الْمُهَذَّبِ
وَ الْفَاضِلِ الْمُقَرَّبِ وَ الْمُطَهَّرِ مِنَ الرِّجْسِ الَّذِي وَرَّثْتَهُ عِلْمَ الْكِتَابِ وَ أَلْهَمْتَهُ فَصْلَ الْخِطَابِ
وَ نَصَبْتَهُ عَلَماً لِأَهْلِ قِبْلَتِكَ وَ قَرَنْتَ طَاعَتَهُ بِطَاعَتِكَ وَ فَرَضْتَ مَوَدَّتَهُ عَلَى جَمِيعِ خَلِيقَتِكَ
اللَّهُمَّ فَكَمَا أَنَابَ بِحُسْنِ الْإِخْلاَصِ فِي تَوْحِيدِكَ وَ أَرْدَى مَنْ خَاضَ فِي تَشْبِيهِكَ وَ حَامَى عَنْ أَهْلِ الْإِيمَانِ بِكَ
فَصَلِّ يَا رَبِّ عَلَيْهِ صَلاَةً يَلْحَقُ بِهَا مَحَلَّ الْخَاشِعِينَ وَ يَعْلُو فِي الْجَنَّةِ بِدَرَجَةِ جَدِّهِ خَاتَمِ النَّبِيِّينَ
وَ بَلِّغْهُ مِنَّا تَحِيَّةً وَ سَلاَماً وَ آتِنَا مِنْ لَدُنْكَ فِي مُوَالاَتِهِ فَضْلاً وَ إِحْسَاناً وَ مَغْفِرَةً وَ رِضْوَاناً
إِنَّكَ ذُو فَضْلٍ عَظِيمٍ وَ مَنٍّ جَسِيمٍ

English Translation

Peace be on you, O my master
O father of Muhammad, Hasan b. Ali,
The rightly-guided guide, mercy and blessings of Allah (be on you).
Peace be on you,
O the representative of Allah and the son of his representatives,
Peace be on you,
O the decisive proof of Allah ,
And the son of his decisive proof ,
Peace be on you,
O the sincerely attached friend of Allah and the son of sincerely attached friends,
Peace be on you,
O the vicegerent of Allah,
And the son of his vicegerents,
And the father of his vicegerent
Peace be on you,
O the son of the last Prophet!
Peace be on you,
O son of the first successor!
Peace be on you,
O son of the Commander of the faithful!
Peace be on you,
O the son of the prime women!
Leader of the worlds.
Peace be on you,
O the son of the guides who showed the right path!
Peace be on you,
O the son of the rightly-guided successors!
Peace be on you,
O the guardian of the God-fearing!
Peace be on you,
O the son of the bountiful Imams!

Peace be on you,
O the support of the believers!
Peace be on you,
O the comforter of the downcast!
Peace be on you,
O the inheritor of the distinguished Prophets!
Peace be on you,
O the custodian of the wisdom of the successor of Allah's messenger!
Peace be on you,
O he who by the command of Allah, invited (mankind) unto Allah
Peace be on you,
O he whose speech was a true reproduction of the book of Allah
Peace be on you,
O the true demonstration of (Allah's) arguments!
Peace be on you,
O the guide of mankind!
Peace be on you,
O the distributor of (Allah's) bounties!
Peace be on you,
O the source of knowledge!
Peace be on you,
O the men through whom (Allah's) compassion reaches mankind!
Peace be on you,
O father of the Awaited Saviour,
For your intelligent son is a clear proof.
Insight in his matters builds up true faith,
Invisible to the searching eyes of the tyrants,
Untraceable in the countries governed by impudent scroundels,
Through him our Lord shall usher in the rennaissance of Islam,

In the wake of persecution and oppression and give
currency to the application of
the Holy Quran, shelved and forgotten for a long time
I bear witness, O my master,
that verily you established the prayers, gave the prescribed
share to the needy,
commanded to do that which is lawful not to do that
which is unlawful,
invited unto the path of your Lord with wisdom and fair
arguments,
And sincerely served Allah till the inevitable came to you.
I beseech Allah in the name of your privileges you enjoy
before Him,
To accept my visitation and appreciate my efforts,
To give favourable answers to my supplications for your sake,
To let me be among the supporters of the truth (among)
its followers, companions, friends and lovers.
Peace be on you and mercy and blessings of Allah,
(be upon you)
O Allah send blessings on our masters, Muhammad and
his Ahl al-Bayt;
Send blessings on Hasan b. Ali who guided people unto
Thy religion,
Invited them unto Thy path,
The sign of guidance,
The torch of piety,
The mine of reason,
The stronghold of intelligence,
The rain of mercy for the human race,
The wisdom-bearing clouds,
The ocean of wisdom,
The inheritor of the Imams,
The witness over the nation,
The near and dear one of Allah,
The thoroughly purified one from uncleanliness,
Who gave him the knowledge of the Book in his inheritance,

Educated him in its brilliant style which distinguishes between truth and falsehood.
Established him as Thy evident sign for the Muslims,
Obedience unto him has been joined with obedience unto Thee,
it has been made obligatory upon all people to love and follow him
O Allah just as he sincerely attached himself to Thy Oneness, repudiated those who rushed into the danger of imitating Thy image, patronised those who believed in Thee,
so bless him, O Lord, with blessings that pursue him to the place where those who have resigned themselves to Thee are found,
and in the paradise raise him to the status of his grandfather,
the last Prophet,
convey to him our greetings and salutations,
and give us on account of our love for him,
Thy bounties, favours, pardon and approval.
Verily, You spread unlimited bounties and Thy gifts are precious.

Ziyarah al-Nahiyah al-Muqaddasah of the 12th Shi'i Imam, Muhammad al-Mahdi

Of the several prescribed *ziyarah* of Imam al-Husayn, one was recited by Imam al-Mahdi and reached his followers through one of his four special deputies. For that reason, it is known as the *ziyarah* that was issued from the sacred side (*Ziyarah al-Nahiyah al-Muqaddasah*). One of the most important features of this *ziyarah* is that in different phrases, Imam al-Mahdi graphically describes the events of Ashura and the agony that Imam al-Husayn and his family faced on that horrific and ominous day.

The text of the *Ziyarah al-Nahiyah* is found in some early *ziyarah* collections such as *al-Mazar al-Kabir*, by Muhammad Ibn Ja'far al-Mashhadi, pp. 496–513. It is also reported in al-Mazar, by al-Mufid as mentioned in *Bihar al-Anwar*, vol. 98, pp. 318–29.

السَّلامُ عَلى ادَمَ صِفْوَةِ اللهِ مِنْ خَليقَتِه،

السَّلامُ عَلى شَيْثٍ وَلِيِّ اللهِ وَ خِيَرَتِه،

السَّلامُ عَلى إِدْريسَ الْقـآئِمِ للهِ بِحُـجَّتِهِ،

السَّلامُ عَلى نُوحٍ الْمُجابِ في دَعْوَتِهِ،

السَّلامُ عَلى هُودٍ الْمَمْدُودِ مِنَ اللهِ بِمَعُونَتِه،

السَّلامُ عَلى صالِحٍ الَّذي تَـوَّجَهُ اللهُ بِكَرامَتِه،

السَّلامُ عَلى إِبْراهيمَ الَّذي حَباهُ اللهُ بِخُلَّتِهِ،

السَّلامُ عَلى إِسْمعيلَ الَّذي فَداهُ اللهُ بِذِبْـحٍ عَظيمٍ مِنْ جَنَّتِه،

السَّلامُ عَلى إِسْحقَ الَّذي جَعَلَ اللهُ النُّبُوَّةَ في ذُرِّيَّتِهِ،

السَّـلامُ عَلى يَعْقُوبَ الَّذي رَدَّ اللهُ عَلَيْهِ بَصَرَهُ بِرَحْمَتِهِ،

السَّلامُ عَلى يُوسُفَ الَّذي نَجّاهُ اللهُ مِنَ الْجُبِّ بِعَظَمَتِهِ،

السَّلامُ عَلى مُوسَى الَّذي فَلَقَ اللهُ الْبَحْرَ لَهُ بِقُدْرَتِهِ،

السَّلامُ عَلى هارُونَ الَّذي خَصَّهُ اللهُ بِنُبُـوَّتِه،

السَّلامُ عَلى شُعَيْبٍ الَّذي نَصَرَهُ اللهُ عَلى أُمَّتِه،

السَّلامُ عَلى داوُدَ الَّذي تابَ اللهُ عَلَيْهِ مِنْ خَطيـئَتِه،

السَّلامُ عَلى سُلَيْمانَ الَّذي ذَلَّتْ لَهُ الْجِنُّ بِعِزَّتِه،

السَّلامُ عَلى أَيُّوبَ الَّذي شَفاهُ اللهُ مِنْ عِلَّتِهِ،

السَّلامُ عَلى يُونُسَ الَّذي أَنْـجَزَ اللهُ لَهُ مَضْـمُونَ عِدَتِهِ،

السَّلامُ عَـلى عُزَيْرٍ الَّذي أَحْياهُ اللهُ بَعْدَ ميتَتِهِ،

السَّلامُ عَلى زَكَرِيّا الصّـابِرِ في مِحْنَتِه،

السَّلامُ عَلى يَحْيَى الَّذي أَزْلَفَهُ اللهُ بِشَهادَتِه،

السَّلامُ عَلى عيسى رُوحِ اللهِ وَ كَلِمَتِهِ،

السَّلامُ عَلى مُحَمَّدٍ حَبيبِ اللهِ وَ صِفْوَتِه،

السَّلامُ عَلى أَميرِالْمُؤْمِنينَ عَلِيِّ بْنِ أَبي طالِبٍ الْمَخْصُوصِ بِأُخُوَّتِهِ،

السَّلامُ عَلى فاطِمَةَ الزَّهْرآءِ ابْنَتِهِ،

السَّلامُ عَلى أَبي مُحَمَّدٍ الْحَسَنِ وَصِيِّ أَبيهِ وَ خَليفَتِهِ،

السَّلامُ عَلَى الْحُسَيْنِ الَّذي سَمَحَتْ نَفْسُهُ بِمُهْجَتِهِ،

السَّلامُ عَلى مَنْ أَطاعَ اللهَ في سِـرِّهِ وَ عَلانِـيَـتِـهِ،

السَّلامُ عَلى مَنْ جَعَلَ اللهُ الشِّـفآءَ في تُرْبَتِهِ،

السَّلامُ عَلى مَنِ الْإِ جابَـةُ تَحْتَ قُـبَّـتِهِ،

السَّلامُ عَلى مَنِ الْأَ ئِـمَّـةُ مِنْ ذُرِّيَّـتِـهِ،

السَّلامُ عَلَى ابْنِ خاتَمِ الْأَ نْبِيآءِ،

السَّلامُ عَلَى ابْنِ سَيِّدِ الْأَوْصِيآءِ،

السَّلامُ عَلَى ابْنِ فاطِمَةَ الزَّهْرآءِ،

السَّلامُ عَلَى ابْنِ خَديجَةَ الْكُبْرى،

السَّلامُ عَلَى ابْنِ سِدْرَةِ الْمُنْتَهى،

السَّلامُ عَلَى ابْنِ جَنَّةِ الْـمَـأْوى،

السَّلامُ عَلَى ابْنِ زَمْـزَمَ وَ الصَّـفا،

السَّلامُ عَلَى الْمُرَمَّلِ بِالدِّمآءِ،

السَّلامُ عَلَى الْمَهْتُوكِ الْخِبآءِ،

السَّلامُ عَلى خامِسِ أَصْحابِ الْكِسْآءِ،

السَّلامُ عَلى غَريبِ الْغُرَبآءِ،

السَّلامُ عَلى شَهيدِ الشُّهَدآءِ،

السَّلامُ عَلى قَتيلِ الْأَدْعِيآءِ،

السَّلامُ عَلى ساكِنِ كَرْبَلآءِ،

السَّلامُ عَلى مَنْ بَكَتْهُ مَلائِكَةُ السَّمآءِ،

السَّلامُ عَلى مَنْ ذُرِّيَّتُهُ الْأَزْكِيآءُ،

السَّلامُ عَلى يَعْسُوبِ الدّينِ،

السَّلامُ عَلى مَنازِلِ الْبَراهينِ،

السَّلامُ عَلَى الْأَئِمَّةِ السّاداتِ،

السَّلامُ عَلَى الْجُيُوبِ الْمُضَرَّجاتِ،

السَّلامُ عَلَى الشِّفاهِ الذّابِلاتِ،

السَّلامُ عَلَى النُّفُوسِ الْمُصْطَلَماتِ،

السَّلامُ عَلَى الْأَرْواحِ الْمُخْتَلَساتِ،

السَّلامُ عَلَى الأَجْسادِ الْعارِياتِ،

السَّلامُ عَلَى الْجُسُومِ الشّاحِباتِ،

السَّلامُ عَلَى الدِّماءِ السّآئِلاتِ،

السَّلامُ عَلَى الأَعْضاءِ الْمُقَطَّعاتِ،

السَّلامُ عَلَى الرُّؤُوسِ الْمُشالاتِ،

السَّلامُ عَلَى النِّسْوَةِ الْبارِزاتِ،

السَّلامُ عَلى حُجَّةِ رَبِّ الْعالَمينَ،

السَّلامُ عَلَيْكَ وَ عَلى ابآئِكَ الطّاهِرينَ،

السَّلامُ عَلَيْكَ وَ عَلى أَبْنآئِكَ الْمُسْتَشْهَدينَ،

السَّلامُ عَلَيْكَ وَ عَلى ذُرِّيَّتِكَ النّاصِرينَ،

السَّلامُ عَلَيْكَ وَ عَلَى الْمَلآئِكَةِ الْمُضاجِعينَ،

السَّلامُ عَلَى الْقَتيلِ الْمَظْلُومِ،

السَّلامُ عَلى أَخيهِ الْمَسْمُومِ،

السَّلامُ عَلى عَلِيِّ الْكَبيرِ،

السَّلامُ عَلَى الرَّضيعِ الصَّغيرِ،

السَّلامُ عَلَى الأَبْدانِ السَّليبَةِ،

السَّلامُ عَلَى الْعِتْرَةِ الْقَريبَةِ،

السَّلامُ عَلَى الْمُجَدَّلينَ فِى الْفَلَواتِ،

السَّلامُ عَلَى النّازِحينَ عَنِ الأَوْطانِ،

السَّلامُ عَلَى الْمَدْفُونينَ بِلا أَكْفان،

السَّلامُ عَلَى الرُّؤُوسِ الْمُفَرَّقَةِ عَنِ الأَبْدانِ،

السَّلامُ عَلَى الْمُحْتَسِبِ الصّابِرِ،

السَّلامُ عَلَى الْمَظْلُومِ بِلا ناصِر،

السَّلامُ عَلى ساكِنِ التُّرْبَةِ الزّاكِيَةِ،

السَّلامُ عَلى صاحِبِ الْقُبَّةِ السّامِيَةِ،

السَّلامُ عَلى مَنْ طَهَّرَهُ الْجَليلُ،

السَّلامُ عَلى مَنِ افْتَخَرَ بِهِ جَبْرَئيلُ،

السَّلامُ عَلى مَنْ ناغاهُ فِي الْمَهْدِ ميكآئيلُ،

السَّلامُ عَلى مَنْ نُكِثَتْ ذِمَّتُهُ،

السَّلامُ عَلى مَنْ هُتِكَتْ حُرْمَتُهُ،

السَّلامُ عَلى مَنْ أُريقَ بِالظُّلْمِ دَمُهُ،

السَّلامُ عَلَى الْمُغَسَّلِ بِدَمِ الْجِراحِ،

السَّلامُ عَلَى الْمُجَرَّعِ بِكَأْساتِ الرِّماحِ

السَّلامُ عَلَى الْمُضامِ الْمُسْتَباحِ،

السَّلامُ عَلَى الْمَنْحُورِ فِى الْوَرى،

السَّلامُ عَلى مَنْ دَفَنَهُ أَهْلُ الْقُرى،

السَّلامُ عَلَى الْمَقْطُوعِ الْوَتينِ،

السَّلامُ عَلَى الْمُحامي بِلا مُعين،

السَّلامُ عَلَى الشَّيْبِ الْخَضيبِ،

السَّلامُ عَلَى الْخَدِّ التَّريبِ،

السَّلامُ عَلَى الْبَدَنِ السَّليبِ،

السَّلامُ عَلَى الثَّغْرِ الْمَقْرُوعِ بِالْقَضيبِ،

السَّلامُ عَلَى الرَّأْسِ الْمَرْفُوعِ،

السَّلامُ عَلَى الأَجْسامِ الْعارِيَةِ فِى الْفَلَواتِ، تَنْهَشُهَا الذِّئابُ الْعادِياتُ،

وَ تَخْتَلِفُ إِلَيْهَا السِّباعُ الضّارِياتُ،

السَّلامُ عَلَيْكَ يا مَوْلاىَ وَ عَلَى الْمَلآئِكَةِ الْمُرَفْرِفينَ حَوْلَ قُبَّتِكَ ، الْحافّينَ بِتُرْبَتِكَ،

الطّآئِفينَ بِعَرْصَتِكَ، الْوارِدينَ لِزِيارَتِكَ،

السَّلامُ عَلَيْكَ فَإِنّي قَصَدْتُ إِلَيْكَ، وَ رَجَوْتُ الْفَوْزَ لَدَيْكَ،

السَّلامُ عَلَيْكَ سَلامَ الْعارِفِ بِحُرْمَتِكَ، الْمُخْلِصِ في وَلايَتِكَ،

الْمُتَقَرِّبِ إِلَى اللهِ بِمَحَبَّتِكَ، الْبَريءِ مِنْ أَعْدآئِكَ،

سَلامَ مَنْ قَلْبُهُ بِمُصابِكَ مَقْرُوحٌ ، وَ دَمْعُهُ عِنْدَ ذِكْرِكَ مَسْفُوحٌ،

سَلامَ الْمَفْجُوعِ الْحَزينِ، الْوالِهِ الْمُسْتَكينِ،

سَلامَ مَنْ لَوْ كانَ مَعَكَ بِالطُّفُوفِ، لَوَقاكَ بِنَفْسِهِ حَدَّ السُّيُوفِ،

وَ بَذَلَ حُشاشَتَهُ دُونَكَ لِلْحُتُوفِ، وَ جاهَدَ بَيْنَ يَدَيْكَ، وَ نَصَرَكَ عَلى مَنْ بَغى عَلَيْكَ،

وَ فَداكَ بِرُوحِهِ وَ جَسَدِهِ وَ مالِهِ وَ وَلَدِهِ، وَ رُوحُهُ لِرُوحِكَ فِدآءٌ، وَ أَهْلُهُ لِأَهْلِكَ وِقآءٌ،

فَلَئِنْ أَخَّرَتْنِى الدُّهُورُ، وَ عاقَني عَنْ نَصْرِكَ الْمَقْدُورُ، وَ لَمْ أَكُنْ لِمَنْ حارَبَكَ مُحارِباً،

وَ لِمَنْ نَصَبَ لَكَ الْعَداوَةَ مُناصِباً، فَلَأَ نْدُبَنَّكَ صَباحاً وَ مَسآءً،

وَ لَأَبْكِيَنَّ لَكَ بَدَلَ الدُّمُوعِ دَماً، حَسْرَةً عَلَيْكَ، وَ تَأَسُّفاً عَلى ما دَهاكَ وَ تَلَهُّفاً،

حَتّى أَمُوتَ بِلَوْعَةِ الْمُصابِ، وَ غُصَّةِ الاِكْتِيابِ،

أَشْهَدُ أَ نَّكَ قَدْ أَقَمْتَ الصَّلوةَ، وَ اتَيْتَ الزَّكوةَ ، وَ أَمَرْتَ بِالْمَعْرُوفِ،

وَ نَهَيْتَ عَنِ الْمُنْكَرِ وَ الْعُدْوانِ، وَ أَطَعْتَ اللهَ وَ ما عَصَيْتَهُ، وَ تَمَسَّكْتَ بِهِ وَ بِحَبْلِهِ فَأَرْضَيْتَهُ،

وَ خَشيتَهُ وَ راقَبْتَهُ وَ اسْتَجَبْتَهُ، وَ سَنَنْتَ السُّنَنَ، وَ أَطْفَأْتَ الْفِتَنَ،

وَ دَعَوْتَ إِلَى الرَّشادِ، وَ أَوْضَحْتَ سُبُلَ السَّدادِ، وَ جاهَدْتَ فِى اللهِ حَقَّ الْجِهادِ،

وَ كُنْتَ للهِ طآئِعاً، وَ لِجَدِّكَ مُحَمَّد صَلَّى اللهُ عَلَيْهِ وَ الِهِ تابِعاً،

وَ لِقَوْلِ أَبـيكَ سامِعاً، وَ إِلى وَصِيَّةِ أَخيكَ مُسارِعاً، وَ لِعِمادِ الدّينِ رافِعاً،

وَ لِلطُّغْيانِ قامِعاً، وَ لِلطُّغاةِ مُقـارِعاً، وَ لِلأُ مَّةِ ناصِحاً، وَ في غَمَراتِ الْمَوْتِ سابِحاً،

وَ لِلْفُسّاقِ مُكافِحاً، وَ بِحُجَجِ اللهِ قآئِماً، وَ لِـلاِْسْلامِ وَ الْمُسْلِمينَ راحِماً،

وَ لِلْحَقِّ ناصِراً، وَ عِنْدَ الْبَلآءِ صابِراً، وَ لِلدّينِ كالِئاً،

وَ عَنْ حَوْزَتِهِ مُرامِياً، تَحُوطُ الْهُدى وَ تَنْصُرُهُ،

وَ تَبْسُطُ الْعَدْلَ وَ تَنْشُرُهُ، وَ تَنْصُرُ الدّينَ وَ تُظْهِرُهُ،

وَ تَكُفُّ الْعابِثَ وَ تَزْجُرُهُ، وَ تَأْخُذُ لِلدَّنِىِّ مِنَ الشَّريفِ،

وَ تُساوي فِى الْحُكْمِ بَيْنَ الْقَوِىِّ وَ الضَّعيفِ، كُنْتَ رَبيعَ الأَيْتامِ،

وَ عِصْمَةَ الأُ نامِ، وَ عِزَّ الاِْسْلامِ، وَ مَعْدِنَ الأَحْكامِ، وَ حَليفَ الاِْنْعامِ،

سالِكاً طَرآئِقَ جَدِّكَ وَ أَبيكَ ، مُشْبِهاً فِى الْوَصِيَّةِ لأَخيـكَ ،

وَفِىَّ الذِّمَـمِ، رَضِىَّ الشِّيَمِ، ظاهِرَ الْكَرَمِ، مُتَهَجِّداً فِى الظُّلَمِ،

قَويمَ الطَّرآئِقِ، كَريمَ الْخَلائِقِ، عَظيمَ السَّوابِقِ، شَريفَ النَّسَبِ، مُنيفَ الْحَسَبِ،

رَفيعَ الرُّتَبِ، كَثيرَ الْمَناقِبِ، مَحْمُودَ الضَّرآئِبِ، جَزيلَ الْمَواهِبِ،

حَليمٌ رَشيدٌ مُنيبٌ، جَوادٌ عَليمٌ شَديدٌ، إِمامٌ شَهيدٌ، أَوّاهٌ مُنيبٌ، حَبيبٌ مَهيبٌ،

كُنْتَ لِلرَّسُولِ صَلَّى اللهُ عَلَيْهِ وَ الِهِ وَلَداً،

وَ لِلْقُرْءانِ سَنَداً مُنْقِذاً :خل وَ لِلأُ مَّةِ عَضُداً، وَ فِى الطّاعَةِ مُجْتَهِداً،

حافِظاً لِلْعَهْدِ وَالْميثاقِ، ناكِباً عَنْ سُبُلِ الْفُسّاقِ وَ :خل باذِلاً لِلْمَجْهُودِ،

طَويلَ الرُّكُوعِ وَ السُّجُودِ، زاهِداً فِى الدُّنْيا زُهْدَ الرّاحِلِ عَنْها،

ناظِراً إِلَيْها بِعَيْنِ الْمُسْتَوْحِشِينَ مِنْها، امالُكَ عَنْها مَكْفُوفَةٌ،

وَ هِمَّتُكَ عَنْ زِينَتِها مَصْرُوفَةٌ، وَ أَلْحاظُكَ عَنْ بَهْجَتِها مَطْرُوفَةٌ،

وَ رَغْبَتُكَ فِى الْآخِرَةِ مَعْرُوفَةٌ، حَتّى إِذَا الْجَوْرُ مَدَّ باعَهُ، وَ أَسْفَرَ الظُّلْمُ قِناعَهُ،

وَ دَعَا الْغَيُّ أَتْباعَهُ، وَ أَنْتَ في حَرَمِ جَدِّكَ قاطِنٌ، وَ لِلظّالِمِينَ مُبايِنٌ،

جَلِيسُ الْبَيْتِ وَ الْمِحْرابِ، مُعْتَزِلٌ عَنِ اللَّذّاتِ وَ الشَّهَواتِ،

تُنْكِرُ الْمُنْكَرَ بِقَلْبِكَ وَ لِسانِكَ، عَلى حَسَبِ طاقَتِكَ وَ إِمْكانِكَ،

ثُمَّ اقْتَضاكَ الْعِلْمُ لِلْإِنْكارِ،

وَ لَزِمَكَ أَلْزَمَكَ :ظ أَنْ تُجاهِدَ الْفُجّارَ، فَسِرْتَ في أَوْلادِكَ وَ أَهالِيكَ،

وَ شِيعَتِكَ وَ مَوالِيكَ وَ صَدَعْتَ بِالْحَقِّ وَ الْبَيِّنَةِ،

وَ دَعَوْتَ إِلَى اللهِ بِالْحِكْمَةِ وَ الْمَوْعِظَةِ الْحَسَنَةِ،

وَ أَمَرْتَ بِإِقامَةِ الْحُدُودِ،

وَ الطّاعَةِ لِلْمَعْبُودِ،

وَ نَهَيْتَ عَنِ الْخَبآئِثِ وَ الطُّغْيانِ،

وَ واجَهُوكَ بِالظُّلْمِ وَ الْعُدْوانِ،

فَجاهَدْتَهُمْ بَعْدَ الْأَيعازِ لَهُمْ الْأَيعادِ إِلَيْهِمْ : خل، وَ تَأْكِيدِ الْحُجَّةِ عَلَيْهِمْ،

فَنَكَثُوا ذِمامَكَ وَ بَيْعَتَك

فَنَكَثُوا ذِمامَكَ وَ بَيْعَتَكَ،

وَ أَسْخَطُوا رَبَّكَ وَ جَدَّ كَ، وَ بَدَؤُوكَ بِالْحَرْبِ،

فَثَبَتَّ لِلطَّعْنِ وَالضَّرْبِ،

وَ طَحَنْتَ جُنُودَ الْفُجّارِ،

وَاقْتَحَمْتَ قَسْطَلَ الْغُبارِ،

مُجالِداً بِذِى الْفَقارِ،

كَأَنَّكَ عَلِيٌّ الْمُخْتارُ،

فَلَمّا رَأَوْكَ ثابِتَ الْجاشِ، غَيْرَ خآئِفٍ وَ لا خاشٍ،

نَصَبُوا لَكَ غَوآئِلَ مَكْرِهِمْ، وَ قاتَلُوكَ بِكَيْدِهِمْ وَ شَرِّهِمْ،

وَ أَمَرَ اللَّعِينُ جُنُودَهُ، فَمَنَعُوكَ الْمآءَ وَ وُرُودَهُ،

وَ ناجَزُوكَ الْقِتالَ، وَ عاجَلُوكَ النِّزالَ،

وَ رَشَقُوكَ بِالسِّهامِ وَ النِّبالِ،

وَ بَسَطُوا إِلَيْكَ أَكُفَّ الاِصْطِلامِ،

وَ لَمْ يَرْعَوْا لَكَ ذِماماً، وَ لاراقَبُوا فيكَ أثاماً، في قَتْلِهِمْ أَوْلِيآءَكَ، وَ نَهْبِهِمْ رِحالَكَ،

وَ أَنْتَ مُقَدَّمٌ فِى الْهَبَواتِ، وَ مُحْتَمِلٌ لِلأَذِيّاتِ،

قَدْ عَجِبَتْ مِنْ صَبْرِكَ مَلآئِكَةُ السَّماواتِ، فَأَحْدَقُوا بِكَ مِنْ كُلِّ الْجِهاتِ،

وَ أَثْخَنُوكَ بِالْجِراحِ، وَ حالُوا بَيْنَكَ وَ بَيْنَ الرَّواحِ،

وَ لَمْ يَبْقَ لَكَ ناصِرٌ، وَ أَنْتَ مُحْتَسِبٌ صابِرٌ، تَذُبُّ عَنْ نِسْوَتِكَ وَ أَوْلادِكَ،

حَتّى نَكَسُوكَ عَنْ جَوادِكَ، فَهَوَيْتَ إِلَى الأَرْضِ جَريحاً، تَطَؤُكَ الْخُيُولُ بِحَوافِرِها،

وَ تَعْلُوكَ الطُّغاةُ بِبَواتِرِها، قَدْ رَشَحَ لِلْمَوْتِ جَبينُكَ،

وَ اخْتَلَفَتْ بِالاِنْقِباضِ وَ الاِنْبِساطِ شِمالُكَ وَ يَمينُكَ، تُديرُ طَرْفاً خَفِيّاً إِلى رَحْلِكَ وَ بَيْتِكَ،

وَ قَدْ شُغِلْتَ بِنَفْسِكَ عَنْ وُلْدِكَ وَ أَهاليكَ،

وَ أَسْرَعَ فَرَسُكَ شارِداً، إِلى خِيامِكَ قاصِداً، مُحَمْحِماً باكِياً،

فَلَمّا رَأَيْنَ النِّسآءُ جَوادَكَ مَخْزِيّاً،

وَ نَظَرْنَ سَرْجَكَ عَلَيْهِ مَلْوِيّاً،

بَرَزْنَ مِنَ الْخُدُورِ، ناشِراتِ الشُّعُورِ عَلَى الْخُدُودِ، لاطِماتِ الْوُجُوهِ سافِراتٍ،

وَ بِالْعَويلِ داعِياتٍ، وَ بَعْدَالْعِزِّ مُذَلَّلاتٍ،

وَ إِلى مَصْرَعِكَ مُبادِراتٍ، وَ الشِّمْرُ جالِسٌ عَلى صَدْرِكَ،

وَ مُولِغٌ سَيْفَهُ عَلى نَحْرِكَ، قابِضٌ عَلى شَيْبَتِكَ بِيَدِهِ،

ذابِحٌ لَكَ بِمُهَنَّدِهِ، قَدْ سَكَنَتْ حَواسُّكَ، وَ خَفِيَتْ أَنْفاسُكَ،

وَ رُفِعَ عَلَى الْقَناةِ رَأْسُكَ، وَ سُبِيَ أَهْلُكَ كَالْعَبيدِ،

وَ صُفِّدُوا فِى الْحَديدِ، فَوْقَ أَقْتابِ الْمَطِيّاتِ،

تَلْفَحُ وُجُوهَهُمْ حَرُّ الْهاجِراتِ، يُساقُونَ فِى الْبَراري وَالْفَلَواتِ،

أَيْديهِمْ مَغْلُولَةٌ إِلَى الأَعْناقِ، يُطافُ بِهِمْ فِى الأَسْواقِ،

فَالْوَيْلُ لِلْعُصاةِ الْفُسّاقِ، لَقَدْ قَتَلُوا بِقَتْلِكَ الإِسْلامَ،

وَ عَطَّلُوا الصَّلوةَ وَ الصِّيامَ، وَ نَقَضُوا السُّنَنَ وَ الأَحْكامَ،

وَ هَدَمُوا قَواعِدَ الأيمانِ، وَ حَرَّفُوا اياتِ الْقُرْءانِ، وَ هَمْلَجُوا فِى الْبَغْيِ وَالْعُدْوانِ،

لَقَدْ أَصْبَحَ رَسُولُ اللهِ صَلَّى اللهُ عَلَيْهِوَ الِهِ مَوْتُوراً،

وَ عادَ كِتابُ اللهِ عَزَّوَجَلَّ مَهْجُوراً، وَ غُودِرَ الْحَقُّ إِذْ قُهِرْتَ مَقْهُوراً،

وَ فُقِدَ بِفَقْدِكَ التَّكْبيرُ وَالتَّهْليلُ، وَالتَّحْريمُ وَالتَّحْليلُ،
وَالتَّنْزيلُ وَالتَّأْويلُ، وَ ظَهَرَ بَعْدَكَ التَّغْييرُ وَالتَّبْديلُ،
وَ الْإِلْحادُ وَالتَّعْطيلُ، وَ الْأَهْوآءُ وَ الْأَضاليلُ،
وَ الْفِتَنُ وَ الْأَباطيلُ، فَقامَ ناعيكَ عِنْدَ قَبْرِ جَدِّكَ الرَّسُولِ صَلَّى اللهُ عَلَيْهِ وَ الِهِ،
فَنَعاكَ إِلَيْهِ بِالدَّمْعِ الْهَطُولِ، قآئِلا يا رَسُولَ اللهِ قُتِلَ سِبْطُكَ وَ فَتاكَ،
وَ اسْتُبيحَ أَهْلُكَ وَ حِماكَ، وَ سُبِيَتْ بَعْدَكَ ذَراريكَ،
وَ وَقَعَ الْمَحْذُورُ بِعِتْرَتِكَ وَ ذَويكَ، فَانْزَعَجَ الرَّسُولُ،
وَ بَكى قَلْبُهُ الْمَهُولُ، وَ عَزّاهُ بِكَ الْمَلآئِكَةُ وَ الْأَنْبِيآءُ،
وَ فُجِعَتْ بِكَ أُمُّكَ الزَّهْرآءُ، وَ اخْتَلَفَتْ جُنُودُ الْمَلائِكَةِ الْمُقَرَّبينَ،
تُعَزّي أَباكَ أَميرَالْمُؤْمِنينَ، وَ أُقيمَتْ لَكَ الْمَاتِمُ في أَعْلا عِلِّيّينَ،
وَ لَطَمَتْ عَلَيْكَ الْحُورُ الْعينُ، وَ بَكَتِ السَّمآءُ وَ سُكّانُها،
وَ الْجِنانُ وَ خُزّانُها، وَ الْهِضابُ وَ أَقْطارُها،
وَ الْبِحارُ وَ حيتانُها، وَ مَكَّةُ وَ بُنْيانُها، :خل وَ الْجِنانُ وَ وِلْدانُها،
وَ الْبَيْتُ وَ الْمَقامُ، وَ الْمَشْعَرُ الْحَرامُ، وَ الْحِلُّ وَ الْإِحْرامُ،
اَللّهُمَّ فَبِحُرْمَةِ هذَا الْمَكانِ الْمُنيفِ ، صَلِّ عَلى مُحَمَّد وَ الِ مُحَمَّد،
وَاحْشُرْني في زُمْرَتِهِمْ، وَ أَدْخِلْنى الْجَنَّةَ بِشَفاعَتِهِمْ،
أَللّهُمَّ إِنّي أَتَوَسَّلُ إِلَيْكَ يا أَسْرَعَ الْحاسِبينَ، وَ ياأَكْرَمَ الْأَكْرَمينَ،
وَ ياأَحْكَمَ الْحاكِمينَ، بِمُحَمَّدخاتِمِ النَّبِيّينَ، رَسُولِكَ إِلَى الْعالَمينَ أَجْمَعينَ،
وَ بِأَخيهِ وَابْنِ عَمِّهِ الْأَنْزَعِ الْبَطينِ ، الْعالِمِ الْمَكينِ، عَلِيّ أَميرِالْمُؤْمِنينَ،
وَ بِفاطِمَةَ سَيِّدَةِ نِساءِ الْعالَمينَ، وَ بِالْحَسَنِ الزَّكِيِّ عِصْمَةِ الْمُتَّقينَ،
وَ بِأَبي عَبْدِاللهِ الْحُسَيْنِ أَكْرَمِ الْمُسْتَشْهَدينَ، وَ بِأَوْلادِهِ الْمَقْتُولينَ،
وَ بِعِتْرَتِهِ الْمَظْلُومينَ، وَ بِعَلِيِّ بْنِ الْحُسَيْنِ زَيْنِ الْعابِدينَ،
وَ بِمُحَمَّد بْنِ عَلِيّ قِبْلَةِ الْأَوّابينَ، وَ جَعْفَرِ بْنِ مُحَمَّد أَصْدَقِ الصّادِقينَ،
وَ مُوسَى بْنِ جَعْفَر مُظْهِرِ الْبَراهينِ، وَ عَلِيِّ بْنِ مُوسى ناصِرِالدّينِ،
وَ مُحَمَّدِبْنِ عَلِيّ قُدْوَةِ الْمُهْتَدينَ، وَ عَلِيِّ بْنِ مُحَمَّد أَزْهَدِ الزّاهِدينَ،
وَ الْحَسَنِ بْنِ عَلِيّ وارِثِ الْمُسْتَخْلَفينَ، وَالْحُجَّةِ عَلَى الْخَلْقِ أَجْمَعينَ،
أَنْ تُصَلِّيَ عَلى مُحَمَّدوَالِ مُحَمَّدالصّادِقينَ الْأَبَرّينَ ، الِ طه وَ يس،
وَ أَنْ تَجْعَلَني فِى الْقِيامَةِ مِنَ الْآمِنينَ الْمُطْمَئِنّينَ، الْفائِزينَ الْفَرِحينَ الْمُسْتَبْشِرينَ،

أَللّهُمَّ اكْتُبْني فِى الْمُسْلِمينَ، وَ أَلْحِقْني بِالصّالِحينَ،

وَاجْعَلْ لي لِسانَ صِدْق فِى الاْخِرينَ، وَانْصُرْني عَلَى الْباغينَ،وَاكْفِني كَيْدَ الْحاسِدينَ،

وَاصْرِفْ عَنّي مَكْرَ الْماكِرينَ، وَاقْبِضْ عَنّي أَيْدِىَ الظّالِمينَ،

وَاجْمَعْ بَيْني وَ بَيْنَ السّادَةِ الْمَيامينِ في أَعْلا عِلِّيّينَ،

مَعَ الَّذينَ أَنْعَمْتَ عَلَيْهِمْ مِنَ النَّبِيّينَ وَالصِّدّيقينَ وَالشُّهَدآءِ وَالصّالِحينَ، بِرَحْمَتِكَ يا أَرْحَمَ الرّاحِمينَ،

أَللّهُمَّ إِنّي أُقْسِمُ عَلَيْكَ بِنَبِيِّكَ الْمَعْصُومِ، وَ بِحُكْمِكَ الْمَحْتُومِ، وَنَهْيِكَ الْمَكْتُومِ،

وَ بِهذَا الْقَبْرِ الْمَلْمُومِ ، الْمُوَسَّدِ في كَنَفِهِ الإِمامُ الْمَعْصُومُ، الْمَقْتُولُ الْمَظْلُومُ،

أَنْ تَكْشِفَ ما بي مِنَ الْغُمُومِ ، وَ تَصْرِفَ عَنّي شَرَّ الْقَدَرِ الْمَحْتُومِ،

وَ تُجيرَني مِنَ النّارِ ذاتِ السَّمُومِ،

أَللّهُمَّ جَلِّلْني بِنِعْمَتِكَ ، وَ رَضِّني بِقَسْمِكَ ،

وَ تَغَمَّدْني بِجُودِكَ وَ كَرَمِكَ ، وَ باعِدْني مِنْ مَكْرِكَ وَ نِقْمَتِكَ ،

أَللّهُمَّ اعْصِمْني مِنَ الزَّلَلِ، وَ سَدِّدْني فِى الْقَوْلِ وَالْعَمَلِ،

وَافْسَحْ لي في مُدَّةِ الأَجَلِ، وَ أَعْفِني مِنَ الأَوْجاعِ وَالْعِلَلِ،

وَ بَلِّغْني بِمَوالِيَّ وَ بِفَضْلِكَ أَفْضَلَ الأَمَلِ،

أَللّهُمَّ صَلِّ عَلى مُحَمَّد وَ الِ مُحَمَّد وَاقْبَلْ تَوْبَتي،

وَارْحَمْ عَبْرَتي ، وَ أَقِلْني عَثْرَتي ، وَ نَفِّسْ كُرْبَتي،

وَاغْفِرْلي خَطيئَتي، وَ أَصْلِحْ لي في ذُرِّيَّتي،

أَللّهُمَّ لاتَدَعْ لي في هذَاالْمَشْهَدِ الْمُعَظَّمِ،

وَالْمَحَلِّ الْمُكَرَّمِ ذَنْباً إِلاّ غَفَرْتَهُ، وَ لاعَيْباً إِلاّ سَتَرْتَهُ،

وَ لاغَمّاً إِلاّ كَشَفْتَهُ، وَ لارِزْقاً إِلاّ بَسَطْتَهُ،

وَ لاجاهاً إِلاّ عَمَرْتَهُ، وَ لافَساداً إِلاّ أَصْلَحْتَهُ،

وَ لاأَمَلا إِلاّ بَلَّغْتَهُ، وَ لادُعاءً إِلاّ أَجَبْتَهُ،

وَ لامَضيقاً إِلاّ فَرَّجْتَهُ، وَ لاشَمْلا إِلاّ جَمَعْتَهُ،

وَ لاأَمْراً إِلاّ أَتْمَمْتَهُ، وَ لامالا إِلاّ كَثَّرْتَهُ،

وَ لاخُلْقاً إِلاّ حَسَّنْتَهُ، وَ لاإِنْفاقاً إِلاّ أَخْلَفْتَهُ،

وَ لاحالا إِلاّ عَمَرْتَهُ، وَ لاحَسُوداً إِلاّ قَمَعْتَهُ،

وَ لاعَدُوّاً إِلاّ أَرْدَيْتَهُ، وَ لاشَرّاً إِلاّ كَفَيْتَهُ،

وَ لامَرَضاً إلاّ شَفَيْتَهُ، وَ لابَعيداً إلاّ أَدْنَيْتَهُ،

وَ لاشَعَثاً إلاّ لَمَمْتَهُ، وَ لا سُؤالا سُؤْلا :ظ إلاّ أَعْطَيْتَهُ،

أَللّهُمَّ إنّي أَسْئَلُكَ خَيْرَ الْعاجِلَةِ، وَ ثَوابَ الآجِلَةِ،

أَللّهُمَّ أَغْنِني بِحَلالِكَ عَنِ الْحَرامِ، وَ بِفَضْلِكَ عَنْ جَميعِ الأَنامِ،

أَللّهُمَّ إنّي أَسْئَلُكَ عِلْماً نافِعاً،

وَ قَلْباً خاشِعاً، وَ يَقيناً شافِياً ، وَ عَمَلا زاكِياً،

وَ صَبْراً جَميلا، وَ أَجْراً جَزيلا،

أَللّهُمَّ ارْزُقْني شُكْرَ نِعْمَتِكَ عَلَيَّ، وَ زِدْ في إحْسانِكَ وَ كَرَمِكَ إلَيَّ،

وَاجْعَلْ قَوْلي فِى النّاسِ مَسْمُوعاً، وَ عَمَلي عِنْدَكَ مَرْفُوعاً،

وَ أَثَري فِى الْخَيْراتِ مَتْبُوعاً، وَ عَدُوّي مَقْمُوعاً،

أَللّـهُمَّ صَلِّ عَلى مُحَمَّد وَ الِ مُحَمَّدالأَخْيارِ ، في اناءِ اللَّيْلِ وَ أَطْرافِ النَّهارِ ،

وَاكْفِني شَرَّ الأَشْرارِ، وَ طَهِّرْني مِنَ الذُّنُوبِ وَ الأَوْزارِ،

وَ أَجِرْني مِنَ النّـارِ، وَ أَحِلَّني دارَالْقَرارِ،

وَ اغْفِرْلي وَ لِجَميعِ إخْواني فيكَ وَ أَخَواتِيَ الْمُؤْمِنينَ وَ الْمُؤْمِناتِ،

بِرَحْمَتِكَ يا أَرْحَمَ الرّاحِمينَ

Supplication in the *qunut* (act of standing in supplication) of the Prayer after the Ziyarat:

لاإلهَ إلاّ اللهُ الْحَليمُ الْكَريمُ ، لاإلهَ إلاَّاللهُ الْعَلِيُّ الْعَظيمُ،

لاإلهَ إلاَّاللهُ رَبُّ السَّماواتِ السَّبْعِ وَ الأَرَضينَ السَّبْعِ، وَ ما فيهِنَّ وَ ما بَيْنَهُنَّ،

خِلافاً لأَعْدآئِهِ، وَ تَكْذيباً لِمَنْ عَدَلَ بِهِ ، وَ إقْراراً لِرُبُوبِيَّتِهِ،

وَ خُضُوعاً لِعِزَّتِهِ ، الأَوَّلُ بِغَيْرِ أَوَّل ، وَالاخِرُ إلى غَيْرِ اخِر،

الظّـاهِرُ عَلى كُلِّ شَيْء بِقُدْرَتِهِ، الْباطِنُ دُونَ كُلِّ شَيْء بِعِلْمِهِ وَ لُطْفِهِ،

لا تَقِفُ الْعُقُولُ عَلى كُنْهِ عَظَمَتِهِ، وَ لاتُدْرِكُ الأَوْهامُ حَقيقَةَ ماهِيَّتِهِ،

وَ لاتَتَصَوَّرُ الأَنْفُسُ مَعانِيَ كَيْفِيَّتِهِ، مُطَّلِعاً عَلَى الضَّمائِرِ،

عارِفاً بِالسَّرآئِرِ، يَعْلَمُ خآئِنَةَ الأَعْيُنِ وَ ما تُخْفِى الصُّدُورُ،

أَللّهُمَّ إنّي أُشْهِدُكَ عَلى تَصْديقي رَسُولَكَ صَلَّى اللهُ عَلَيْهِ وَ الِهِ وَ إيماني بِهِ،

وَ عِلْمي بِمَنْزِلَتِهِ، وَ إنّي أَشْهَدُ أَنَّهُ النَّبِيُّ الَّذي نَطَقَتِ الْحِكْمَةُ بِفَضْلِهِ،

وَ بَشَّرَتِ الأَ نْبِيآءُ بِهِ، وَ دَعَتْ إلَى الإقْرارِ بِما جآءَ بِهِ،

وَ حَثَّتْ عَلى تَصْديقِهِ، بِقَوْلِهِ تَعالى: «اَلَّذي يَجِدُونَهُ مَكْتُوباً عِنْدَهُمْ فِى التَّوْرِيةِ وَ الْأنْجيلِ يَأْمُرُهُمْ بِالْمَعْرُوفِ وَ يَنْهيهُمْ عَنِ الْمُنْكَرِ وَ يُحِلُّ لَهُمُ الطَّيِّباتِ وَ يُحَرِّمُ عَلَيْهِمُ الْخَبائِثَ وَ يَضَعُ عَنْهُمْ إِصْرَهُمْ وَ الْأَغْلالَ الَّتي كانَتْ عَلَيْهِمْ»

فَصَلِّ عَلى مُحَمَّدٍ رَسُولِكَ إِلَى الثَّقَلَيْنِ، وَ سَيِّدِ الْأَنْبِياءِ الْمُصْطَفَيْنَ،

وَ عَلى أَخيهِ وَ ابْنِ عَمِّهِ، اللَّذَيْنِ لَمْ يُشْرِكا بِكَ طَرْفَةَ عَيْنٍ أَبَداً،

وَ عَلى فاطِمَةَ الزَّهْراءِ سَيِّدَةِ نِساءِ الْعالَمينَ،

وَ عَلى سَيِّدَيْ شَبابِ أَهْلِ الْجَنَّةِ الْحَسَنِ وَ الْحُسَيْنِ ، صَلاةً خالِدَةَ الدَّوامِ،

عَدَدَ قَطْرِ الرِّهامِ، وَ زِنَةَ الْجِبالِ وَ الْأكامِ ، ما أَوْرَقَ السَّلامُ،

وَ اخْتَلَفَ الضِّياءُ وَ الظَّلامُ، وَ عَلى آلِهِ الطّاهِرينَ، الْأَئِمَّةِ الْمُهْتَدينَ، الذّآئِدينَ عَنِ الدّينِ،

عَلِيّ وَ مُحَمَّد وَ جَعْفَر وَ مُوسى وَ عَلِيّ وَ مُحَمَّد وَ عَلِيّ وَالْحَسَنِ وَ الْحُجَّةِ الْقَوّامِ بِالْقِسْطِ،

وَ سُلالَةِ السِّبْطِ،

أَللّهُمَّ إِنّي أَسْئَلُكَ بِحَقِّ هذَا الْإمامِ فَرَجاً قَريباً،

وَ صَبْراً جَميلا، وَ نَصْراً عَزيزاً ، وَ غِنىً عَنِ الْخَلْقِ ، وَ ثَباتاً فِى الْهُدى،

وَ التَّوْفيقَ لِما تُحِبُّ وَ تَرْضى، وَ رِزْقاً واسِعاً حَلالا طَيِّباً ، مَريئاً داراً سآئِغاً،

فاضِلا مُفَضِّلا صَبّاً صَبّاً ، مِنْ غَيْرِ كَدٍّ وَ لا نَكَد،

وَ لا مِنَّة مِنْ أَحَد، وَ عافِيَةً مِنْ كُلِّ بَلآءٍ وَ سُقْمٍ وَ مَرَض،

وَ الشُّكْرَ عَلَى الْعافِيَةِ وَ النَّعْماءِ، وَ إِذا جآءَ الْمَوْتُ فَاقْبِضْنا عَلى أَحْسَنِ ما يَكُونُ لَكَ طاعَةً،

عَلى ما أَمَرْتَنا مُحافِظينَ حَتّى تُؤَدِّيَنا إِلى جَنّاتِ النَّعيمِ،

بِرَحْمَتِكَ يا أَرْحَمَ الرّاحِمينَ،

أَللّهُمَّ صَلِّ عَلى مُحَمَّد وَ آلِ مُحَمَّد، وَ أَوْحِشْني مِنَ الدُّنْيا وَ آنِسْني بِالْآخِرَةِ،

فَإِنَّهُ لايُوحِشُ مِنَ الدُّنْيا إِلاّ خَوْفُكَ، وَ لايُؤْنِسُ بِالْآخِرَةِ إِلاّ رَجآؤُكَ،

أَللّهُمَّ لَكَ الْحُجَّةُ لاعَلَيْكَ، وَ إِلَيْكَ الْمُشْتَكى لامِنْكَ،

فَصَلِّ عَلى مُحَمَّد وَ آلِهِ وَ أَعِنّي عَلى نَفْسِىَ الظّالِمَةِ الْعاصِيَةِ،

وَ شَهْوَتِىَ الْغالِبَةِ، وَاخْتِمْ لي بِالْعافِيَةِ،

أَللّهُمَّ إِنَّ اسْتِغْفاري إِيّاكَ وَ أَنَا مُصِرٌّ عَلى مانَهَيْتَ قِلَّةُ حَياء،

وَ تَرْكِىَ الِاسْتِغْفارَ مَعَ عِلْمي بِسَعَةِ حِلْمِكَ تَضْييعٌ لِحَقِّ الرَّجآءِ،

أَللّـهُمَّ إِنَّ ذُنُوبي تُؤْيِسُني أَنْ أَرْجُوَكَ ، وَ إِنَّ عِلْمي بِسَعَةِ رَحْمَتِكَ يَمْنَعُني أَنْ أَخْشاكَ ،

فَصَلِّ عَلى مُحَمَّد وَ الِ مُحَمَّد ، وَ صَدِّقْ رَجائي لَكَ ،

وَ كَذِّبْ خَوْفي مِنْكَ ، وَ كُنْ لي عِنْدَ أَحْسَنِ ظَنّي بِكَ يا أَكْرَمَ الاْكْرَمينَ،

أَللّهُمَّ صَلِّ عَلى مُحَمَّد وَ الِ مُحَمَّد وَ أَيِّدْني بِالْعِصْمَةِ،

وَ أَنْطِقْ لِساني بِالْحِكْمَةِ، وَ اجْعَلْني مِمَّنْ يَنْدَمُ عَلى ما ضَيَّعَهُ في أَمْسِهِ،

وَ لايَغْبَنُ حَظَّهُ في يَوْمِهِ ، وَ لا يَهُمُّ لِرِزْقِ غَدِهِ،

أَللّهُمَّ إِنَّ الْغَنِيَّ مَنِ اسْتَغْنى بِكَ وَ افْتَقَرَ إِلَيْكَ ،

وَ الْفَقيرَ مَنِ اسْتَغْنى بِخَلْقِكَ عَنْكَ ، فَصَلِّ عَلى مُحَمَّد وَ الِ مُحَمَّد،

وَ أَغْنِني عَنْ خَلْقِكَ بِكَ ،

وَ اجْعَلْني مِمَّنْ لا يَبْسُط كَفّاً إِلاّ إِلَيْكَ ،

أَللّـهُمَ إِنَّ الشَّقِيَّ مَنْ قَنَطَ وَ أَمامَهُ التَّوْبَـةُ وَ وَرآءَهُ الرَّحْمَـةُ،

وَ إِنْ كُنْتُ ضَعيفَ الْعَمَلِ فَإِ نّي في رَحْمَتِكَ قَوِيُّ الأْمَلِ،

فَهَبْ لي ضَعْفَ عَمَلي لِقُوَّةِ أَمَلي،

أَللّـهُمَ إِنْ كُنْتَ تَعْلَمُ أَنْ ما في عِبادِكَ مَنْ هُوَ أَقْسى قَلْباً مِنّي وَ أَعْظَمُ مِنّي ذَنْباً،

فَإِ نّي أَعْلَمُ أَنَّهُ لامَوْلى أَعْظَمُ مِنْكَ طَوْلا،

وَ أَوْسَعُ رَحْمَةً وَ عَفْواً، فَيامَنْ هُوَ أَوْحَدُ في رَحْمَتِهِ، إِغْفِرْ لِمَنْ لَيْسَ بِأَوْحَدَ في خَطيئَتِهِ،

أَللّـهُمَّ إِنَّكَ أَمَرْتَنا فَعَصَيْنا، وَ نَهَيْتَ فَمَا انْتَهَيْنا،

وَ ذَكَّرْتَ فَتَناسَيْنا، وَ بَصَّرْتَ فَتَعامَيْنا،

وَ حَذَّرْتَ فَتَعَدَّيْنا، وَ ما كانَ ذلِكَ جَزآءَ إِحْسانِكَ إِلَيْنا،

وَ أَنْتَ أَعْلَمُ بِما أَعْلَنّا وَ أَخْفَيْنا،

وَ أَخْبَرُ بِما نَأْتي وَ ما أَتَيْنا،

فَصَلِّ عَلى مُحَمَّد وَ الِ مُحَمَّد وَ لاتُؤاخِذْنا بِما أَخْطَأْنا وَ نَسينا،

وَ هَبْ لَنا حُقُوقَكَ لَدَيْنا، وَ أَتِمَّ إِحْسانَكَ إِلَيْنا،

وَ أَسْبِلْ رَحْمَتَكَ عَلَيْنا،

أَللّهُمَّ إِنّا نَتَوَسَّلُ إِلَيْكَ بِهذَا الصِّدّيقِ الإْمامِ،

وَ نَسْئَلُكَ بِالْحَقِّ الَّذي جَعَلْتَهُ لَهُ وَ لِجَدِّهِ رَسُولِكَ وَ لِأَبَوَيْهِ عَلِيّ وَ فاطِمَـةَ ، أَهْلِ بَيْتِ الرَّحْمَةِ،

إِدْرارَ الرِّزْقِ الَّذي بِهِ قِوامُ حَياتِنا، وَ صَلاحُ أَحْوالِ عِيالِنا،

فَأَنْتَ الْكَرِيمُ الَّذي تُعْطي مِنْ سَعَة،

وَ تَمْنَعُ مِنْ قُدْرَة، وَ نَحْنُ نَسْئَلُكَ مِنَ الرِّزْقِ مايَكُونُ صَلاحاً لِلـدُّنْيا، وَ بَلاغاً لِلْآخِرَةِ،

أَللّهُمَّ صَلِّ عَلى مُحَمَّد وَ الِ مُحَمَّد،

وَ اغْفِرْلَنا وَ لِوالِدَيْنا،

وَ لِجَميعِ الْمُـؤْمِنينَ و الْمُؤْمِناتِ، وَ الْمُسْلِمينَ وَ الْمُسْلِماتِ الْأَحْياء مِنْهُمْ وَالْأَمْواتِ

وَ اتِنا فِى الدُّنْياحَسَنَةً وَفِى الأخِرَةِ حَسَنَةً وَقِنا عَذابَ النّار،

At this point, pilgrims complete their prayer, recite the *tasbih* (invocation) of Lady Fatimah and place the side of their faces on the ground, saying the following forty times:

سُبْحانَ اللهِ وَ الْحَمْدُ للهِ وَ لاإلهَ إلاَّ اللهُ وَاللهُ أَكْبَرُ

Then pilgrims embrace the inner shrine, kiss it, and say:

زادَ اللهُ في شَرَفِكُمْ ، وَالسَّلامُ عَلَيْكُمْ وَ رَحْمَةُ اللهِ وَ بَرَكاتُهُ

Finally, they pray for themselves, their parents and for whomsoever they wish.

English Translation by Vahid Majd

Peace be upon Adam, the chosen one of Allah from among His creation.

Peace be upon Seth (*Shaith*), the friend of Allah and His elite.

Peace be upon Enoch (*Idris*), who established (religion) on behalf of Allah by His authority.

Peace be upon Noah (*Nuh*), whose invocation (for punishment) was answered.

Peace be upon Hud, who was assisted through Allah's aid.

Peace be upon Salih, whom Allah crowned with His generosity.

Peace be upon Abraham (*Ibrahim*), whom Allah endowed with His friendship.

Peace be upon Ishmael (*Isma'il*), whom Allah ransomed with a great sacrifice from His Heaven.

Peace be upon Isaac (*Is'haq*), in whose progeny Allah placed prophethood.

Peace be upon Jacob (*Ya'qub*), for whom Allah restored his sight by His mercy.

Peace be upon Joseph (*Yusuf*), whom Allah rescued from the well by His majesty.

Peace be upon Moses (*Musa*), the one for whom Allah split the sea with His Power.

Peace be upon Aaron (*Harun*), whom Allah distinguished with his prophethood.

Peace be upon Jethro (*Shu'aib*), whom Allah made victorious over his people.

Peace be upon David (*Dawud*), to whom Allah turned (in mercy) after his mistake.

Peace be upon Solomon (*Sulaiman*), for whom Allah made the Jinn subservient by His majesty.

Peace be upon Job (*Ayyub*), whom Allah cured after his (prolonged) illness.

Peace be upon Jonah (*Yunus*), for whom Allah fulfilled the purport of His promise.

Peace be upon Ezra (*Uzair*), whom Allah brought to life after his death.

Peace be upon Zechariah (*Zakariyya*), who remained patient in his tribulations.

Peace be upon John (*Yahya*), whom Allah drew near (his rank) by his martyrdom.

Peace be upon Jesus (*Isa*), the spirit of Allah and His word.

Peace be upon Muhammad, the beloved of Allah and His elite.

Peace be upon the Leader of the Faithful, Ali Ibn Abi Talib, who was exclusively selected for brotherhood to him (the Prophet).

Peace be upon Fatima al-Zahra, his daughter.

Peace be upon Abu Muhammad al-Hasan, the executor of (the will of) his father, and his successor.

Peace be upon al-Husain, who sacrificed himself up to the last drops of the blood of his heart.

Peace be upon him, who obeyed Allah secretly and openly.

Peace be upon whom Allah placed a cure in the soil of his place (of martyrdom).

Peace be upon the one under whose dome answer (to supplications) is guaranteed.

Peace be upon the one in whose descendants are the Imams (after him).

Peace be upon the son of the seal of the prophets.

Peace be upon the son of the chief of the executors.

Peace be upon the son of Fatima, the radiant.

Peace be upon the son of Khadija, the great.

Peace be upon the son of the lote-tree in the outermost boundary (of Heaven).

Peace be upon the son of the Garden of refuge.

Peace be upon the son of Zamzam and al-Safaa.

Peace be upon him, who was saturated in (his) blood.

Peace be upon him, whose tents were violated.

Peace be upon the fifth of the People of the Cloak.

Peace be upon the loneliest of the lonely.

Peace be upon the (greatest) martyr of all martyrs.

Peace be upon him, who was slain by the individuals of illegitimate birth.

Peace be upon the one who is at rest in Karbala.

Peace be upon the one for whom the heavenly Angels wept.

Peace be upon the one whose descendants are the pure.

Peace be upon the chief of the religion.

Peace be upon the places of the (divine) proofs.

Peace be upon the Imams, the masters (of mankind).

Peace be upon the bloodstained chests.

Peace be upon the parched lips.

Peace be upon the plucked souls.

Peace be upon the snatched spirits.

Peace be upon the stripped corpses.

Peace be upon the pallid bodies.

Peace be upon the gushing bloods.

Peace be upon the dismembered limbs.
Peace be upon the heads raised upon lances.
Peace be upon the women (forcibly) exposed.
Peace be upon the Proof of the Lord of the worlds.
Peace be upon you and upon your pure ancestors.
Peace be upon you and upon your martyred sons.
Peace be upon you and upon your children who aided (you).
Peace be upon you and upon the accompanying Angels.
Peace be upon the slain and the oppressed one.
Peace be upon his poisoned brother (Imam al-Hasan).
Peace be upon Ali, the elder (*Ali al-Akbar*).
Peace be upon the suckling infant (*Ali al-Asghar*).
Peace be upon the plundered bodies.
Peace be upon the family and children who were nearby (the place of martyrdom) [who where without support among strangers].
Peace be upon the mangled corpses (left) in the desert.
Peace be upon those who were left far from their homeland.
Peace be upon those who were buried without shrouds.
Peace be upon the heads severed from the bodies.
Peace be upon the bereaved and the patient one.
Peace be upon the oppressed one who was without a helper.
Peace be upon the inhabitant of the purified soil.
Peace be upon the possessor of the lofty dome.
Peace be upon him, whom the Almighty purified.
Peace be upon him, of whom Gabriel (*Jabra'il*) was proud.
Peace be upon the one to whom Michael (*Mika'il*) spoke tenderly in the cradle.
Peace be upon the one whose pact was broken.
Peace be upon the one whose rights and dignity were violated.
Peace be upon the one whose blood was shed unjustly.
Peace be upon the one who was bathed in the blood of his wounds.
Peace be upon the one who tasted the spears raining down over his body.
Peace be upon the one against whom people came together and made lawful the shedding of his blood.
Peace be upon the one slaughtered in public.

Peace be upon the one who was buried by the strangers from (nearby) villages.
Peace be upon the one whose aorta was severed.
Peace be upon the defender who had no helper.
Peace be upon the grey hair that was dyed (with blood).
Peace be upon the cheek that struck the dust.
Peace be upon the butchered body.
Peace be upon the front teeth that were beaten with a rod.
Peace be upon the head raised (upon a lance).
Peace be upon the unclothed corpses in the desert, bitten by wild wolves and around whom the beasts of prey prowled.
Peace be upon you, O my master, and the Angels who flutter around your dome,
surround your grave, circumambulate your courtyard, and come for your visitation.
Peace be upon you! Indeed, I intended your visitation, and I am hopeful of achieving the prosperity that is with you.
Salutations to you,
Salutations from he who recognises your sanctity, is a sincere (believer) in your guardianship, seeks nearness to Allah through your love, and is aloof from your enemies,
Salutations from the one whose heart is wounded due to the tribulations you have suffered, and whose tears flow in your remembrance,
Salutations from the one who is distressed, grief-stricken, distracted, and yielding,
Salutations from the one, who, had he been present with you in that plain, would have shielded you from the sharpness of the swords with his body and sacrificed his last breath for you, would have struggled beside you, helped you against the aggressors, and redeemed you with his soul, body, wealth, and children,
(Salutations from the one) whose soul is a sacrifice for yours and whose family is a shield for yours.
But as I have been hindered by the course of time and as (Allah's) decree has prevented me from helping you,
and as I could not fight those who fought you, and was not able to show hostility to those who showed hostility to you,

I will, therefore, lament you morning and evening, and will weep blood in place of tears, out of my anguish for you and my sorrow for all that befell you,
until I meet death from the pain of the catastrophe and the choking grief.
I bear witness that you certainly established prayer, gave alms,
enjoined good, forbade evil and transgression,
obeyed Allah, never disobeyed Him, and held fast to Him and to His rope.
Then, you pleased Him, held Him in awe, were attentive towards Him, and were responsive to Him,
established the customs (of the Prophet (PBUH&HF)), extinguished turmoil (in religion),
invited people to rectitude, clarified the ways of righteousness, and truly strove in the way of Allah.
You were an obedient one to Allah,
a follower of your grandfather, Muhammad, peace be upon him and his family,
heedful of the saying of your father,
quick to execute the will of your brother,
an erector of the pillars of the religion, a suppressor of tyranny,
an advancer on the transgressors, and a sincere exhorter for the nation,
a traveller into mortal throes,
a warrior against the wretched, and a maintainer of Allah's proofs (on earth),
compassionate towards Islam and Muslims,
a champion of truth and most patient in adversity,
a protector for the religion, and a defender of its domain.
You safeguarded the right path and supported it,
spread justice and promoted it,
advocated the faith and manifested it,
restrained and reproached the frivolous,
took back (the rights) of the lowly from the privileged,
and were equitable in your arbitrations between the weak and the strong.
You were the springtime of the orphans, the protection of humanity, the glory of Islam,

the treasure of divine laws, and a relentless ally of benevolence.
You pursued the path of your grandfather and your father,
resembled your brother in will,
were loyal to your obligations, possessed pleasant manners,
embodied generosity, and spent the darkness (of night) in prayer.
You were the straightest path, the most generous of the creation, and had the brightest record.
You were of great ancestry, noble descent, and lofty rank.
You possessed plentiful merits, praiseworthy manners, and were abundant in endowments.
You were forbearing, upright, always turning (to Allah), generous, knowledgeable, strong,
a martyred Imam, grieved, repentant with earnest prayers (to Allah), dearly loved, and awesome.
You were to the Messenger, peace be upon him and his family, a son,
for the Quran, an authority [a saviour],
and for the nation, a support.
You were diligent in obedience,
a protector of the covenant and oath,
keeping away from the paths of the debauched,
sparing no effort (in fulfilling the duties),
performing prolonged bowing and prostrations,
abstaining from the world, like one who is departing from it,
looking upon it (the world) through the eyes of one estranged (from it).
Your desires from it (the world) were abstentious,
your efforts were far-removed from its embellishments,
your glances removed from its joys,
and your desire for the hereafter was well-known,
even when tyranny became widespread,
injustice removed its veil,
wickedness called upon its followers,
and you were residing in the sanctuary of your grandfather,
detached from the oppressors,
sitting in the house and the prayer niche,
unattached to (worldly) pleasures and carnal desires,

and renouncing evil in your heart and on your tongue to the extent of your strength and ability.
Then the knowledge demanded you for disavowal (of falsehood),
and made it incumbent on you to struggle against the deviant.
Therefore, you set out in company of your children, kinsfolk, followers, and supporters,
disclosed the truth and clear proofs,
summoned people towards Allah with wisdom and fine exhortation,
ordered the establishment of the limits of divine law, and the obedience to the One Who should be worshipped,
and forbade (people) from wickedness and oppression.
But, they confronted you with injustice and aggression.
Therefore, you resisted them after advising them and stressing over (divine) proofs against them.
However, they violated your (divine) rights and oath.
angered your Lord and your grandfather,
and initiated battle against you.
Hence, you stood firm to spear and strike,
pulverised the soldiers of the transgressors, and stormed (courageously) into the dust of the battle,
fighting with Thulfaqar as if you were Ali, the chosen one.
So when they saw you firm, fearless, and courageous,
they set up their most malicious deceptions against you, and fought you with their deceit and viciousness.
The accursed one (Umar Ibn Sa'd) commanded his soldiers, and thus, they prevented you from reaching or receiving water.
They rushed to engage you in combat, descended swiftly upon you,
showering you with arrows and stones,
and moving towards you with uprooting hands.
Neither they respected your rights, nor were they mindful of retribution for slaying you and your companions, and plundering your belongings.
You were in the front line of the storm (of battle), enduring afflictions.
Indeed, the angels of the heavens were astonished by your patience.
The enemy then surrounded you from all sides,
weakened you by inflicting wounds,

prevented you from taking any repose,
and you had no helper remaining.
You were bereaved yet patient,
defending your women and children,
until they caused you to fall from your horse.
You fell to the ground, wounded,
horses trampled you with their hooves,
tyrants raised their swords against you,
the sweat of death appeared on your forehead,
and you continually clenched and unclenched your hands,
secretly gazing upon your caravan and tents,
while trapped by yourself away from your children and family.
(At that time,) your horse distractedly galloped towards your camp, neighing and crying.
When the women saw your horse distraught,
and observed your saddle contorted,
they came from the tents,
dishevelling their hair,
striking their now unveiled cheeks,
calling you by lamenting and wailing,
being humiliated after being honoured,
hastening to where you lay wounded.
At that time Shimr was sitting on your chest,
quenching his sword with (the blood of) your throat,
grabbing your beard with his hand,
as he slew you with his sword.
Your faculties faded,
your breath became shallow and ceased,
and your head was raised onto a spear.
Your family were captured like slaves,
bound with iron chains atop camels,
with midday heat scorching their faces.
They were driven across deserts and wastelands,
with their hands chained to their necks,
and were paraded around the markets.
Woe be unto the wicked transgressors!

Certainly, by killing you, they have killed Islam,
disrupted (the truth of) prayer and fasting,
revoked the (prophetic) customs and the (divine) laws,
destroyed the pillars of faith,
distorted the verses of the Quran,
and brutally rushed into tyranny and aggression.
Certainly, (by this event,) the Messenger of Allah (PBUH&HF) was wronged, left alone, and denied vengeance,
the Book of Allah, the mighty and the majestic, was again abandoned,
truth was betrayed when you were forcibly overcome,
And with your loss, call for Allah's glorification and His Unity,
His prohibitions, sanctions, revelation, and interpretation were lost.
After you, alteration, distortion, infidelity, abandonment (of the Islamic laws), vagary, misguidance, turmoil and falsehood became prevalent.
The announcer of your martyrdom came near the grave of your grandfather, the Messenger,
gave the news to him with tears flowing, saying:
O the Messenger of Allah! Your brave grandson was slain,
and abuse of your family and supporters was deemed lawful.
After you, your progeny were captured,
and adversity befell your family and your offspring.
Indeed, the Messenger became distressed and his depressed heart wept,
The Angels and the prophets offered their condolences to him for your martyrdom,
Your mother, al-Zahra, became distressed and bereft of you,
Legions of favoured Angels came in waves to offer their condolences to your father, the Leader of the Faithful,
Mourning commemorations were held for you in the utmost exalted place Heaven,
and the dark-eyed Maidens (of Paradise) hit their own heads and faces in grief,
The skies and their inhabitants wept,
as did Paradise and its keepers,
the mountains and their surroundings,
the oceans and their fishes,
the heavens and their servants,

the House (*Ka'ba*), and the Station (of Abraham),
the Sacred Monument,
and Mecca and its sanctuary.
O Allah! By the sanctity of this exalted place (the tomb of Imam al-Husain (PBUH)),
bestow blessings upon Muhammad and the family of Muhammad,
assemble me in their company,
and admit me to Paradise by their intercession.
My Allah! I implore You, O He who is the quickest of the reckoners!
O the most generous of the generous and the wisest of judges!
By Muhammad, the seal of the prophets, Your Messenger to all the worlds,
By his brother and cousin, the uprooter of hidden polytheism, the distinguished and learned, Ali, the Prince of the Faithful,
By Fatima, the chief of women of the worlds,
By al-Hasan, the purified one and the protection of the pious,
By Abi Abdillah, al-Husain, the most honored martyr,
By his slain children and oppressed family,
By Ali Ibn al-Husain, the ornament of the worshippers,
By Muhammad Ibn Ali, the direction of those who turn to Allah,
By Ja'far Ibn Muhammad, the most truthful,
By Musa Ibn Ja'far, the discloser of the proofs,
By Ali Ibn Musa, the helper of the religion,
By Muhammad Ibn Ali, the exemplar of those who accepted guidance,
By Ali Ibn Muhammad, the most ascetic,
By Hasan Ibn Ali, the inheritor of the appointed ones,
By the Proof upon all creation (al-Mahdi),
Bless Muhammad and the family of Muhammad,
the most truthful and devoted ones (who are) the family of *Taha* and *Yasin*,
and place me on the Day of Judgement among those who are safe, confident,
triumphant, happy, and felicitous.
O Allah! Destine me to be amongst the submitters,

Join me with the righteous,
Ordain for me (offspring with) truthful tongue among the last generation,
Make me victorious over the transgressors,
Suffice me the deception of the envious,
Turn away from me the evil plans of the schemers,
Hold back from me the hands of the oppressors,
Gather me with the blessed masters in the utmost exalted place of Heaven,
along with whom You have bestowed favour, from among the prophets, the truthful, the martyrs, and the righteous,
By Your mercy, O the most merciful of the merciful.
O Allah! I implore You by Your infallible Prophet,
by Your definite judgement, and Your concealed preventive wisdom,
by this grave which is the place of congregation and in which lies the infallible Imam, the slaughtered, and the oppressed,
that You dispel from me all that grieves me,
divert from me the harm of the decisive foreordained plan,
and give me refuge from the Hellfire with scorching winds.
My Allah! Honor me with Your bounties,
Make me content with Your apportionment,
Encompass me with Your munificence and generosity,
And keep me far off from Your requital scheme and Your wrath.
O Allah! Protect me from errors,
Make me firm in speech and action,
Extend for me the period (of life),
Relieve me from pain and ailments,
Make me achieve, through my masters and Your grace, the best of wishes.
O Allah! Bless Muhammad and the family of Muhammad and accept my repentance and my return,
Have mercy upon my weeping,
Lessen my lapses,
Relieve my distress,
Forgive me my mistake,

And improve my (righteousness) through my children.
My Allah! Do not leave for me, in this exalted and honoured place of martyrdom, any sin but that You forgive,
Nor any defect but that You conceal,
Nor any grief but that You remove,
Nor any sustenance but that You extend,
Nor any (spiritual) status but that You cause to prosper,
Nor any corruption but that which You correct,
Nor any wish but that You fulfil,
Nor any supplication but that You answer,
Nor any pressure but that You relieve,
Nor any dispersed (believers) but that You reunify,
Nor any matter but that You complete,
Nor any wealth but that You increase,
Nor any character but that You improve,
Nor any charity but that You repay,
Nor any condition but that You cause to improve,
Nor any envious (one) but that You suppress,
Nor any enemy but that You destroy,
Nor any evil but that You suffice,
Nor any ailment but that You cure,
Nor any distant (one) but that You bring near,
Nor any scattering but that You reunite,
Nor any request but that You grant.
O Allah! I ask You for the goodness of this transitory world,
and the reward of the hereafter.
O Allah! Suffice me with what You made lawful from the unlawful,
and with Your grace from all other creatures.
My Allah! I ask You for beneficial knowledge,
a humble heart,
unequivocal certitude,
pure action,
beautiful patience,
and a bountiful reward.
O Allah! Grant me gratitude of Your blessing upon me,
Increase Your favour and munificence on me,

Make my speech amongst people effective,
my deeds elevated and worthy of being delivered to You,
my righteous works followed (by others),
and my enemy quelled,
O Allah! Send blessings upon Muhammad and the family of Muhammad, the best of the creations, day and night,
Spare me from the evil of the wicked,
Purify me from sins and burdens,
Give me refuge from Hell-fire,
Settle me in the House of rest (Paradise),
And forgive me and all my faithful brothers and sisters,
By Your mercy, O the most merciful of the merciful!

Notes

1. Majlisi: Bihar al-Anwar, volume 99, no. 63.
2. Ibid volume 99, no. 67.

SECTION 3

AN EXPERIENCE OF A PILGRIM: VISITING THE SAMARRA SHRINE

Sayyid Qamar Abbas

This section includes a personal experience of a pilgrim who visited Samarra and performed the *ziyarah* of the shrines of the 10th and 11th Shi'i Imams. It is intended to give readers an insight into what Shi'i pilgrims experience when they perform *ziyarah*.

Setting off

2009 was drawing to a close but at the same time, the year 1431 A.H had begun in the Islamic calendar. It was 28th December 2009 or 11th Muharram 1431 and I had woken up at 4:00 in the morning in the city of Karbala. The tiredness and spiritual experience of the previous day was still fresh. The day before, I had observed millions of people commemorating the martyrdom of Prophet Muhammad's grandson, Husayn, in Karbala. They came in thousands and millions, marching to the mausoleum of Husayn, chanting 'Labbayk Ya Husayn' (I am here, O Husayn). They were remembering Husayn's call on tenth Muharram 1370 years ago on this very ground where he stood in the afternoon, after his family and companions were killed, raising his voice saying, 'Is there anyone to help us?' Now, with my pilgrim group, I made my way to a bus station. Our destination was Samarra.

Samarra is about 125 kilometres (78 miles) north of Baghdad. It took our bus about 5 hours to get to Samarra. On the way, we stopped at 'Balad', a town where the son of Ali al-Hadi, Muhammad is buried. It was now about 8:00 in the morning. We grabbed a bite to eat and then proceeded. As our bus approached Samarra, the images of security forces became more and more abundant. That was nothing surprising. In fact, it would have been essential to have heavy security there in light of the bombings at Samarra's famous mausoleum in February 2006 and June 2007. Our ultimate destination that day was the same mausoleum. Our bus stopped at a fair distance and we were asked to leave any digital equipment, including cameras and mobile phones, inside the bus. I got off and walked on the built road between iron bars for some distance before entering a gate. Here the sides were blocked by huge concrete barriers. I was stopped and body searched. As I walked between those barriers, my heart raced and my mind slipped into the past.

The Samarra shrine

I entered the last gate and looked upwards. What I saw was the debris of the bombed domes on the right and a heavily damaged shrine in front of me. Construction work was in process. I was now looking at the damaged shrine which holds the graves of Imams Ali-al-Hadi and Hasan-al-Askari. Right opposite the shrine was the rubble. Many people out of their love for the place were climbing over the small fence and gathering pieces of rubble as a holy souvenir. I looked at that but simply could not do that. I just turned back to the shrine.

It was almost midday. As I walked towards the holy shrine, the call for prayers reverberated in the air. Masjid al-Askari is well-known for housing both the Shi'a and Sunni at the time of prayers. Security guards checked us again and I walked towards the ablution rooms. People were entering the mosque from the south western main gate. I also hurried to the gate as the grouping (jamaat) started congregating in the main courtyard. I joined the congregation and raised my hands saying, 'God is greatest.'

After the prayers, I turned to face the room, which houses the graves of Ali al-Hadi and Hasan al-Askari. The Shi'a are recommended to call their names with the phrase 'Alayhi-salaam' (Peace be upon him). There was calm in the air. Most of the Shi'a were still in Karbala whereas locals were busy at their jobs. Outside the main hall, there are wall hangings with writings of tributes to both leaders. The Shi'a believe that to enter their shrines one must obtain permission, which is called 'idhn al-dukhool', as these leaders are kept alive in spirit by God. It would be an infringement of their household to enter without permission. The main door of the hall was still damaged but I read the proper wordings of the idhn al-dukhool and entered the main hall. There was a division between men and women, clearly marked by 'al-nisa' (women) and 'al-rijal' (men). Different to all shrines of the Shi'a, where graves are surrounded by silver grills, this one was surrounded by wooden walls covered in green cloth. They have not been able to finish reconstructing the grill. It just dawned on me that the wall also surrounds al-Askari's sister, Lady Hakima and his wife, Lady Narjis. My arm stretched and with trembling hands, I placed it on the wall, saying 'Salaam my imam.'

Although not overwhelming, it still had a lot of people inside the shrine. There was a group of pilgrims reciting poetic lamentations in Farsi as it was the month of Muharram. The wooden wall seemed to be the only distance between me and the Imams who had walked on this earth. History reports that they were buried in the house that they lived in. I looked around . . . so this was the place, where they are not just buried but actually lived. I was conscious of the fact that people were approaching the wooden wall after their prayers. I had to move to make way for them. There was a feeling of fragility to the wall. Unlike Karbala or Najaf, where there are silver and iron grills around the sarcophagus, it was weaker. I paid my respect and moved to the far end. There was a small hall there. I found myself a small corner and sat there. Time for reflection . . . so this was the place, where Al-Hadi and Al-Askari used to see their loving companions. This was the place where the ladies, Hakima and Narjis, would be engaged in activities of daily living. I shut my eyes and tried hard to catch some voices from the past.

My eyes suddenly opened. An old Arab was standing next to me. His finger was pointing to the inner side of the dome and its walls. He was surrounded by a small group. He obviously was explaining to those pilgrims how the domes were blown away by bombs in 2006 and 2007. It was now the end of 2009 but the domes were still a long way from repair. I looked around and I could see the builders' dilemma. There were hundreds of thousands of people coming in and out, every day, all the time. Some, like today, were clearly overwhelmed by the seriousness of damage to the complex. Some were awed by the experience to be so near to their Imams. Some obviously were lamenting the Imams' grandfather, Husayn b. Ali. I again shut my eyes.

I saw their house. Al-Hadi must have been so lonely in this house with only his wife to keep him company. I remembered my 8th Imam, Ali al-Ridha. He is buried in Mashhad, Iran and we remember him as 'gharib al-ghuraba', meaning a stranger among the strangers. I sadly thought to myself that the same title is appropriate for al-Hadi as well. This was the house he would have seen his successor, al-Askari, running around as a child. He would have helped his wife, Haditha, in looking after him. He would have shared his domestic issues with Haditha, as they had none but each other in this strange town. My eyes wondered around. Is this town still a strange one for Al-Hadi? Does he still lie here and feel lonely? Is that how his dome was blown up - no one accepting any responsibility and the whole town staying hush? I wondered where the 'gayamin' (the traditional guards of shrine) were when the bombing happened. It is claimed that they were relieved of their duties just before the explosion took place. How lonely then and how lonely now!

Samarra felt quite peaceful yet distinctly sad. There were lots of people walking in but they were also taken aback with the destruction of the shrine. They quietened as they walked inside the main hall; their body language changing from excitement in paying homage to their Imam to utter sadness to find their Imam's last resting place like this! I recalled Karbala and Najaf's hubbub. Later I was to see a different kind of peace in Kadhimain where al-Hadi's father and great grandfather rested. But here, it felt like an empty house, prison-like! I wondered if al-Hadi had ever seen a peaceful home! Now it was time to leave. I stood up but not before I recalled my recollection of the lonely Imam's demise.

Farewell

As I started walking towards the main gate, my son asked, 'Abu (Dad)! All the imams were known as per their qualities. What does al-Askari mean?' Even the reply to such question recalls the oppression of the son and father. I started saying, 'Well! Samarra was a garrison town. The army lived here and this area was specifically known as al-Askar meaning the garrison. These two, father and son together are called al-Askariyyain, meaning the ones who were garrisoned. But you know what? Al-Askari would not even know life outside al-Askar–he was 4 years old when he arrived here. A little child would not even know what is happening to his family, just because they belonged to progeny of Prophet! He then lived here and died.' I then pointed to the wooden wall. 'Look son! He is now sleeping next to his father. Forever, he was to stay in al-Askar.'

I got to the main gate of the shrine. I turned around. It is a tradition in my family that you do not turn your back on the Imam. I tried to follow that. Walking backwards, the sight of the wooden wall which surrounded the graves of al-Hadi, al-Askari and two noble ladies was getting smaller and smaller. This was my first journey to Samarra. I quietly prayed, 'O Allah! Please do not make this my last one.' Now I had to turn left to leave the shrine. I turned. The wooden wall disappeared from my eyes.

I now turned to the small blue dome on the side of grand mausoleum. This was very different to any dome I had observed at the shrines of any Imam. I recalled that the Prophet's dome in Madinah was green but all the others in Najaf, Karbala, Mashhad, Kadhimain and Damascus were golden. Even the shape was a bit elongated. Under it was a small building and people were now heading towards this place in abundance. There was an air of loyalty in them. This was called 'sardab', the place where al-Askari's son and the twelfth Shi'i Imam, Muhammad al-Mahdi, was seen for the last time, only to be concealed by God.

It was a steep staircase downwards and quite a narrow one too! I was now literally rubbing my shoulders with all the pilgrims and lovers of al-Mahdi as I descended. The sound of recitation and lamentation was getting louder as I took my last steps. I was in a basement full of men and women praying, most of them in black. However, I found one thing interesting. It was normal to expect prayers in an Imam's shrine but this was al-Mahdi's house. It certainly wasn't obligatory to come or consider the area within the remit of a shrine. I came to only one conclusion. People came here out of their love for al-Mahdi. There was a bond between all of us. As I avoided bumping into people who were trying to pray or contemplate, the group leader pulled me and showed me an area. He said, 'This was the area where the twelfth Imam was seen for the last time. So difficult it was for him that the caliph's soldiers were waiting to kill him outside, so he never came out of here. Allah protected him by vanishing him.'

So this was the place where the final infallible was last ever seen. I looked at the small glass protected area in Sardab. This was the place of our last contact with spirituality. This was the place, where the Shi'a virtually became leaderless. I wondered how the people in and around Samarra felt at that time. They must have been so used to having Al-Hadi and then Hasan al-Askari around that it must have felt weird, suddenly not to have that spiritual cloak over the town. I looked around. People were now slowly gathering and making their way to the top of another staircase as more and more people were entering the entrance. They were all waiting for the day when al-Mahdi reappears and the world becomes meaningful again for them. I looked around for the last time and started walking upstairs. I began my farewell to Samarra.

I came out of Sardab and turned towards the main gate. 'Doctor! Have some tea!' It was one of the group companions. I made my way to a small platform where people from my group were sitting on wooden benches. It was traditional Arab tea, without milk, in a tiny cup. I gulped it. I could not resist but turned around once more. My eyes became transfixed on the damaged dome. I looked to the blue sky on this sunny day and said, 'My Imam! Call me again. Let this not be my last trip!' My lips trembled. 'I think we must move. We need to get to Kadhimain before maghrib (sunset)', I heard our group guide say. My eyes went back for one last visit to the dome. I leaned on my 12 and 9 year old boys. I whispered and they heard patiently, 'Sons! Recognise this. Even if I cannot live long enough to come back, you do as I did and convey my salutation to these two leaders.'

CONTRIBUTORS

Sayyid Qamar Abbas is Deputy Medical Director at St Clare Hospice in Hastingwood, Essex and has postgraduate degrees in History, Medical Ethics and Palliative care. He is also the Principal of the Shi'a Ithna Ashari Madrassah of Essex and member of the Faith Forum of Essex. He is currently compiling a book on Shi'i heritage.

Pascal Missak Abidor is a PhD Candidate at McGill University's Institute of Islamic Studies. He holds a BA from McGill University in Middle Eastern Studies and Political Science and an MSc in Islamic and Middle Eastern Studies from the University of Edinburgh, and from 2008 to 2009 he was a research scholar at the Council for British Research in the Levant, Amman.

Sayyid Fadhil Bahrululoom is Director of the Centre for Islamic Shi'a Studies. Since 2003, he has been pursuing higher studies at the Islamic seminary in Qum. He teaches at the Islamic College, London and serves as the Director for the Ahlulbayt Foundation, London. He has published several works in Arabic and English including *The Hajj Guide.*

Usam Ghaidan is a Conservation Architect for UNESCO at the Department of Focal Point for Culture (Holland/Iraq). He is also a member of the Royal Institute of British Architects (R.I.B.A) and the Centre for Islamic Shi'a Studies, London.

Amal Imad received her MA in Muslim Cultures from the Institute for the Study of Muslim Civilisations, Aga Khan University. Her area of interests includes contemporary challenges encountered by European Muslims and function of religious traditions in modern-day Muslim societies.

Sajad Jiyad is Researcher at the Centre for Islamic Shi'a Studies (CISS) specialising in Middle Eastern History and Politics. He completed his BSc in Economics and Politics from University of London and obtained his MA from the Islamic College in London. He currently teaches at the Islamic College and frequently presents conference papers.

Alastair Northedge is Professor of Islamic Art and Archaeology at Université de Paris 1 (Panthéon-Sorbonne). He has worked in Syria, Jordan, Saudi Arabia, Kazakhstan and Turkmenistan and conducted projects at Amman in Jordan and Ana in Iraq, in addition to Samarra. He is author of Studies on Roman and Islamic Amman, joint author of *Excavations at Ana*, and has recently published *Historical Topography of Samarra.*

Imranali Panjwani is a Tutor and PhD candidate in the Theology and Religious Studies faculty at King's College London. Educated at the University of Sheffield, The College of Law and Al-Mahdi Institute in Birmingham, he has worked for the Centre for Islamic Shi'a Studies in London as its Research Co-ordinator.

Peter Sluglett teaches modern Middle Eastern history at the University of Utah, Salt Lake City. He has written extensively on the history of Iraq and Lebanon in the twentieth century and more broadly on the urban social history of the Middle East between the eighteenth and twentieth centruries, including *Britain in Iraq: Contriving King and Country* (I.B.Tauris, 2003).

Charles R. H. Tripp is Professor of Politics at the School of Oriental and African Studies (SOAS), University of London. Author of *A History* *of Iraq* (2007, 3rd edition), he is a noted expert on the Middle East and modern Iraq.

Reidar Visser is Research Fellow at the Norwegian Institute of International Affairs and the editor of the Iraq website www.historiae.org. His books include *Basra, the Failed Gulf State: Separatism and Nationalism in Southern Iraq* and (edited with Gareth Stansfield) *An Iraq of Its Regions: Cornerstones of a Federal Democracy?*

GLOSSARY

Abbasids The Abbasid dynasty held the Caliphate, with Baghdad as its capital, from 750 when they overthrew the Umayyads until 1258.

Adhan Arabic word for the call to prayer

Ahl al-Bayt In Arabic, this phrase literally means 'people of the house' and refers to the Prophet Muhammad's family and descendents. In particular, this includes the Prophet Muhammad, Ali, Fatimah, Hasan and Husayn. For Twelver Shi'a, the *Ahl al-Bayt* are the rightful successors of the Prophet.

Akhbaris A minority of Shi'a, who believe only the twelve Imams can interpret the Qur'an – only their exegesis, preserved in their *hadith*, can be used to derive laws and religious rulings.

Ali (around 600 – 40/661). Ali b. Abi Talib was the son-in-law and cousin of the Prophet Muhammad. He was the fourth of the *Rashidun* (rightly guided) Caliphs, and ruled from 656 until he was assassinated by the Kharijites in 40/661. He was also the first Shi'i Imam, believed to have been designated as the Prophet's successor at *Ghadir al-Khumm* in 632.

Ali al-Hadi (212/828 – 254/868). The tenth Shi'i Imam, born in Madinah and killed in Samarra. He is considered a martyr as he is believed to have been poisoned by the Abbasid caliph al-Mu'tazz or, according to some accounts, al-Mu'tamid.

Amilis Shi'i clerics from the southern Lebanese region of Jabal Amil, who have close ties to the Iraqi shrine cities, such as Najaf and Samarra.

al-Askariyyain Shrine Located in Samarra, it holds the tombs of tenth Imam Ali al-Hadi, eleventh Imam Hasan al-Askari, Ali al-Hadi's sister Hakima and

Hasan al-Askari's wife Narjis. The shrine, and religious and scholarly traditions that have developed around it, make Samarra an important pilgrimage site for Shi'a. The tombs began to be developed into a shrine in 4th/10th century by the Hamdanids and then the Buyids. It was partially destroyed by bomb attacks in 2006 and 2007, which are seen as an important causal factor in the wave of sectarian violence that followed Iraq. It is also known as al-Askariyya or al-Askari shrine.

Ashura The day that Shi'a commemorate and mourn the martyrdom of Husayn at the Battle of Karbala in 61/680. It is marked on 10 Muharram, in the Islamic Calendar.

Ba'athism Secular political philosophy that has been the official ideology of totalitarian regimes in both Iraq and Syria. It was developed by Syrian thinker Michel Aflaq in the 1940s, as a form of socialist Arab nationalism. The Ba'ath party took power in Iraq in 1968, and was the ruling party of Saddam Hussein until he was overthrown by the US-led invasion of 2003.

Caliph Holder of the Caliphate and ruler of the Islamic Empire. 'Caliph' is the Arabic for 'representative' – i.e. God's representative on Earth. After the first four *Rashidun* (rightly guided) Caliphs, the title was held by the Umayyads, Abbasids, Fatimids and Ottomans.

Coalition Provisional Authority Set up after the toppling of Saddam Hussein, this US-led body took control of Iraq in April 2003 and was led by American diplomat Paul Bremer until authority was transferred back to Iraq in June 2004, through an interim government (selected by the CPA). It has been widely criticised as having badly managed the aftermath of the fall of Saddam Hussein, in particular the decision to disband the Iraqi army.

Da'wa Literally meaning 'inviting', it refers to the act of calling people to Islam.

Faqih A jurist who exercises *ijtihad* in order to deduce laws.

Fatwa Religious edict or formal legal opinion, issued by a recognised religious authority.

Fiqh Literally meaning 'understanding', it refers to the subject of Islamic jurisprudence.

Ghadir al-Khumm In Arabic, this means 'the Pond of Khumm'. It is here that Shi'a believe the Prophet Muhammad designated Ali as his successor and the first Imam of the Muslim community in 632.

al-Ghayba The Arabic word for 'occultation'. In Shi'a belief, it refers to the occultation of the twelfth Imam, Muhammad al-Mahdi, who went into minor occultation at the age of four in 259/874. During this period he had contact with his followers through various appointed representatives. Al-Mahdi entered into the current major occultation in which there are no appointed representatives, at the age of approximately 72.

Ghilman Turkish slave soldiers, who, under the Abbasids gained increasing political power and caused much unrest in the Empire's capital Baghdad.

Hadith Sayings, deeds and tacit approval of the Prophet Muhammad that have been compiled by *ulama* and now serve as a key source of Islamic law. Different schools of law have different sets of Hadith.

Hajj Pilgrimage to Mecca, that all Muslims must strive to perform as one of the five pillars of Islam.

Hasan (3/625 – 50/670). Al-Hasan b. Ali b. Abi Talib was the second Shi'i Imam, grandson of the Prophet and son of Ali and Fatima. He was killed in 670, believed to have been poisoned by his wife on instruction of Muawiyah I, and is remembered in Muslim tradition as a martyr.

Hasan al-Askari (232/846 - 260/874). The eleventh Shi'i Imam, born in Madinah and killed in Samarra. He is considered a martyr as his death is believed to have been caused by poison ordered by the Abbasid caliph, al-Mu'tamid.

Hawza Shi'i religious seminary, where students are trained in classical subjects such as *fiqh, kalam, hadith and tafsir.*

Husayn (4/626 – 61/680). Al-Husayn b. Ali b. Abi Talib was the third Shi'i Imam, grandson of the Prophet, son of Ali and Fatima, and brother of Hasan (the second Shi'i Imam). He was killed by Yazid I's forces at the Battle of Karbala in 61/680.

Ijaza The Arabic word for 'license to teach' or 'permission to transmit', it is part of Imami religious sciences given by well-established jurists to their pupils. It also refers to the certification given to a qualified jurist to employ *ijtihad* for the purpose of deriving judicial decisions.

Ijma The Arabic word for 'consensus', it is one of the tools used by scholars to derive Islamic law.

Ijtihad The employment of effort to derive a law from its sources within one's human comprehension. According to the Shi'a, these sources are the *Qur'an, Sunnah* (Prophetic and Imami tradition), *Ijma* (consensus) and *Aql* (intellect).

Sunni jurists differ on the last source which, according to them, is *Qiyas* (analogy).

Ithna-Ashariyyah See: *Twelver Shi'ism*

Imam For the Shi'a, the Imam is a member of the *Ahl al-Bayt* and the true leader of the community, even if not recognised by the political ruler of the time.

Imamah Meaning 'leadership', it is a central concept in Shi'i theology and belief, as the *Imamah* represents a continuous line of divinely ordained leadership from the Prophet, through his descendents. It is considered by Shi'a to be the true seat of leadership for Muslims, that has been usurped over the centuries by corrupt rulers.

Iran-Iraq war (1980–88). War fought between Iran and Iraq.

ISCI Islamic Supreme Council of Iraq, previously the Supreme Council for the Islamic Revolution in Iraq (SCIRI). The ISCI is a Shi'a Iraqi political party, led by Ayatollah Muhammad Baqir al-Hakim, until his assassination in 2003, and now by Ammar al-Hakim. It has become a powerful political force in post-Saddam Iraq.

Kadhimayn Area in northern Baghdad in which the shrines of the seventh Imam Musa al-Kadhim and ninth Imam Muhammad b. Ali al-Taqi are located.

Karbala Iraqi city located south-west of Baghdad. It is a centre of Shi'i learning and pilgrimage, as the site of the Battle of Karbala and location of Husayn's shrine.

Karbala, the Battle of On 10 Muharram 61/680, Husayn and his relatives and followers were killed by Caliph Yazid b.Mu'awiyah's forces. This battle and Husayn's martyrdom are of great significance to Shi'a, and it is commemorated and mourned every year through Ashura.

Khums Arabic word for 'a fifth.' In the Shi'i legal system, it is a form of taxation incumbent upon all Shi'a, in addition to almsgiving *(zakat).*

Madrasa Arabic word for 'school'. Traditionally, the *madrasa* provided religious (Islamic) instruction to boys.

Madinah (Medina) The second most holy city in Islam, located in Saudi Arabia. It is the burial place of Prophet Muhammad and was his home after the *Hijra* in 622. It is also the birth place of all Twelver Shi'i Imams, except the twelfth.

Makkah (Mecca) The most holy city in Islam, located in the Hijaz region of Saudi Arabia. It is the birthplace of the Prophet and the destination for the Hajj.

Nouri al-Maliki (1950 –). Prime Minister of Iraq since 2006, and leader of the Iraqi Dawa Party.

Mashhad Iranian city east of Tehran, and a holy location for Shi'a as home to the shrine of eighth Imam Ali b. Musa al-Ridha.

al-Mahdi Meaning 'the Guided One' in Arabic, it is the name given to the twelfth Imam, who is believed to have gone into occultation at the age of 4 in 259/874, to escape death. Shi'a belief says he will return to save humanity.

Marja taqlid Literally 'source of imitation' in Arabic, and known as *marja-i taqlid* in Persian. It is the title given to a Shi'i figure of religious authority who is to be emulated and who's role it is to give guidance to the Muslim community and make legal decisions.

Mirza Shirazi (1815 – 95). Muhammad Hasan Husayni al-Shirazi was an important religious Shi'i jurist of the nineteenth century. Born in Shiraz, he spent 20 years in Najaf before establishing his own *hawza* in Samarra, that attracted students and development to the city in his time, and becoming the *marja taqlid*. He is known for his role in the Tobacco Protest of 1890–91.

Mu'awiyah I (602 – 61/680). The first Caliph of the Umayyad dynasty, he ruled between 40/661 and 61/680. According to Shi'i history, Mu'awiyah agreed with Hasan that his brother Husayn would succeed him as Caliph, but he reneged on this deal by appointing his son Yazid as successor instead.

Mujtahid Meaning the 'one who strives' in Arabic, it has come to acquire the same definition as *faqih* – i.e. a jurist who exercises *ijtihad* in order to deduce laws.

Muqtada al-Sadr (1973 –). Iraqi Shi'i cleric and political figure who gained increasing power and notoriety after the 2003 US-led invasion of Iraq, in particular for his militia the Mahdi Army. He is the son of populist cleric Muhammad Baqir al-Sadiq al-Sadr, who was imprisoned and then executed by the Ba'athist regime in 1999.

Najaf Iraqi city south of Baghdad and a great centre of Shi'i learning and pilgrimage. This city is home to the tomb of Ali, as well as many religious figures and *hawzas* over the centuries.

Rawda Translated from Arabic as the 'sanctuary' of a shrine, it is the enclosed area around the tomb.

Riwaq Translated from Arabic as 'portico' or 'vestibule', it is an architectural feature common to Shi'i shrines.

Saddam Hussein (1937 – 2006). Leader of the Iraqi Ba'ath party and of Iraq from 1979, until he was overthrown by the US-led invasion of 2003. He was convicted of crimes against humanity and executed in Iraq in 2006.

Sahn Arabic for 'courtyard', it is a common feature of Shi'i shrines.

Samarra City in the north of Baghdad, situated on the east bank of the River Tigris in the Salah al-Din Governorate. It is home to al-Askariyyain shrine.

Sanduq Arabic for 'box' or 'container', it refers to the covering of a grave.

SCIRI Supreme Council for the Islamic Revolution in Iraq, now the *ISCI*.

Shariah Literally meaning 'way' or 'path', it has come to refer to the code of conduct and body of rules guiding the life of a Muslim.

Sunnah Literally meaning 'trodden path', it refers to the model, conduct and practice of Prophet Muhammad. For the Shi'a, this also includes the actions of his descendants, specifically the twelve Imams.

Surra Man Ra'a Original Arabic name for city of Samarra, meaning 'delighted who beholds it', which was later shortened to its modern name.

Tafsir (Qur'anic) exegesis.

Tanzimat Ottoman nineteenth century reforms

The Tobacco Protest (1890 – 91). A protest movement in Iran led by Shi'i clerics against a concession granted in the tobacco industry by Nasir al-Din Shah to Great Britain in March 1890.

Taqiyyah Arabic word meaning 'religious dissimulation,' referring to the practice of concealing one's faith from threat or persecution.

Taqlid Meaning 'imitation.' It is the act of committing one's self to follow the rulings of a *mujtahid* in whom one has placed his/her trust, even if he/she does not act in accordance with those rules subsequently.

Twelver Shi'ism Known as *Ithna Ashariyyah* in Arabic, this branch of Shi'ism takes its name from the belief in the divine leadership of twelve Imams, carried through the line of the Prophet Muhammad, and the occultation of the twelfth Imam Muhammed al-Mahdi.

UIA The United Iraqi Alliance is a Shi'i political bloc, with its two largest parties as the Islamic Dawa Party and the Supreme Islamic Iraqi Council.

Ulama (pl. of *alim*) Arabic word for Islamic scholars.

Umayyads The Umayyad dynasty held the Caliphate, with Damascus as its capital, from 661 until they were overthrown by the Abbasids in 750.

Ummah Muslim community of believers across the world.

Usul al-Fiqh The Arabic for 'principles of jurisprudence', this is a core part of traditional Islamic scholarship and a science through which laws are derived from the core Islamic sources (Qur'an, Sunnah, Ijma and Aql).

Usulis Usulis take their name from their belief that the Qur'an and Hadith should be interpreted through *usul al-fiqh*. Most Shi'a are Usulis and this school of thought contrasts with Akhbarism.

Ziyarah The Arabic for 'visitation', which can refer specifically to the visitation of a shrine. It also refers to giving salutations to a saint from afar.

SELECT BIBLIOGRAPHY

English Language Works

Abisaab, Rula, *Converting Persia: Religion and Power in the Safavid Empire* (New York, 2004)

Abrahamian, Ervand, *Iran between Two Revolutions* (New Jersey, 1982)

Al-Amini, Ibrahim, *Al-Imam al-Mahdi: The Just Leader of Humanity* (London, 1996)

Al-Majlisi, Muhammad (trans. Hassan Allahyari), *The Book of Occultation: Kitab al-Ghaibah* (Qum, 2003)

Al-Marashi, Ibrahim & Durlacher, Katherine, *Iraqi Perceptions of UK and American Policy in Post-Saddam Iraq* (The Nathan Hale Foreign Policy Society, nd). Available online at: http://www.foreignpolicysociety.org/iraq.pdf

Al-Mufid, Muhammad (trans. I.K.A Howard), *Kitab Al-Irshad: the Book of Guidance* (London, 1981)

Al-Muzaffar, Muhammad (trans. Jasim al-Rasheed), *Imam al-Sadiq* (Qum, 1998)

Al-Nawbakhti, Hasan (trans. Abbas Kadhim) *Kitab Firaq al-Shi'a* (London, 2007)

Al-Sadr, Muhammad Baqir (trans. Mujahid Husayn), 'A Discussion concerning the Mahdi', *Al-Tawhid: A Journal of Islamic Thought and Culture*. Available online at: http://www.al-islam.org/al-tawhid/default.asp?url=mahdi/discussion.htm

Al-Sadr, Muhammad Baqir (trans. Arif Abdul Hussain & Hamid Algar), *Principles of Islamic Jurisprudence* (London, 2003)

Al-Shawi, Ibrahim, *A Glimpse of Iraq* (London, 2006)

Allawi, Ali, *The Occupation of Iraq: Winning the War, Losing the Peace* (London, 2007)

Ali, Sayyid Amir, *A Short History of Saracens,* (London, 1916)

Ammanat, Abbas., 'In Between the Madrasa and the Marketplace: The Designation of Clerical Leadership in Modern Shi'ism', in Said Amir Arjoman, ed., *Authority and Political Culture in Shi'ism* (New York, 1988)

An-Nu'mani, Ibn Abu Zaynab (trans. Abdullah Al-Shahin), *Al-Ghayba: Occultation* (Qum, 2003)

Avery, Peter et al., *The Cambridge History of Iran* (Cambridge, 2003)
Axtmann, Roland, *Liberal Democracy into the Twenty-First Century: Globalization, Integration and the Nation-State* (New York, 1997)
Bahmanpour, Muhammad, 'The Book of Imam Ali (Kitabu Ali): al-Jamiah', *Journal of Shi'a Islamic Studies*, 1:1 (2008), pp. 3–28
Bashkin, Orit, *The Other Iraq: Pluralism and Culture in Hashemite Iraq* (Palo Alto, 2009)
Bauman, Zygmunt, *Postmodern Ethics* (Oxford, 1993)
Bayhom-Daou, Tamima, *Shaykh Mufid* (London, 2005)
Beazeley, George Adam, 'Aerial Oblique of Samarra - Surveys in Mesopotamia During the War', *The Geographical Journal*, 55:2 (1920), pp. 109–127
Bilmes, Linda, & Joseph Stiglitz, *The Three Trillion Dollar War: The True Cost of the Iraq Conflict* (New York, 2008)
Budge, Wallis, *By Nile and Tigris* (London, 1920)
Burton, Michael, & John Higley, *Elite Foundations of Liberal Democracy* (Lanham, 2006)
Cady, Linell & Brown, Delwin, *Religious Studies, Theology and the University: Conflicting Maps and Changing Terrain* (New York, 2002)
Chalabi, Tamarra, *The Shi'is of Jabal 'Amil and the New Lebanon: Community and Nation State 1918–1943* (New York, 2006)
Cordesman, Anthony H. & Davies, Emma, *Iraq's Insurgency and the Road to Civil Conflict* (Connecticut, 2008)
Deringil, Selim., 'The Struggle Against Shi'ism in Hamidian Iraq; a Study in Ottoman Counter-Propaganda', *Die Welt des Islams*, 30 (1990), pp. 45–62.
Donaldson, Dwight M, *The Shi'ite Religion: A History of Islam in Persia and Irak* (London, 1933)
Ende, Werner., 'The Flagellations of Muharram and the Shi'ite *'Ulama'*, *Islam*, 55 (1978), pp. 19–36
——, 'From Revolt to Resignation: The Life of Shaykh Muhsin Sharara' in Asma Afsaruddin & A.H. Mathias Zahniser (ed.s), *Humanism, Culture, and Language in the Near East* (Winona Lake, 1997), pp. 61–70
Eppel, Michael, 'The Elite, the *Effendiyya*, and the Growth of Nationalism and Pan-Arabism in Hashemite Iraq, 1921–1958', *International Journal of Middle East Studies*, 30:2 (1998), pp. 227–50
Eich, Thomas, 'Patterns of the 1920 Rising in Iraq: The Rifaiyya Tariqa and Shiism', *Arabica*, 56:1 (2009), pp. 112–19
Fernea, Robert A., 'Land Reform and Ecology in Post revolutionary Iraq', *Economic Development and Cultural Change*, 17: 3 (1969), pp. 356–81
Foulk, Vincent L., *The Battle for Fallujah: Occupation, Resistance and Stalemate in the War in Iraq* (London, 2006)
Fuccaro, Nelida, *The Other Kurds: Yazidis in Colonial Iraq* (London, 1999)
Fuller, Graham & Francke, Rend Rahim, *The Arab Shi'a: The Forgotten Muslims* (New York, 1999)

Gabbay, Rony, *Communism and Agrarian Reform in Iraq* (London, 1978)
Gagnon, Valere Philip, *The Myth of Ethnic War: Serbia and Croatia in the 1990s* (London, 2004)
Galbraith, Peter, *The End of Iraq: How American Incompetence Created a War Without End* (New York, 2006)
Gheissari, Ali & Nasr, Vali, *Democracy in Iran: History and the Quest for Liberty* (New York, 2006)
Gleave, Robert, *Inevitable Doubt: Two Theories of Shi'i Jurisprudence* (Leiden, 2000)
Hashim, Ahmed S., *Insurgency and Counter-Insurgency in Iraq* (New York, 2006)
Heazle, Michael & Islam, Iyantul, *Beyond the Iraq war: the Promises, Pitfalls and Perils of External Interventionism* (Cheltenham, 2006)
Hitti, Philip K., *History of the Arabs* (London, 2002)
Howard, Ian K. A., "Tahdhib al-Ahkam' and 'Al-Istibsar' by Al-Tusi', *Al-Serat: A Journal of Islamic Studies*, 2:2 (1976). Available online at: http://www.al-islam.org/al-serat/default.asp?url=Tusi-howard.htm
Hussain, Jassim M., *The Occultation of the Twelfth Imam: A Historical Background* (London, 1982)
Ibn Battuta, Muhammad (ed. Tim Mackintosh-Smith), *The Travels of Ibn Battutah* (London, 2003)
Inati, Shams, *Iraq: Its History, People and Politics* (New York, 2003)
Isin, Engin Fahri & Wood, Patricia K., *Citizenship and Identity* (London, 1999)
Jabar, Faleh, *The Shi'ite Movement in Iraq* (London, 2003)
Jones, J. F., 'Steamship Voyage to the North of Baghdad, in April 1846', *Journal of the Royal Geographical Society of London,* 18 (1848), pp. 1–19
Keddie, Nikki, *Religion and Rebellion in Iran: The Iranian Tobacco Protest of 1891–1892* (New York, 1966)
Kerkuklu, Mofak Salman, *The Turkmen City of Tuz Khurmatu* (Turkey, 2008)
Kinneir, John MacDonald, *Journey through Asia Minor, Armenia and Koordistan in the Years 1813 and 1814* (London, 1818)
Kymlicka, Will, *Multicultural Citizenship: A Liberal Theory of Minority Rights* (New York, 1996)
Lalani, Arzina, *Early Shi'i Thought: The Teachings of Imam Muhammad al-Baqir* (London, 2004)
Lamb, Harold, *The Crusades: the Flame of Islam* (New York, 1930)
Lambton, Ann, 'The Tobacco Regie: Prelude to Revolution I', *Studia Islamica* 22 (1965), pp. 119–157
Lapidus, Ira M., *A History of Islamic Societies* (Cambridge, 2002)
Le Strange, Guy, *The Lands of the Eastern Caliphate* (New York, 2006)
Leaman, Oliver & Nasr, Syed Hossein (ed.s), *History of Islamic Philosophy* (London, 2003)
Litvak, Meir, 'Madrasa and Learning in Nineteenth-Century Najaf and Karbala', in Rainer Brunner & Werner Ends (ed.s), *The Twelver Shia in Modern times: Religious Culture & Political History* (Leiden, 2001), pp. 58–78

Litvak, Meir, *Shi'i scholars of Nineteenth Century Iraq: The 'Ulama' of Najaf and Karbala'* (Cambridge, 1998)

Longrigg, Stephen Hemsley, *Iraq 1900 to 1950* (Oxford, 1953)

Lorimer, John Gordon, *Geographical and Statistical Gazetteer of the Persian Gulf, Oman and Central Arabia* (Reading, 1908)

Maalouf, Amin (trans. Barbara Bray), *In the Name of Identity (*New York, 2000)

Makdisi, Ussama, *The Culture of Sectarianism: Community, History, and Violence in Nineteenth-Century Ottoman Lebanon* (Los Angeles, 2000)

Masters, Bruce, *Christians and Jews in the Ottoman Arab World: the Roots of Sectarianism* (Cambridge, 2001)

Mervin, Sabrina, 'The Clerics of Jabal Amil and the Reform of Religious Teaching in Najaf Since the Beginning of the Twentieth Century', in Rainer Brunner & Werner Ende (ed.s), *The Twelver Shia in Modern times: Religious Culture & Political History* (Leiden, 2001), pp. 79–86

Modarressi, Hossein, *An Introduction to Shi'i law* (London, 1984)

Momen, Moojan, *The Lives of the Imams and Early Divisions Among the Shi'is: An Introduction to Shi'i Islam* (London, 1985)

Morley, David & Robins, Kevin, *Spaces Of Identity: Global Media, Electronic Landscapes And Cultural Boundaries* (New York, 1995)

Mussavi, Ahmad Kazemi, 'The Institutionalization of *Marja'-i Taqlid* in the Nineteenth Century Shi'ite Community', *Muslim World* 83 (1994), pp. 279–99

Nakash, Yitzhak, *Reaching for Power: The Shi'a in the Modern Arab World* (New Jersey, 2007)

——, *The Shi'is of Iraq* (Oxford, 1995)

——, 'The Struggle for Power in Iraq', *Dissent* (Summer 2003). Available online at: http://www.dissentmagazine.org/article/?article=485

Nasr, Vali, *The Shia Revival: How Conflicts Within Islam Will Shape the Future* (New York, 2006)

Newman, Andrew & Ispahany, Batool, *Islamic Medical Wisdom: The Tibb al-Aimma* (London, 1990)

Noorbaksh, Mehdi, 'Shiism and Ethnic Politics in Iraq', *Middle East Policy*, 15:2 (2008), pp. 53–55

Northedge, Alastair, *The Historical Topography of Samarra* (Oxford, 2005)

Panjwani, S. & Panjwani, I., *Islamic Metaphysics in Bioethics: Animal-Human Experimentations* (London, 2010)

Pilger, John, *The New Rulers of the World* (London, 2002)

Qurashi, Baqir Shareef (trans. Abdullah al-Shahin), *The Life of Imam Hasan al-Askari* (Qum, 2005)

Roberts, Richard H., *Religion, Theology and the Human Sciences* (Cambridge, 2002)

Said, Edward W., *Orientalism* (London, 1985)

Shadid, Anthony, *Night Draws Near: Iraq's People in the Shadow of America's War* (New York, 2005)

Shah-Kazemi, Reza, *Justice and Remembrance: Introducing the Spirituality of Imam Ali* (London, 2007)
Simon, Reeve S., *Iraq between two World Wars; the Creation and Implementation of a Nationalist Ideology*, (New York, 1986)
Sluglett, Peter, *Britain in Iraq: Contriving King and Country* (New York, 2007)
Talhami, Ghada Hashem, 'The Zanj rebellion reconsidered', *International Journal of African Historical studies*, 10:3 (1977), pp. 443–461
Taylor, Charles, *Sources of the Self: The Making of the Modern Identity* (Cambridge, 2008)
Visser, Reidar, 'Historical Myths of a Divided Iraq', *Survival*, 50:2 (2008), pp. 95–106
——, 'Iraqi Minorities Get Special Representation in the Provincial Elections Law', *Historiae.org*, (2008). Available online at: www.historiae.org/minorities.asp
Weiss, Max., 'The Cultural Politics of Shi'i Modernism: Morality and Gender in Early twentieth-Century Lebanon,' *International Journal of Middle East Studies*, 39:2 (2007), pp. 249–270
Wilson, Mary C., *King Abdullah, Britain and the Making of Jordan* (Cambridge, 1987)
Young, Iris Marion, *Justice and the Politics of Difference* (New Jersey, 1990)

Arabic Language Works

Al-Arbili, Al-Fath, *Kashf al-Ghama* (Beirut, 1985)
Al-Amili, Al-Hur, *Wasa'il al-Shi'a* (Qum, 1993)
Al-Amiri, Thamir Abd al-Hasan, *Mawsu'at al-Asha'ir al-Iraqiyya* (Baghdad, 1992)
Al-Bihbahani, Wahid, *al-Dama'a al-Sakiba fi-Ahwal al-Nabi wa al-Ishra al-Tahira* (Beirut, 1989)
Al-Barrak, Fadhil, *al-Madaris al-Yahudiyya wa al-Iraniyya fi al-Iraq* (Baghdad, 1984)
Al-Fadhli, Abd al-Hadi, *Tarikh al-Tashri al-Islami* (Qum, 2006)
Al-Haythami, Hasan, *Majma al-Zawa'id* (Beiruit, 1988)
Al-Hilli, Hasan b. Yusuf b. Mutahhar, *Khulasat al-Aqwal (Qum,* 2002)
Al-Juburi, Kamil Salman, *Sayyid Muhammad Kazim al-Yazdi* (Qum, 2006)
Al-Khalili, Ja'far, *Mawsu'at al-Atabat al-Muqaddasa* (Beiruit, 1987)
Al-Kulayni, Muhammad, *al-Kafi* (Tehran, 1978)
Al-Majlisi, Muhammad Baqir, *Bihar al-Anwar* (Beirut, 1983)
Al-Maududi, Sayyid Abu al-A'la, *Khilafat wa Mulukiyat* (Lahore, 1965)
Al-Najafi, Muhammad al-Qasim Husayni, *Thawrat al-Tanzih* (Beirut, 1996)
Al-Sadr, Hasan, *Takmilat Amal al-Amil* (Qum, 1985)
Al-Tabarasi, Ahmad, *al-Ihtijaj* (Najaf, 1966)
Al-Tusi, Muhammad b. al-Hasan, *Fihrist Kutub al-Shi'a wa Usuluhum wa Asma al-Musannifin wa Ashab al-Usul* (Qum, 2000)
——, *Talkhis al-Shafi* (Qum, 1974)

Al-Saduq, Muhammad, *Uyun Akhbar Al-Ridha* (Qum, 2006)
Al-Samarra'i, Yunis, *Tarikh Madinat Samarra* (Baghdad, 1968)
Al-Suyuti, Jalal al-Din, *Tarikh al-Khulafa* (Beirut, 1993)
Al-Wardi, Ali, *Lamahat Ijtima'iyya min Tarikh al-Iraq al-Hadith* (Baghdad, 1969)
Al-Ya'qubi, Ahmad, *Tarikh al-Ya'qubi* (Beirut, 1960)
Arab, Muhammad Mahmud, a*l-Sarra fi Ahwal Samarra* (London, 2006)
Athir, Ali b., *al-Kamil fi al-Tarikh* (Beirut, 1966)
Ibn Kathir, Ismail, *al-Bidaya wa al-Nihaya* (Beirut, 1993)
Ibn Maja, Muhammad, *Sunan ibn Maja* (Texas, 2007)
Mahallati, Zabih Allah, *Maathir al-Kubara fi Tarikh Samarra* (Qum, 2005)
Mahbuba, Ja'far, *Madi al-Najaf wa Hadiruha* (Najaf, 1955–58)
Sharaf al-Din, Abd al-Husayn, *Bughyat al-Raghibin fi Silsal Al Sharaf al-Din* (Beirut, 1991)
Shustari, Nurullah, *Majalis al-Mu'minin* (Beirut, 1989)

French and German Language Works

Al-Amin, Muhsin (trans. Mervin, Sabrina & Al-Amin, Haitham), *Autobiographie D'Un Clerc Chiite du Gabal 'Amil* (Damascus, 1998)
Babakhan, Ali, *L'Irak 1970–1990: Déportations des chiites* (Paris, 1994)
Eich, Thomas, *Abu l-Huda as-Sayyadi: Eine Studie zur Instrumentalisierung sufischer Netzwerke und genealogischer Kontroversen im spätosmanischen Reich* (Berlin, 2003)
Harling, Peter, 'Saddam Husayn et la débâcle triomphante: Les ressources insoupçonnés de Umm al-Ma'ârik', R*evue du Monde Musulman et de la Méditerranée,* 117–118 (July 2007), pp. 157–78
Luizard, Pierre-Jean, *La Formation de l'Irak Contemporain: Le Rôle Politique des Ulémas Chiites à la Fin de la Domination Ottomane et au Moment de laCconstruction de l'Etat Irakien,* (Paris, 1991)
——, 'Le Mandat Britannique en Irak: Une Rencontre entre Plusieurs Projets Politiques', in Nadine Méouchy & Peter Sluglett (ed.s), *The British and French Mandates in Comparative Perspectives/Les Mandats Français et Anglais dans une Perspective Comparative* (Leiden, 2003), pp. 363–64
Mervin, Sabrina, *Un Réformisme Chiite, Ulémas et lettrés du Jabal 'Âmil (actuel Liban-Sud) de la fin de l'Empire ottoman à l'indépendance du Liban* (Paris, 2000)

INDEX